Bootstrap

Bootstrap

Lessons Learned Building a Successful Company from Scratch

Kenneth L. Hess

S-Curve Press · Carmel, California

Published by:
S-Curve Press
P.O. Box 5038
Carmel, CA 93921-5038

Printed in the United States of America

2001: First Edition.
2007: Second Printing.

ISBN-10: 0-9711873-0-4
ISBN-13: 978-0-9711873-0-6

Library of Congress Control Number 2001 132080

Library of Congress Cataloging-in-Publication Data

Hess, Kenneth L.
    Bootstrap : lessons learned building a successful company from
scratch / Kenneth L. Hess
    x, 301 p.; 24 cm.
    Includes bibliographical references and index.
    ISBN 0-9711873-0-4
    1. Banner Blue Software (Firm)—History. 2. New business
enterprises—United States—Management. 3. Entrepreneurship—United
States. 4. Computer software industry—United States—History. I.
Hess, Kenneth L. II. Title.
    HD62.5 .H477 2001
                                                        2001132080

This book is printed on acid-free paper.

www.KLHess.com/bootstrap/

To Connie and Amber

Table of Contents

Preface

This book recounts my many experiences founding, running, and ultimately leaving a business—and the lessons I learned in doing so.

Although my company, Banner Blue Software, was a technology start-up, most of what I learned applies to virtually any business or organization. In fact, the longer I ran my own show, the more respect I acquired for the individual who founds any business—from a bakery shop to an automobile dealership.

The book is arranged chronologically, allowing the reader to share my experiences in the order they happened. While this makes for a better story, several readers of my early drafts suggested that I summarize the lessons I learned to make for easier reference. I thought that was a good idea, and I have included such a summary in Appendix A.

Most of the individuals mentioned in this book are still actively pursuing a career, so I have chosen to be sensitive in my use of proper names. If I in any way communicate a negative opinion about an individual's performance, or if I think a reader may see my comments as negative, then I do not identify the person by name. As I circulated early drafts of the book for comments, I learned that this convention has a disadvantage. People try to guess who I am talking about, and often they guess wrong. All I can do is caution the reader about making the same mistake. Of course, any judgment I make about another person is simply my opinion, and readers with a different perspective than my own may come to an entirely different conclusion.

During the writing of this book I contracted the services of two professional editors. The first, Kim Mullin, worked with me chapter by chapter as I wrote the book. No matter how horrible my initial draft, Kim always had a suggestion for how to fix it. Her efforts greatly improved this work and it has been a pleasure working with her.

Once the book was complete, Kristin Barendsen filled the role of copy editor. Her critical and experienced eye caught a number of errors that I had missed. Kristin also made numerous suggestions for improvement that went well beyond simple copy editing. I want to thank her for displaying initiative in so many ways.

Between the periods of writing and editing, I sought feedback from readers on each of the book's three major drafts much like I would for a piece of computer software. The breadth and quality of comments was remarkable and literally hundreds of changes resulted. I offer my sincerest thanks to everyone who helped me. In alphabetical order, they are: Scott Alberts, Monty Allen, Rob Armstrong, Mark Bailey, Darrell Boyle, Shirley Buccieri, Barry Chodak, John Cogan, Courtney Corda, Paul DeBry, Lauren Dutton, Robert Ferrara, John Glynn, Kaarin Graham, Gina Han, Dan Handalian, Jo-L Hendrickson, Connie Hess, Geof Indrajo, Chris Kocher, Claire LaBeaux, Igal Ladabaum, Jeff Levinsky, Fred MacDonald, Chuck McMinn, John Neer, Linda Hess Nelson, Lori Olds, Ann Peckenpaugh, Peter Robinson, Alma Rodoni, Heidi Roizen, and Andria Strelow.

I want to especially thank John Neer for helping me improve a chapter I found particularly difficult to write. The episode I was describing was very emotional for me, and John helped to bring the relevant issues into focus.

Once it was written and edited, Tina Lanese moved the book effortlessly through the process of publication. I told her that I wanted her to "just take care of it" and she did.

Of course, this book would not have been possible without the many contributions and sacrifices of Banner Blue's employees. Without them, there would have been nothing to write about. The fact that some Banner Blue employees are mentioned and some are not is more a matter of the lessons I was trying to illustrate than the relative contribution of any particular employee.

I also want to thank my parents, Phyllis and Richard Hess. They instilled in me the values that have served as a foundation for all my endeavors. Finally, more than anyone else, I want to thank my wife Connie and daughter Amber for allowing me to pursue my dreams. For that story, you need to read the book.

1

Should I Start My Own Company?

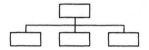

After several hours of intense design work, I feel good about the new database product I am building. Today I solved a number of engineering issues that had perplexed me for over a week. I cannot think of a more satisfying way to spend a Saturday morning.

I always enjoy stepping back to reflect on my creative accomplishments, studying how the pieces mesh to form something new and useful. But today my mind reflects back much farther than usual, to the time sixteen years ago when I founded Banner Blue Software. Driven by the need to control my own fate and excited by dreams of financial independence, I developed a product, grew a company, and fulfilled my dreams of wealth before I left just a few short years ago. So why am I working on a new product at all, let alone on a Saturday morning?

Most would call me a successful Silicon Valley entrepreneur, having bootstrapped a thriving company from little more than the ideas in my head and the money in my bank account. I had pursued wealth as the means to a new life with the freedom to pursue any endeavor. But after more than a decade of toil and a measure of good fortune I found the results of my achievement to be very different from my expectations. Since leaving my colleagues at Banner Blue, I have found that what makes me happy is not wealth or the freedom it brings, but working with bright people to analyze markets, create new products, and build a company. To my surprise, I enjoy the entrepreneurial process more than the final reward.

So I have come full circle. The product I work on today is for a new company, my second start-up, which I founded only months ago.

I have learned many lessons in the last sixteen years, and I want to share them with those who might also seek to explore the unknowns of their professional and personal lives. I want to offer my thoughts on what it is to be an entrepreneur, to found a successful start-up, to gain the wealth of your dreams—and to realize that what is really important is not wealth or how fast you obtain it, but the journey itself and how you conduct yourself along the way.

My path to entrepreneurship began many years before I founded my first company. Little did I know it at the time, but the activities I enjoyed as a youth honed the skills that were invaluable to me as a businessman.

Learning to Build Things

I love to create. My father was a mechanical engineer and our ancestors going back ten generations were machinists, mechanics, or locksmiths. Since I was old enough to hold a tool from my father's well-equipped shop, I have been creating and building hundreds of different things. I built a push-car for riding around the driveway, dozens of machines with my Erector Set, five Soap Box Derby racers, a firecracker cannon, what may well have been the first Christmas tree illuminated with fiber optics, numerous rockets, a crystal radio, several pieces of furniture, a cloud chamber for tracking subatomic particles, a refracting telescope with a German equatorial mount, a camera copy stand, a darkroom easel, a garage for my father, a microscope, and much, much more.

I always knew exactly what I wanted, and if I wanted something, I figured out a way to build it. Because I had limited funds, I became creative at scrounging for and using available parts in whatever I constructed. If I needed a tool that was too dangerous for me to use, my father would operate it for me with his hand on top of mine.

Sometimes my projects had problems. A neighborhood kid accidentally ran over me in my own push-car, leaving a two-inch scar on my right knee. It was the hard way to learn that the car needed brakes. Being extremely impatient, I hated to draw plans before I started building—it took too much time! My dad was an excellent draftsman and he always drew a sketch before building anything. He tried to teach me to do the same, but instead I liked to just visualize everything in my head, then hammer away. As the things I built became more and more complex, the lack of adequate plans became troublesome. I remember when I first tried my telescope mount. As I swung it around the polar axis, it clanged into another part of the mount and I had to rebuild it so I could look at the whole sky. Eventually, I learned what my father had been trying to teach me: it's important to have a plan.

My father also taught me about craftsmanship. "If a job is worth doing, it's worth doing right," he told me again and again. Both his plans and the things he constructed always looked much more polished than mine, and his work served as a goal for me. Every year I got closer to the high standard he set.

I did not know it then, but I was already displaying my most fundamental character traits: I knew what I wanted, I wanted it done right, and I wanted it yesterday. I was goal-oriented, competitive, and creative in my means of achievement.

I entered Stanford University as a chemistry major, but soon switched to engineering. Computers were still new at the time and they fascinated me, so I concentrated in product design and computer science. It seemed I could program a computer to do anything (except conjure up a date for the weekend), a powerful appeal to someone who likes to build things.

In other classes I was able to study the art of creating. One of my college instructors, Egon Loebner, taught me his analytical method for systematically inventing new things in any field. The local patent library provided source material for the class. In one exercise, I selected several existing patents for which I estimated the pool of potential inventors. I found that only a handful of individuals were likely to have the required combination of knowledge, skill in applying the knowledge, and motivation. This emphasized to me the importance of being the world expert in the chosen area of invention. Having an idea was the easy part. Understanding all existing and related inventions, separating new ideas from old, deciding what was possible, deciding what was valuable to someone, implementing the idea—those were the difficult things that only an expert could accomplish. I learned that doing my homework was as important as preparing a good set of plans.

Do I Have What It Takes?

Throughout my education during the 1960s and 1970s, I evaluated a variety of career opportunities, primarily in the areas of science and technology because those were my favorite subjects. During junior high school I wanted to become an aeronautical engineer; then in high school I settled on being a chemist. It was not until college that I first considered becoming an entrepreneur.

Vern Anderson, a Stanford instructor teaching a seminar called "Ethical Problems of American Businessmen," was the first person to put this idea in my head. Vern was a successful entrepreneur and his enthusiasm for starting a business shined through in every class. I also saw in Vern the financial independence that comes with a successful company. With my own company I could create new, unique products and attain the financial freedom that would allow me to pursue my other interests.

Although creative freedom and a big pot of money sounded pretty good, everyone else I knew worked for a large company, so entrepreneurship was uncharted territory. Vern's example to the contrary, dozens of articles in newspapers and popular magazines had formed my image of an entrepreneur. Most of these entrepreneurs had created giant companies (since giant companies are the ones that attract attention in the popular press), and as people, they did not seem to be much like me. Some were scientists or inventors with an obsession, others were performers or self-promoters, and many had become legends. I was not any of those things. I also wanted to raise a family, and I noted that many of these entrepreneurs had broken marriages and spoiled kids. While I liked the idea of being an entrepreneur, I was not sure that I could be successful. Vern did seem to be more like me, and he had a wonderful family, but he was only an example of one. Besides, and perhaps most importantly, I did not have a good idea for a product.

What I did have was lots of questions: What personal qualities does it take to found a successful business, and do I have them? What education and experience is the best preparation for becoming an entrepreneur? How do I find a good product idea? How do I obtain the money to start a company? Could I run a successful business and still have a normal family life?

If I wanted to be an entrepreneur, I had a great deal to learn. With the vague objective of starting my own company—a company doing or building what, I did not know—I began to educate myself.

Learning About Industry

After graduating in 1974, I took a job as a production supervisor in Intel's original semiconductor manufacturing plant, Fab 1, in Mountain View, California. Two of the best-known entrepreneurs in the industry, Robert Noyce and Gordon Moore, had founded Intel only five years earlier. The company's primary product was a semiconductor memory chip for use in computers. I accepted this position because I thought that learning to manage the twenty people in my group would be a good step toward starting my own company, and I certainly did receive many lessons.

One of the first things I had to handle was a layoff caused by poor business conditions. My manager, Lynn Brewer, had anticipated the need to reduce our workforce before we received any corporate directive, so we were able to transfer several people to a booming part of the company. Because of Lynn's prescience, I do not believe we actually had to terminate anyone, although many areas of the company did. Nonetheless, that experience made a lasting impression on me. Never again did I want to watch the frightened eyes of someone whose life was changing unexpectedly with a transfer to someplace they knew nothing about. In the future, I would always do all that I could to avoid repeating the experience.

I came from a different world than many of my employees. Most of them had families and a large number of them were immigrants from the Philippines, while I was a young, arrogant kid just out of college. It took me a while to learn that I could not do my job without the respect of key people, and it took me a while longer to realize that just being smart was not going to earn that respect. I found that I won more admiration baking pumpkin pies for a potluck dinner than I did when I set up the plant's new computer. Over time my employees and I learned that our motivations and desires in life were not as different as we had thought.

I also quickly learned the importance of discipline among my team because it was almost nonexistent when I started. At first, I tended to procrastinate about personnel problems, repressing my displeasure when someone was not performing. Gradually, however, I became much more proactive. I put troublemakers on formal, written warning and ultimately I had to fire several people. Day by day, my shift improved. I learned how to delegate authority and develop the skills of people who worked for me. I read several books about management and took a class about supervision, but I learned the most on the job.

After a year as a production supervisor, I received a promotion to run the entire afternoon shift in the plant, so I was the senior manager in the building after the executives went home for dinner. The wholesale change in staff reporting to me was an opportune learning experience. I found out that it was much easier to set a particular level of discipline from the outset than it was to start out relaxed and then try to increase the level of discipline over time. I must have been doing something right, because soon my subordinates were bringing me my favorite donuts and occasionally preparing a dinner for their bachelor boss.

Intel ran by focusing on objectives and meeting them, and this style was an excellent fit with my personality. As a production facility, we had shipment targets that we had to meet on a weekly basis. I enjoyed staying late until we had finished the job because it gave me a sense of accomplishment. At the time, there was almost no automation in the process and we hand-carried the semiconductor wafers we manufactured from machine to machine. One day I was personally carrying a box of wafers that we needed to meet our target for the week when I accidentally bumped into a piece of equipment. The wafers, whose value was equal to several months of my salary, fell to the floor, every single one shattering into tiny pieces.

Nothing like this had happened to a manager in my experience at Intel, but I knew the company was not afraid to fire someone. I also knew our manufacturing plant had not missed a production commitment since I began my job, and my accident had placed that record in jeopardy. These facts did nothing to help the knot in the pit of my stomach.

Surprisingly, no one expressed anger toward me, and instead of allowing me to be fired, the entire team rallied to save my skin. To replace those wafers and meet our shipment targets we had to pull a set of wafers from far back in the production process, performing many more operations on them than we typically did in the time we had available—yet we succeeded. This episode was a lesson in the value of a results-oriented business philosophy. Intel did not worry about blame; it just got the job done. Of course, my colleagues did not soon let me forget the episode; it was the source of much ribbing for many weeks to come.

Something else that I will never forget is the day that my boss Lynn received a note from legendary manager Andy Grove, then Intel's vice president of operations, about what he felt was our excessive consumption of sulfuric acid at one of the processing steps. On the one hand, I thought someone in his position should have better things to do than worry about twenty dollars in potential cost savings by someone three or four levels lower in the organization. Yet, I also knew that he sent the note to serve as an example of what he wanted us to pay attention to, and he was successful—we did begin to pay more attention. Later I would work under many managers too reticent to send that kind of message, if they even took the occasion to look at such levels of detail. Ultimately, my conclusion was that Andy got better results from his organization than the other managers did from theirs.

At Intel, I not only learned about business philosophies and how to manage people, but I also saw firsthand how technology moved from the development stage to production. In the space of two years we moved from heavy production of 1K random access memory chips, to production of 4K chips, to pre-production runs of 16K chips. All of the products we built used a metal-oxide semiconductor technology. Each transition was fraught with problems that engineers worked out one by one. This was another good lesson for me, because I saw that even in a well-managed company, technology development is not always a smooth process. Every day the developers used the scientific method of isolating the problem, hypothesizing a solution, and testing the hypothesis to move ever closer to a workable process.

While Intel struggled to develop its new process, the trade press hyped other new, supposedly superior technologies such as silicon-on-sapphire. It concerned me that Intel applied such a weak development effort to silicon-on-sapphire, but as time passed, silicon-on-sapphire never achieved any lasting importance for commercial products and Intel continued to grow. What I learned was that the trade press focused on the limited advantages of silicon-on-sapphire, and that they were unaware of the inherent manufacturing difficulties. At the same time, the trade press ignored the rapid improvements occurring in metal-oxide semiconductor technology that soon negated most advantages silicon-on-sapphire had to offer. Intel's management knew these things and invested their resources accordingly. So, I learned that the technology receiving the most publicity was not always the one that wins. In the future, I would often have to choose among different technologies and I would think back to these first lessons of how complex technologies evolve.

After two years at Intel, I had found that my results-oriented personality was a good fit in the business world, and I had learned innumerable management lessons. I also felt my steep learning curve was leveling off and I was no longer progressing toward my goal of starting my own business. So, I decided to leave Intel and return to school to obtain a Master of Business Administration (MBA) degree at Harvard.

At the same time, I was working on another important aspect of my life—the personal side. In April 1976, I began dating a woman I met at Intel, Connie Irish. People who know me do not use the word *romantic* to describe me, but Connie tells me I was exceptionally romantic during those months before I left for business school. She decided to move to Boston with me.

Transition: Business School, Marriage, and a New Job

While at Intel, I had mostly learned about manufacturing and management, but at business school, I finally saw all of the aspects of running a business. Marketing was new to me and especially interesting. Marketing classes taught me about determining the needs and wants of the customer, communicating the benefits of the product, and setting prices. At business school, I also found that I was better than almost anyone at making sense from a collection of numbers describing a business. Encouraged by my success, I became quite competitive at applying my analytical skills whenever I could.

Between the first and second year of business school, Connie and I married. Before the ceremony, we had come to an important agreement. She would help support me while in business school, then I would return the favor, supporting her while she completed her undergraduate degree. After our education was complete, we both wanted to have children and we reached an understanding that one of us, probably Connie, would stay home with them while they were young. We also may have discussed my plans to start a business, but in no great detail at that time.

Connie and I had a simple marriage ceremony at my parents' home in Ohio, attended by a number of friends, including an Intel contingent who came all the way from California. With another expensive year of business school looming ahead, an extravagant honeymoon was not in the budget, but we scraped together enough money to spend a wonderful week at Disney World in Florida before I started my summer job at Teradyne in Boston, Massachusetts.

After completing business school in 1978, I accepted a marketing job with Hewlett-Packard in Palo Alto, California, and Connie went back to school. The optoelectronics division I was to work for manufactured a variety of products based on light-emitting diodes (LEDs). I felt that this marketing job would give me a comprehensive overview of an entire business and balance well with my previous experience in manufacturing, thus putting me one step closer to having my own business. On the other hand, it was unlikely that I would find any entrepreneurial opportunities in the area of light-emitting diodes, so my decision to work for Hewlett-Packard reflected a trade-off.

Fortunately, my decision proved to be a wise one. One of the first things I became immersed in was the pricing of our products. Hewlett-Packard negotiated the pricing for the vast majority of large transactions. I participated in hundreds of deals, developing a "street sense" for qualifying the people with whom we did business—were they interested in a long-term relationship or just looking for the cheapest price today before switching to our competitors tomorrow? It was a great introduction to an entirely new aspect of running a business.

The Power of Analysis

At Hewlett-Packard I also had the opportunity to test my analytical skills on real-world business situations, and I found that I enjoyed modeling market behavior. I describe my technique in detail, because it is adaptable to many situations, and it also provides an interesting insight into my personality.

Building a model of market behavior has some similarity to assembling a puzzle. Imagine trying to assemble a jigsaw puzzle of a house. You begin by picking out all of the pieces with at least one straight side; these comprise the border of the puzzle. Then, staring at the ultimate objective, a picture of the completed puzzle on the cover of the package, you might look for a unique feature of the house, let's say a chimney. Sorting through the immense pile of pieces, you search for those that contain a portion of the chimney. Gradually, the chimney takes shape. When a piece does not fit, you try another and another. After roughing out the chimney, you move on to another unique feature, a door or a window, and so the process repeats. To summarize, assembling a puzzle involves finding the *border*, the edge of the picture; it involves *analysis*, breaking the picture into smaller features that are easier to deal with; and it involves *iteration*, repetitively trying new pieces when one does not fit.

Constructing a business model is also a puzzle, and assembling it involves a similar process of defining a border, performing analysis, and iterating theories. Once completed, the model represents a useful picture analogous to the jigsaw puzzle, in this case an abstract picture of how the business can improve itself. The model might suggest new product features desired by customers, new distribution channels where customers would prefer to purchase, or markets the company should avoid. Unfortunately, when building a business model, the picture you seek is not on a box. You can describe every market with many equally valid models, yet have no a priori idea which one is best. Because there is more than one correct answer, creativity becomes as important as analysis in finding the best solution.

When I examine a market, my goal is to find a picture that gives me an advantage over the one used by competitors, a picture that indicates what action I should take. Once I have this picture, I can use it to formulate a strategy for beating my competitors—a vision.

For example, while I was working with light-emitting diode products at Hewlett-Packard, my manager assigned me the task of analyzing competitive technologies for constructing display devices. Our business had been under intense pricing pressure from competitors manufacturing vacuum fluorescent and liquid crystal displays (LCDs). We needed to understand the impact of those technologies several years into the future. Would light-emitting diode displays be able to compete, or would this large segment of our business disappear? The situation was so urgent that the division manager assigned a task force of individuals to assist me.

My manager's assignment provided the border for my puzzle. My team collected and organized detailed technical information about our own products and those of competitors. This information represented the pieces in our puzzle. Then we began a process of analysis lasting a number of weeks.

Traditional methods of analyzing the display market revolved around the type of information being displayed, the type of device using the display, and the geographical location of our customers. Some products displayed only numbers, as would a digital clock.

Others displayed both numbers and letters, as required by most computer applications. Asian markets building low-cost consumer products were extremely price sensitive. These traditional methods of analyzing the display market showed no meaningful technology trends, so they had limited value in solving my puzzle. At the time, most of the competing technologies had a successful presence in each of these markets. What I wanted to know was which technologies would be successful in the *future,* and why.

If in doubt about how to analyze something, I drive down to the lowest possible level in search of an element *common* to all the pieces. Then I compare each of the pieces, looking for a *difference* in the behavior of the common element. Finally, I come back up level by level, analyzing each one for interesting information. I use the word *level* to signify a layer in a hierarchical structure. For example, if our jigsaw puzzle of a house had four chimneys instead of just one, I would have examined the chimneys at a lower, more detailed level. Perhaps the chimneys differ in their construction material or architectural detail. If so, I could sort the puzzle pieces accordingly.

In the case of display technologies, I examined several alternatives before provisionally deciding that the lowest useful level of analysis was the picture element. A picture element is the smallest dot or line that, when combined with other dots or lines, appears as a number or character on the display. Many digital clocks use displays comprising seven line segments, or picture elements, for each possible digit. If the clock activates two vertical picture elements, one on top of the other, the viewer sees the numeral 1. If the clock activates all seven picture elements, the viewer sees an 8.

Having identified picture elements as a very low-level feature common to all display technologies, the next step was to compare picture elements in some enlightening way to uncover differences in their behavior from one technology to another.[1] Comparing the cost for a picture element in each of the different technologies seemed like a natural thing to do. I found that the cost per picture element across the different technologies seemed somehow related to the height of the complete character, but the data was confusing. Sometimes one technology was the cost leader, sometimes another, and I could not predict which one it would be. In other words, the pieces of the puz-

---

[1] It is helpful that there are not many things to compare to at a sufficiently low level of analysis. There are the six primary dimensions from physics (time, mass, length, temperature, voltage, and charge), bits and bytes from computer science, people (as in per capita), and, of course, there is always money.

zle did not fit together, so I began to iterate. I did not record the many combinations I tried, but I worked on the problem for several weeks. I kept iterating. Finally, I did some back-of-the-envelope calculations, looking at the area of each character (height times width). Bingo!

After I discovered this relationship, the underlying cause was obvious to me. Some of the display technologies have a manufacturing process such that a fixed area of the display, say one square centimeter, costs about the same amount of money no matter how many picture elements the manufacturer jams into that space. As the resolution of these displays increased, the cost of the entire display would stay relatively flat while the cost for each picture element would fall (more picture elements in the same area). Other display technologies, like Hewlett-Packard's light-emitting diodes, had a manufacturing process that was almost independent of the area. Every light-emitting diode picture element cost about the same amount of money, regardless of the area of the display. So, as the resolution of a light-emitting diode display increased, the cost would skyrocket, depending on how many picture elements the designer added.

It took me weeks to discover this fact because relatively low resolution clock and calculator displays comprised the bulk of the market at the time. It just so happened that the costs of the various technologies were roughly equivalent at this low resolution, hiding the likely behavior of the technologies as the market evolved.

With this low-level insight in hand, I analyzed progressively higher levels of the market. From picture elements I moved up to examine the market for display components, sub-assemblies, and products actually shipped to end users: clocks, scientific instruments, and computers. All evidence pointed to strong demand for higher and higher display resolution—more picture elements in a fixed area.

I had my team polish up the numbers and prepared a presentation for my manager. By solving the puzzle and building a model, I had found a picture of the market that enabled me to create a strategy for a competitive advantage. I recommended that Hewlett-Packard abandon efforts to develop high-resolution light-emitting diode displays. We would find ourselves falling farther behind in cost no matter how hard we worked and no matter how great our achievements. If the company wanted to enter the fast-growing, high-resolution markets, we would have to develop an alternative display technology.

This kind of work played to my analytical strengths, my creativity, and my personality. Fitting puzzle pieces together is an example of pattern matching, and I have an innate desire to establish patterns in almost anything I observe. Because of my impatience, I do not belabor any one prospective pattern. I try another and another until a pattern fits. At the same time, I am comfortable with the inherent uncertainty of assembling a puzzle without prior knowledge of the picture. If one attempt fails it does not bother me—I am confident I will succeed with my next try.

My initial success in modeling markets gave me additional confidence and spurred me to try solving more complex problems. Then, gradually, all of this experience taught me what to look for, magnifying my initial advantage. The quality of information often determines my success, but when a pattern appears or a model coalesces, to me it is a thing of tremendous beauty.

From time to time, I used my weekends to investigate business possibilities, constructing market models in other industries. I had lunch with my instructor from Stanford, Vern Anderson, and he suggested that software was an ideal market for an entrepreneur because the monetary investment required to start a software company was exceptionally low.

I had always loved working with computers, and as I studied different business opportunities, I found myself dwelling on Vern's suggestion. So, to learn more about software firsthand, in 1981 I transferred to a division of Hewlett-Packard that manufactured minicomputer software. While I was there, the personal computer revolution took root.

Pervasive Newness—The Personal Computer Revolution

For the next three years I learned all I could about personal computer software. I regularly read a collection of trade journals, and I also read books and played with all the software I could find. I attended trade shows where computer and software manufacturers demonstrated their wares, and conferences where industry luminaries described how they became successful. As part of my job at Hewlett-Packard I talked with dozens of customers about their needs for office software and their experiences with products they already owned. I also looked at alternative ways to categorize the needs of the market and prepared dozens of sales forecasts.

My forecasts convinced me that the personal computer software industry was only beginning its growth. An S-curve (with size on the vertical axis and time on the horizontal axis) describes the growth of almost anything, whether biological, physical, or economic. Growth starts erratically as the new thing fights for a toehold in its environment. If successfully established in spite of the odds against it, growth accelerates exponentially. The new thing becomes a feature of the environment against which other new things must compete. Eventually, the new thing approaches its proper size and growth slows.

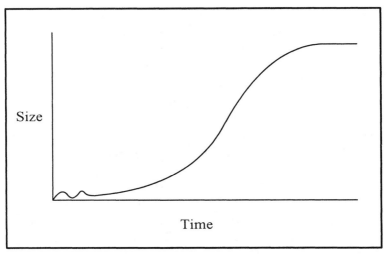

FIG. 1. AN S-CURVE DESCRIBES THE GROWTH OF ALMOST ANYTHING.

Over the course of the previous several years, I had graphed and analyzed dozens of markets, including automobiles, appliances, and electric power production. My experience from those exercises told me that explosive growth of short duration defines a fad, and fads generally do not obtain great size relative to the economy. In 1982, the personal computer software industry had already exceeded the duration of a fad. Instead, its growth rate and duration suggested that it was at the lower part of the S-curve. I concluded that it should grow for decades, becoming a significant component of the economy.

At this time, the personal computer software industry comprised hundreds of young companies, seemingly one on every block. Among the oldest was Microsoft, established in the mid-1970s, but the vast majority were less than five years old. Perhaps ten of these companies had as many as a hundred employees, none had a thousand. The typical company had fewer than ten employees, and every day seemed to bring a new start-up. I especially enjoyed following Software Publishing Corporation because I knew some of the people who had left Hewlett-Packard to join the company and I had heard the company's high-energy founder, Fred Gibbons, speak about the economics of his business.

Growth estimates for the year 1982 showed the sales revenues of Microsoft increasing over 50 percent, Digital Research over 200 percent, and Software Publishing Corporation over 400 percent. The average sales growth of all personal computer software companies combined probably exceeded 100 percent. Driving the growth was a diverse collection of products, strategies, and competencies that represented a market of unique vitality. The more I studied the industry, the more it appealed to me.

Fast growth excited me because it was synonymous with capital appreciation. Rapid sales increases meant soaring company valuations and wealth for the founders—and the desire to create wealth remained my primary reason for wanting to become an entrepreneur. I thought that if I concentrated on becoming independently wealthy as a young man, I would later have the freedom to pursue my other interests—astronomy, photography, history, philosophy, public policy, and building things—without concern for the income they might generate. At the time, I was certain that I would want to enter government in some capacity after I completed my business career. My strategy was the classic one of deferred gratification.

Gold-rush analogies were abundant among my colleagues. It seemed that everyone else in Silicon Valley also wanted to strike it rich. They joined start-up companies in return for a big block of stock options. If the company went public, they made a fortune, at least by their standards. Of course, stories about fool's gold were also common. Many companies attempting to capitalize on this market failed; ironically, they were often the companies in which financiers had invested the most. Personally, I never considered that I might fail.

Notwithstanding my desire for wealth, the *pervasive newness* of the personal computer software industry also attracted me. Newness permeated every aspect of the industry as entrepreneurs were creating all the elements from scratch. To many individuals this type of atmosphere was scary, but we all obtain satisfaction from some activities where others may only find apprehension—skydiving, traveling in distant countries, performing on stage. To me, pervasive newness was an opportunity to innovate and express my creativity.

I realized that if I were to found a company in the personal computer industry at that time, I would have limited ability to establish the defining principles of the industry. It was too late to be a pioneer. At the same time, I occasionally worried that the computer software industry might be too complex to understand as thoroughly as other markets I had modeled. But, so long as the industry was chaotic, I felt I would have an advantage over others in figuring out the proper course to take. If I did not have a comprehensive understanding of the marketplace, at least I would have valuable insights. As far as I could tell, I was in the right place at the right time to capitalize on my professional strengths and to work creating products that I enjoyed.

Wanting to Have Children

Meanwhile Connie had been working extremely hard at San Jose State University, receiving a Bachelor of Science degree in Interior Design with Great Distinction. After graduating, she began her new career at Ambiance Associates, a firm that designed interiors for commercial buildings. We were hoping that she would become pregnant, but unfortunately that did not happen.

After a reasonable period of time, we consulted an infertility specialist and began a long, dehumanizing process to find the root of the problem. At one point, Connie was in the hospital for almost a week to correct something that "may or may not" have been the cause. The fertility field at that time was much more art—or, it seemed black magic—than science. Nonetheless, we kept at it, often attending appointments together for the various consultations and procedures, our hope fading a little bit with each one. Fortunately, our health insurance covered most of the expense. Every time I blew out the candles on my birthday cake, pulled a turkey wishbone, or prayed, I was hoping for children.

The Final Impetus

During 1982, a friend and I seriously considered starting a company to produce software that would train people how to use other software they had purchased. But, I had doubts about the long-term viability of the software training market, so I decided not to take the plunge. Then in 1983 I became frustrated with my manager at Hewlett-Packard and decided to leave, although at the time I still did not feel ready to start my own company.

Instead, I decided to join Symantec, a company with an exciting product idea to create a personal computer database program that would respond to natural language queries. Instead of learning how to operate a complex program, Symantec offered users the promise of typing simple questions like, "How many widgets are in the warehouse?" Unfortunately, an exciting product idea turned out to be all that Symantec had during 1983.

Sometimes one sees the right course more clearly when the wrong one is available as a counter-example, so Symantec served as a valuable contrast for me. During the one year I worked at Symantec, the company suffered enormous management turnover, having two different presidents and three different engineering leaders. Unfocused and totally dysfunctional, the company wrote no shippable programming code during the entire time that I was there, even though as many as twenty-five engineers were on staff. The venture capitalist Pierre Lamond concluded that the company was unwilling or unable to do the things start-ups had to do. He said during a fundraising presentation we made, "You are a start-up in disguise."

In my opinion, Symantec had far too many people who simply did not know how to do the tasks required for success. Reflecting the immaturity of the personal computer software industry at that time, Symantec's well-regarded senior managers had tasted success at other organizations, but as was quite common, they left to join Symantec without knowing the recipe for duplicating that success. Perhaps they had just been lucky in their previous employment. Whatever the case, I am not a gambler—I wanted to succeed through calculation.

My studies at business school, my experience at Intel and Hewlett-Packard, and my readings in business publications had refined my image of a successful entrepreneur. In the first place, the successful high-technology entrepreneur understood the technology. Andy Grove at Intel literally wrote the book, *Physics and Technology of Semiconductor Devices*, and even late in his career, Bill Hewlett initiated and mentored the project to build the first scientific handheld calculator to fully replace the slide rule, the HP-35. In the personal computer software industry, both Bill Gates of Microsoft and Mitch Kapor of Lotus Development had written some of the code in their products. Technology was driving the pervasive changes in the industry and a technical background gave the entrepreneur an advantage in establishing a vision. Because these entrepreneurs understood the underlying technology, they knew what they *could* build. They also had proved that they understood the needs of their customers, thus they knew what they *should* build. Finally, they had developed a process for turning their ideas into products.

I had never been the general manager of any organization, and I had not performed many of the important tasks that founding a company would require. Several of the Symantec executives had. What made me think that I would be more successful than they were? Did I know the recipe? I was increasingly confident that I did.

I observed that many of Symantec's problems stemmed from a lack of vision. The product concept was very exciting, but soon after my arrival, the work of a marketing colleague showed that the underlying technology was incapable of meeting some very basic customer requirements. From that point on, Symantec had a new and different strategy on a regular, almost weekly basis. In other words, the vision was not complete to begin with and the management response to the deficiency communicated uncertainty rather than improvement, chaos rather than stability. It was impossible to ship a product if one day the company wanted a product that performed one function and the next day decided the product should do something entirely different. It was my belief that I could use my analytical skills to create a complete vision, avoiding the trap that had captured Symantec.

The contrast between Hewlett-Packard and Symantec also crystallized my business values, particularly in the areas of personnel policies and spending. As strategies changed, layoffs at Symantec were frequent and poorly planned. They hired one employee, laid him off, re-hired him, and laid him off again in the space of several months. This disregard for individuals was repugnant to me. Hewlett-Packard would have done everything possible to avoid a layoff. At the same time, I saw innumerable examples of excess at Symantec. There was unproductive spending for toys like projection TVs and extravagant amounts of office space far before the company required it. I simply would not run a company in this fashion. I could only hope that my philosophy would aid my success.

As Symantec struggled, employees increasingly shifted their allegiance from management to the venture capitalists who had funded the company. Several employees openly told me that a manager might leave tomorrow, but Symantec's venture capitalists would be around forever, perhaps at the very next company at which the employee worked.

Indeed, venture capitalists of outstanding reputation had funded Symantec and they were a constant source of ideas for correcting the company's myriad problems. Many of the ideas were good, some bad. The venture capitalists expected the executives of the company to take the good ideas and reject the bad, but the executives appeared to take them all. Rather than filtering input from the financiers, they swallowed it whole. A self-reinforcing spiral ensued where management abrogated control to the venture capitalists who were trying to protect their investment, causing even more employees to shift allegiance. I could not imagine trying to manage a company in such an environment, with loyalties split between the executives on the inside and investors on the outside.

Day by day, I was learning a crucial personal lesson—the importance of control to my happiness. I had spent years learning about business and the personal computer software market. Daily, my confidence in my own judgment increased, but at Symantec I was unable to exercise it. Often I felt that I knew what to do, but I rarely had the freedom to act. As I witnessed the horrible scene of a management team that had lost control, I concluded that it was a fate even worse than never having had control in the first place.

I wanted to be in charge. I wanted to create my own world. My Symantec experience taught me that control was as important as creation.

Without committing myself to leave Symantec, I actively began preparing to found my own company. I wanted a good option if Symantec did not turn around. I had no intention of building a product that competed with anything contemplated by Symantec; therefore, I saw no conflict of interest and no need to tell them what I was doing in my spare time.

Deciding to Pull Myself Up by the Bootstraps

Most new companies have outside investors of one kind or another, perhaps as many as three companies out of four. Some number of those without investors would dearly like to have them, but they simply cannot obtain funding for one reason or another.

Technology companies are no different, and Symantec's strategy was quite typical—hand over a large equity stake to venture capitalists in return for cash. Some of the earliest personal computer software companies had started without outside investors, but self-funding was becoming increasingly rare among new entrants to the market like Symantec. These newer companies came to the conclusion that the increasingly crowded marketplace required elaborate products followed by heavy spending to establish distribution. Lotus Development had utilized large amounts of capital to launch its product 1-2-3.

Yet, my desire to retain control biased me against using venture capital. I did not formally analyze my needs for financing. My *feelings* about this matter were just that—instinctive and somewhat emotional, based as they were on my experiences at Symantec. Although self-financing never seems to be in favor, I certainly would not be the first person to try it. Perhaps naively, I was comfortable bucking the conventional wisdom about what it took to start a software company.

The term for a company founded with no outside investors and minimal resources is a *bootstrap*. Clearly, bootstrapping the company would establish constraints on the type of product I could offer and the way I could sell it, but to me, it seemed like a fair trade-off in return for complete control over my company.

During February and March of 1984, my business approach started taking form. I decided that in order to do a bootstrap, my product needed to meet several important criteria:

1. I wanted it to be a unique, creative product first in its market niche.

2. I wanted it to create obvious value for the user by saving large quantities of time in an important task—a productivity product that the customer was waiting for someone to offer.

   It would have been expensive to convince a customer they had a problem when they did not already know it, and money was something I did not have. Several heavily capitalized software companies had recently failed because of that exact strategy, trying to persuade people to do something new, just because their product made it easy. On the other hand, ThinkTank, a niche program that automated the creation and editing of common outlines, was enjoying success because customers were looking for a better tool to perform that task. What I wanted was a productivity tool for a job that people performed in spite of the job's difficulty. The absence of direct competitors and obvious customer value would help the product sell itself.

3. The product also had to be buildable in about one work year. I did not have enough money for anything more complex.

There were also market reasons to keep the product simple. The combination of rapid market changes, no competition, and high customer need would permit me the luxury of a minimalist product strategy. I could design an elegant, simple product, then ship it quickly. The objective was to include only features essential to the primary task of the software, ruthlessly excluding anything that was not a certain requirement of the target user. I would not need to worry about meeting the features of a competitor, because there would not be one. Then, I would aggressively and proactively obtain feedback from users to learn the strengths and weaknesses of the product. Following that, I would rapidly revise and ship a new version of the product, continuing this process indefinitely.

If instead I tried to develop a perfect, robust product, the risk grew that development time would exceed the validity of my original market insight. While vainly trying to create perfection, a competitor would come to market first, the customer would meet his needs in some other way, or like Symantec I would bite off more than I could chew. My experience had taught me that it was far better to keep things simple.

Additionally, but unrelated to my bootstrap financing, I wanted the product to have high performance. Responsiveness and interactivity were key ingredients in making personal computers successful against larger, time-shared computers.

Although I have learned many requirements, advantages, and disadvantages of a bootstrap since the time I formulated these criteria, they form the core of my product thinking to this day.

Searching for product ideas, I looked at existing software made for both larger computers and smaller handheld calculators. I ana-

lyzed my experience at Hewlett-Packard and as a computer user myself. The result was a list that included possible programs to automate business travel expense reports, produce office organization
charts, prepare timesheets, make calendars, help control a computer
printer, print project schedules in the form known as a GANTT chart,
assist in preparing salary evaluations, print graph paper, prepare bul-
let charts for corporate presentations, and make maps. I also considered a clock program and a collection of financial utilities or calculators. Some of these ideas were not first in their niche, still others
would not result in significant time savings. Some would take too
long to develop, some not long enough, meaning that it would be too
easy for a competitor to imitate. The clear winner was a program to
make office organization charts. I called it OrgChart.

An organization chart consists of a group of boxes, each containing the name and title of an individual in the organization. A line
connects each individual to his manager's box. These hierarchical
diagrams are simple, but were difficult to produce using the tools of
that era. At the time, most people drew organization charts using a
pen and ruler. Then they used a typewriter to add the names and titles. A few people used word processors, spreadsheet programs, or
crude drawing programs to prepare the charts.

While I was at Hewlett-Packard, I had seen the need for
OrgChart in several contexts. Hewlett-Packard used organization
charts extensively, so I had firsthand knowledge of how and why
someone produces such charts. I had even made them myself. Hewlett-Packard also produced a software and hardware product combination for creating box and line diagrams, with the resulting chart
printed on a pen plotter. You had to manually place every box, word,
and line, so it was slow, but the results looked very professional,
much better than drawing by hand. Obviously, the product could
make organization charts and that's why many customers purchased
it—in spite of a cost equal to about six months of an engineer's salary.

To me, the number of customers purchasing Hewlett-Packard's
time-consuming, expensive package suggested a large, latent demand
for a product to produce organization charts. Hewlett-Packard had
toyed with the idea of a minicomputer program specifically to make
these charts, but nothing ever came of it.

Other companies had produced drawing programs for personal
computers similar to the one manufactured by Hewlett-Packard. For
example, Decision Resources had introduced a program called Dia-

gram Master that they marketed for the production of flow charts, organization charts, and decision-tree diagrams. I do not recall the details of the product, but I thought this multi-purpose drawing program was too expensive and poorly suited for producing organization charts, in spite of the manufacturer's claims. I never considered it a viable competitor to what I envisioned.

I was confident that a personal computer program could automate the drawing of boxes and lines around the names and titles input by the user. I would price the product so that it would cost a day's pay, about 20 percent of the cost of word processing and spreadsheet software and a tiny fraction of what Hewlett-Packard charged for its drawing program. Because it would run on a customer's existing personal computer hardware, OrgChart would be ten times more cost-effective than any other solution, no matter how a customer evaluated the proposition. I knew that when choosing a tool, people often turn to the most familiar one even if it does a poor job. I needed to offer a solution that was ten times cheaper to counter this inertia. If OrgChart offered superior results *and* dramatic cost-savings, then it would sell itself. Nothing less would suffice.

"Sell itself?" It was dangerous to conclude that my product would do this. At the time there was no software similar to OrgChart. It was both a new idea and a new category. The closest successful programs were vaguely grouped as "accessories": ProKey was a "macro" program to store repetitive keystrokes, Norton Utilities was famous for the capability to unerase mistakenly erased files, Sideways allowed spreadsheets to be printed in landscape orientation on the page (printers of the time could not do this themselves), Banner Maker was for creating signs, Copy II PC allowed the user to duplicate copy-protected software, Micro Cookbook was a recipe program, and there were some calculator programs.

The only thing these programs had in common was their price, which was in the range I was contemplating for OrgChart. Collectively, the accessory programs represented about 5 percent of the software market and that share was growing. Copy II PC was by far the most successful of the group, with Sideways a distant second. Of course, these two programs were also the least similar to OrgChart.

It was also difficult to obtain distribution for these products. Computer stores only wanted to sell hardware and high-priced software. However, in October of 1983 Software Publishing Corporation had started a catalog called "Power Up," carrying only accessory software such as these programs. At the time I had no information about their level of success, but I was watching them carefully.

In the absence of successful products to emulate, I was betting on a well-educated hunch. My analysis of the market told me that the environment would change. As the number of computer users grew and their experience increased, I believed that niches like making organizational charts would become good business opportunities. Several months later I took the time to formalize this thinking, but for now my hunch was good enough. I was having fun and I started to design my product.

The next year was a period of intense and highly varied work that I enjoyed almost without exception. Because I had chosen to do a bootstrap, my limited funds required me to learn and do things on my own rather than hire expensive employees and consultants. Over the next several months I would investigate the features required by the product, design the product, recruit someone to program the product, prepare a budget, analyze the market, and learn to program, all while continuing my day job and trying to have children.

Because I love to learn about and create new things, this exhausting list actually represents one of the most fulfilling periods of my life. I was embarking on my largest creation up to that time, and almost every day brought a renewed sense of accomplishment. The details about this time period illustrate not only the intensity of the work, but also some of the lessons applicable to a wide range of start-ups.

The Product Development Life Cycle

To turn an idea into a finished product, technology companies follow a sequence of steps called a *product development life cycle*. Each step in the product development life cycle consists of a document, such as a design specification, or a procedure, such as a reliability test. Each step moves the product incrementally towards completion. Because the personal computer software industry was so new it had no consensus on the steps in the life cycle, so I chose to loosely follow the life cycle developed by Hewlett-Packard for its minicomputer software.[2]   Hewlett-Packard's process called for steps to investigate, design, code, and test the product.

In April of 1984, I wrote the product requirements document for OrgChart, a document which Hewlett-Packard would have considered part of their investigation phase. It was concise and to the point:

PRODUCT DESCRIPTION

OrgChart is a tool optimized for one specific task—making organization charts.

Organization charts are a universal requirement of modern business. Their production is an ideal application of the personal computer, yet the market is now poorly served. With OrgChart the user should be able to achieve substantial time savings over manual and existing computer methods when the chart is first constructed. Even greater time savings are possible when the chart is subsequently edited.

OrgChart has three major modules: a tree editor, an automatic formatter, and a printer/plotter driver. The tree editor is analogous to a text editor; however, it operates on nodes and branches, the stuff of an organization chart, instead of words and paragraphs. Hiring and firing, the insertion or deletion of a node, is comparable to a text editor's insertion or deletion of a word. Transferring a department, the movement of a branch, is comparable to a text editor's block move, and so forth. In addition to capabilities such as these, the editor provides the means to navigate about the chart inter- and intra-level. This special editor makes it simple for the user to change or even do "what ifs" with the organization's structure.

The automatic formatter follows a set of built-in rules to lay out the chart without user intervention (although several defaults may be specified in advance by the user). This module lets the computer do what it does best—math.

The third module, the printer/plotter driver, supports output of the chart to popular hard copy devices.

COMPETITION

Competitive products are exclusively of the "You draw it!" variety. Approximately 15 are currently on the market. These products treat the computer as a new medium to draw on; this is fine

---

[2] Over time, Banner Blue evolved the product development life cycle to closely match our needs. Appendix B contains a description of the development process as it came to be in maturity.

for some applications but poorly serves those who want to make an organization chart. The text processor is again a good analogy. Imagine how unsatisfied one would be if a text processor only recorded handwriting on a graphics tablet. Input would be as slow as writing on paper, probably slower. Editing would be next to impossible; erasing and re-entering would be the rule. To aid in alignment the product would draw horizontal lines on the screen! Of course this type of text processor would be unsatisfactory, just as the current organization chart tools are. To make matters worse, existing hardware has a screen too small and resolution too coarse to allow anything but a small piece of the chart to be legibly viewed at one time. OrgChart rectifies all of these deficiencies because of its superior metaphor.

MARKET OPPORTUNITY

By the close of 1984 the installed base of IBM personal computers and compatibles will be 3 million units and monthly sales will approach 200,000. Most systems are in the hands of business users. These numbers make even niche markets financially appealing.

OrgChart has the opportunity to be a totally unique product that performs a task required of almost every manager or his/her secretary. This market is smaller than that for general purpose productivity tools such as spreadsheets, but the lack of viable competition and overall size of the personal computer market makes it highly attractive for a small software company. Entry costs should be low.

DESIGN OBJECTIVES

Three objectives dominate the development of OrgChart: quality of output, ease of learning, and performance. The need for high-quality output is self-evident—these charts are being made for presentation purposes and nothing else. Since the product may be used infrequently relative to others, ease of learning/relearning must take precedence over ease of use. This objective can be met through craftsmanship, emulation of already popular user interfaces, and thorough prototyping. Fortunately, OrgChart's text editor metaphor inherently provides substantial improvements in ease of use over its competitors. Finally, as with all personal computer products, performance is of primary concern, especially of the user interface.

In a tabular format, the product requirements document went on to describe minimum specifications in eighteen different areas, including chart capacity, organizational structures, reporting relationships between employees, and automated procedures for sizing the chart to the space available. A second column listed optional requirements in descending order of importance: important, highly desirable, and desirable. A sample organization chart showed key terminology.

It was now May 1984. With the product requirements document complete, I began writing the first draft of the external product specification, one of the most important design documents in the product development life cycle. An external product specification describes the operation of the product from the user's viewpoint. For OrgChart it also specified the hard copy output. I did not review the external product specification with my father, but it would have pleased him to see that I was finally drawing up plans before I began to build.

The external product specification showed drawings of each screen in the program as it would appear to the user. I meticulously mapped out the behavior of every key the user could press in response to each screen (at that time the keyboard was the only means for interacting with mainstream business software). Some inputs led to incorrect or out-of-range conditions and I identified these potential error conditions so that the software could handle them properly. The external product specification also described every command the user could invoke with a menu or special keys. Editing commands permitted easy updates to a chart. Printing commands gave the user control over a chart's appearance.

In order for the program to automatically draw professional-looking charts, the external product specification specified forty-three rules for producing an organization chart, most of which I formulated after examining dozens of sample charts (I actually found a book on organization charts at the Stanford library). For example, one rule stated, "At a given level, all boxes are the same size."

Creating the design for a totally new product in a new, niche category offered many challenges, but I enjoyed every one of them. Software was the ultimate Erector Set! For example, it was not obvious what editing features a tree editor should have. What if I left out an important one? I used the process of analogy to ensure that I had a complete design. I listed all the editing features of a typical word processor, which was a class of software over a decade old and well-refined in comparison to other personal computer software. Then in a second column I specified the analogous tree editor function, if any. Of course, the tree editor also had some unique features. For example, the concept of promoting a box from one level to another did not exist in a word processor of the time, because text was linear, not hierarchical.

In June I sought comments on the draft product requirements document and external product specification from a colleague at Hewlett-Packard, Wayne Chin. Wayne did not like some of the limitations I had specified, such as a maximum of twenty-five characters for each individual's name. "Hate to have limitations," he wrote. This was a prescient comment that I later wished I had heeded. All in all, however, he thought the documents looked good.

One of my motives for having Wayne review the documents was to interest him in doing the programming. Unfortunately, he enjoyed the security of his position at Hewlett-Packard. OrgChart was too risky for him to quit his job and too big a project to accomplish in his limited spare time.

Next I prepared a budget. In anticipation of starting a company, I had been saving money to the point of causing friction with Connie. She felt I was being obsessive. In a way, because I had chosen to do a bootstrap, Connie was my investor. The money that I put into the company was money that we could have spent on other things. For me to start a company she had to defer gratification, and for that reason her assent to my plan was important for our marriage.

I began an open dialog, essentially a financial negotiation, with Connie about quitting my job and starting a company. Connie insisted that I agree to keep a cushion in our savings no matter what happened. It was okay for me to start a business, but she did not want to risk losing our home. I readily agreed, obtaining Connie's full support for my start-up. Allowing for these adjustments, my budget showed that I had about a year to ship a product. It surprised me to see how long we could survive without income when I did not have to pay income taxes. Savings were after-tax dollars; they bought much more than a dollar of salary did. It also occurred to me at this time that taking a leave of absence from Symantec rather than quitting outright would reduce my risk even more, but I was not ready to take this final step just yet.

At that time, I saw my position as one of tremendous freedom. In the past, I had viewed being fired as equivalent to failure, but now I consciously thought about how it would be a blessing in disguise, forcing me to do what I was not quite ready to do on my own—start a company.

The work became more technical as my venture progressed. My first formal schedule called for a product mock-up, a study of computer organization and data structures, self-instruction in the C programming language, a more rigorous software market analysis, selection of a programmer, and a preliminary design of the internal structure of the program. I wanted to complete this work by the end of September.

Although it was not on my schedule, I started thinking about a name for my company. I did not want a coined name, the fad at the time being made-up words ending with an "x," like "Xidex." Quite independently of my company planning, I had done some genealogical research at the Stanford Library to help my mother, and found an obituary of my great-grandfather, George Franklin Hess. Through this obituary, I discovered that George had been superintendent of motive power for the Wabash Railroad. It turned out that my manager at Symantec was a railroad buff, so he loaned me a book about the Wabash featuring photographs of many trains. The convention was to name trains and the Wabash was quite creative in that regard, with names like the *Blue Bird*, the *Detroit Arrow*, the *Banner Blue Limited*, and many more. The name that stuck in my mind was *Banner Blue*. I thought it was catchy and I liked the idea of a family connection for my company's name. I decided Banner Blue was it.

Meanwhile, I was still working long hours at Symantec. Because of the company's many problems, executives worried about good people leaving. I had not told anyone at Symantec about my OrgChart project, so when the chief executive officer decided to chat with me about my career plans, he caught me off guard, and I was somewhat uncomfortable. During our conversation, he asked if I would commit to stay at Symantec if he fired a particularly incompetent senior manager who had been a significant factor in the company's lack of success. I did not want to divulge my moonlighting on OrgChart, and I could not think fast enough to come up with anything else to say—so I answered affirmatively. Given my advanced progress with OrgChart, this was a poor course to choose, for every day was bringing me closer to resignation. I had let the chief executive officer extract a commitment I did not want to make and was unlikely to keep.

In retrospect, I simply should have disclosed that I was working to start my own company, or at the very least I should have declined

to make a commitment about my continued employment. Since my
days at Symantec I have often been on the other side of similar situations. Many people naturally fear what will happen if they discuss
entrepreneurial ambitions or a career change with their manager. On
the contrary, an employee gains my respect when he tells me his
plans and loses my confidence when he dissembles. If you are
working with honest people, it pays to be open and honest with them.
I did the wrong thing in this case.

On July 8, 1984, I completed the first mock-up of OrgChart. It
showed exactly how OrgChart would look, but had no smarts. I used
a scripting program to display a series of screens on the computer in a
predetermined sequence. Any keystroke advanced the simulation to
the next screen. Despite its limitations, I could step through several
operations and obtain feedback from others about how the program
behaved. As it turned out, it uncovered an important flaw in my design. When a customer entered data about the organization, the user
interface was too much like a static, paper form, making it difficult to
know what portion of the chart the program displayed at any given
moment. As a result the user was unsure how to proceed from one
step to the next. One of my highest three objectives was ease of
learning, so I would have to make improvements.

Preparing a Formal Market Analysis

While I considered an improved design, I was also working on my
software market analysis. Fortunately the analysis supported my earlier hunch about what was happening. According to Michael Porter
in his book *Competitive Strategy*, the state of competition in an industry depends on five basic forces: the threat of new entrants, the
threat of substitute products, the bargaining power of buyers, the bargaining power of suppliers, and rivalry among existing firms. The
relative strength of these forces determines the industry's ultimate
profit potential. I decided to analyze the state of the personal computer software industry along these lines, then examine likely shifts
in the same forces.

During 1984, the industry was wildly profitable. From my eight-
page analysis I expected profits to level off, although they could remain high in some market niches. I also thought the biggest opportunities were available to people who opened new market segments,
because the barriers to entering an existing market segment were too

high. It seemed the best strategy was to develop an entirely new product such as OrgChart.

Looking forward, how would the market change? I collected raw data from a variety of publications and market research firms, sorting out the good from the bad by looking for independent sources that were in close agreement. Then, I developed my sales forecasts to show sales of personal computers relative to total potential sales, a comparison that yielded much more information than either number by itself. Given the uncertainty in both numbers, I also made my projections at three levels—one I considered low, one high, and one the most likely. The most valuable projections were those that held constant across all three of these sales forecasts; in other words, they were insensitive to the uncertainties in my forecasts. My resulting analysis found that the primary dynamic was the increasing penetration of the business personal computer, and from this I was able to draw several conclusions.

The first conclusion was that the installed base of all personal computers was now larger than annual sales. The second conclusion was that replacement sales would outnumber first-time personal computer purchases within a three- to five-year period (assuming a five-year product life). Finally, the experience level of the average personal computer owner would double from eighteen to almost thirty-six months during this same time. From these conclusions I expected a number of consequences. The most important were these:

1. After-market software (bought well after the purchase of a computer) and upgrade software (purchased to improve the performance of software already owned) would become a larger proportion of the market. At the same time, the large installed base would make some niches attractive business opportunities for unique but limited-appeal products. Both trends would be favorable to a product like OrgChart.

2. Slowing hardware sales would force successful, full-service retailers to become serious about selling software and the large installed base would be an incentive to create software-only stores. All else remaining equal, shelf space for software would tend to increase. Thus, a major hurdle for a new software company would fall. It would be easier than ever to break onto the shelf of the retailer.

3. Increasing customer experience would make the average consumer more qualified to compare and judge software. The questions would shift from whether to buy to what to buy. It was likely that traditional methods of differentiating one product from another such as quality, value, and convenience would become more important.

4. At the time, competitors were almost gentlemanly to each other. The reaction of companies to new competitors and the rivalry among existing competitors would likely increase.

I was taking a very long-term view of the industry. I did not even consider a short-term strategy. I did not know whether a long-term view was good or not, but to me it seemed natural.

I was also being contrarian; many of my conclusions were at odds with the prevailing wisdom. At the time, most experts thought the future belonged to large, integrated programs combining spreadsheets and word processors, programs like Symphony by Lotus Development and Ovation by Ovation Technologies. As formerly successful companies like VisiCorp, Sorcim, and Digital Research terminated large numbers of employees because of falling sales during the first half of 1984, many experts thought the golden age of software was over. They concluded that the next round of success would go to large software companies with the financial muscle to shower retailers with lavish marketing budgets, effectively buying shelf space.

My contrary opinions actually made me more confident, but being contrarian was certainly no guarantee of success. There were infinitely many ways to fail when going against conventional wisdom. Nonetheless, I had observed throughout my young career that "what's hot" in the minds of the *cognoscenti* often falls flat, probably as often as not. "Hotness" started in the mind of an industry leader— it was something he *wanted* to have happen. Very often it reflected desire, not merit or certainty. Driven by public relations, the desire entered a marketplace of ideas where the buyers were also industry leaders. The winning desire became "hot." People talked about the idea, wrote about the idea, and sometimes made a livelihood promoting the idea. Ultimately, the desire became a product. Then the real market determined whether the idea was good or bad. Starting with the silicon-on-sapphire technology during my days at Intel, I noted a low correlation between hot ideas and successful products.

Work, Work, Work

Late in July 1984, I started yet another task, teaching myself the C programming language. Over a period of about seven weeks I went through several books and wrote numerous practice applications. *The C Programming Language* by Kernighan and Ritchie had many simple text analysis exercises and most of my programs expanded on those examples.[3]

I was working every waking hour. My job at Symantec took forty-five to fifty hours a week plus another five or six hours of commute time. OrgChart was consuming every other free moment. The situation reminded me of a conversation several years earlier with an entrepreneur flying in the seat next to me. He described how his only time away from his business was the three hours he spent reading the Sunday paper from cover to cover. Yet, he said he would not trade it for anything. At the time, I thought he had an obsession; now I felt the same way as he did.

Naturally, all this work led to stress with Connie. She was generally supportive of my objectives, but had priorities of her own and obviously wanted some of her activities to include me. When she talked me into a social activity I often had her drive to our destination while I worked in the passenger seat.

Then, out of the blue, after several years of frustration and medical attention, we surprisingly found that Connie was pregnant. Our hopes of having children had almost evaporated; now we were exuberant. I went to every medical appointment with Connie, and in August she had her first ultrasound. The fetal heart had just started beating, a single pixel on the monitor blinking on and off. We nicknamed the baby "Twinkle."

Because we had agreed that Connie would quit her job to care for our children, the pregnancy placed additional pressure on my budget and deepened Connie's concern. Now neither one of us would be working if I started the company, but the numbers still looked okay. My obsessive money-saving had paid off.

---

[3] My computer was an original IBM Personal Computer with two 360-KB floppy diskette drives and a 256-KB motherboard expanded to 512 KB. Its Intel 8088 processor had a clock speed of 4.77 MHz and the monitor could display graphics at a resolution of 640 x 200 pixels.

I still had not told anyone at Symantec about my budding plans to form my own company, but I had persuaded my manager at Symantec to give me a leave of absence starting at the end of September. I felt I had accomplished as much as I could on OrgChart while still working for someone else. The time off would allow me to complete the work necessary to decide whether to proceed.

I started my leave in September and immediately turned my attention to the problems with OrgChart's user interface. I intently read Paul Heckel's pioneering book, *The Elements of Friendly Software Design*. From it I was better able to define the problem with OrgChart's user interface. Again I found myself using the technique of analogy to set a direction when everything facing me was new.

Heckel's work convinced me that OrgChart needed to create the illusion that the user was seeing his organization chart on the monitor even though that was not possible with the computers of the time. The existing user interface was far from this ideal. The user just filled out a series of computerized forms. I drew an analogy between the techniques of an animated movie and the techniques available to me on the IBM personal computer. Then, with these new ideas in mind, I changed the shape of the forms in the program to look like the boxes in an organization chart. I also added animation between forms to create the illusion that the user was shifting his perspective from one part of the chart to another.

To test these new concepts I eventually built another mock-up that allowed me to quickly change the speed of the animation and other characteristics. I tweaked these variables for some time to come, but I had found the fundamental improvement. The program would be easy to learn and now I was proud of my design.

Meanwhile I continued to interview candidates to program OrgChart. One suggested that I do it myself, commenting that I would be 50 percent as efficient as anyone else I found, maybe better. It was an intriguing idea, but instead I chose an engineer who had worked at Symantec. He had good experience and it was easy to work with him. He would do the work during the evening and on weekends since what I could pay him only amounted to supplemental income. He did not have his own computer, so I would have to procure one for him.

Decision Time

In October, Connie had another ultrasound. The pregnancy was going well and so was OrgChart.

Strangely, as I worked on OrgChart I realized that the desire to accumulate wealth was no longer my primary objective, although it was still very important. Instead, I increasingly found that my desire to create and control my own environment held sway. In contrast to working for others, the freedom that this project allowed me was almost intoxicating.

I had chosen to produce an entirely new software application in an entirely new category. I planned to price my product at a level most software companies deemed unprofitable and I was uncertain how I would sell it. It was by far the most complex thing I had ever attempted to build. I intended to do this with my own limited funds at a time when financiers were investing large sums of money in seemingly every new software company. Yet I was totally and completely confident of success.

I had studied and analyzed this market for years—I knew in which direction it was going. I had been wielding tools since I was a toddler—I knew I could build OrgChart and a company to sell it. Most importantly, I had been consuming every spare moment with this project for eight months, and I loved the sense of creation and the total control over my own fate. This was the right thing for me.

Although I could not imagine failing—what if I did? I had money in the bank and I could find a job in a matter of days. I decided that the worst possible outcome of bootstrapping my own company was preferable to staying at Symantec. At that moment the risk of proceeding reached zero. I decided to go!

2

Betting on Change — The Founding of Banner Blue Software

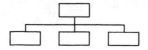

Ironically, Symantec was about to turn the corner and become a highly successful company. At just about the time I made my decision to start Banner Blue, Symantec merged with CE Software, whose founder, Gordon Eubanks, brought to the table many of the things Symantec had been lacking: a successful development process, engineers experienced at developing personal computer software, a more complete and realistic product vision, and a steadying influence. Nonetheless, it was too late for me to change my mind. I was having the time of my life working on OrgChart, and I no longer cared what happened at Symantec.

When I resigned, my decision visibly upset the chief executive officer, and rightfully so—I had told him I would stay if he fired the incompetent senior manager and he had. I have always taken commitments seriously, but in this case I had simply made a mistake. I had indicated a willingness to stay under certain circumstances, when in fact the issue was much more complex than that. I had known for sure that I would leave if Symantec retained the vice president of engineering, but my staying truly depended on both my business plans and the prospects for Symantec. Now, I did not want to abandon my plans for Banner Blue just so I could say that I had never reneged on a commitment. I felt bad, but I resolved to move forward and not make the same mistake again.

Finally, I was in business for myself, and the first few months proved to be a thorough lesson in exactly what having your own business means. The unending list of tasks to accomplish, compounded by the pervasive newness of the industry, provided constant stimulation and challenge. With Connie pregnant, any moment of calm at work probably meant a surprise was brewing at home. As an independent businessperson, there was little outside direction or structure in my life, so I could only look to myself to provide occasional islands of stability. Most days I loved my new situation—but not every day.

On the evening of October 23, 1984, my first day in business for myself, I was reading the trade journal *PC Magazine* and saw an advertisement about a product called PC-OrgChart from NorFork Systems. I was in total shock. I had carefully chosen a niche where I would be the first player and therefore without competitors. Now, on my first day in business, someone had announced a competitive product many months before I would be able to ship a program—and they had stolen my product name as well! I ordered the program the first thing the next morning and asked that it be shipped to me overnight.

When the package arrived, I ripped it open. The user manual was the first thing I saw. It was not very attractive, but in those days that did not mean much about the quality of the software. Some good programs had very unprofessional documentation and vice versa. I loaded the program into my computer, began playing with it, and immediately a sense of relief came over me. The program queried the user for every piece of information, one by one. For example,

ENTER   NAME   OF   DEPTARTMENT   [sic]   HEAD:

ENTER NUMBER OF DIRECT REPORTS: __

DATA DRIVE WILL DEFAULT TO YOUR 'd' DRIVE, IF DEFAULT IS APPROPRIATE PRESS ENTER KEY.

The design was easy to learn, but hopelessly tedious and inflexible to use. Correcting the simplest typographical error required nine steps. In addition, it had no options for controlling the appearance of the chart, and the user interface contained several misspelled words.

The low quality of the NorFork Systems program reduced my anxiety, yet I had learned how quickly a competitor could appear.

While the newness of the personal computer software industry attracted me, this was truly one aspect I could do without. Throughout the day I reflected on NorFork Systems and finally said aloud to myself, "This guy should be worried about my program, not I about his."

However, because of NorFork Systems' product, I had to choose a new name for my own. After a great deal of thought, I settled on the name Org. I did not like it as well as OrgChart, but under trademark law I had no claim to my original choice.

Testing Twinkle

On October 29, Connie and I went to a doctor who specialized in performing amniocentesis, a procedure wherein the physician inserts a large needle into the amniotic sac to withdraw amniotic fluid for genetic analysis. The procedure was common for pregnant women older than thirty-five, but there was a small risk that it might accidentally terminate the pregnancy, so we were both rather anxious. An ultrasound image allowed me to watch as the doctor inserted the needle, and I saw Twinkle jump to the other side of the womb, out of harm's way. Then the doctor withdrew the fluid, removed the needle, and—relieved—we were on our way.

The procedure could tell us Twinkle's gender, but we asked the doctor to keep it a secret. Genetic testing of a fetus was relatively new at the time, and we decided to be old-fashioned about our pregnancy—we would wait until our baby was born to find out whether it was a boy or a girl. In early November 1984 we got the word that Twinkle's genes showed no abnormalities, and we were both ecstatic.

Programming Org

In order for work to begin, I needed to find a computer for Org's programmer. Fortunately, my friend Brett Walter was willing to loan me one for a few months. On the day that the programmer was to start work, he rang the doorbell and I answered, ready to hand him the computer. But before I could say hello, he blurted out that he could not write the program because his wife did not like the idea of him programming during all of his spare time. He was sorry, but he said his only choice was to decline the job.

In all of my hiring experience, I have found that such changes of heart are extraordinarily frequent. Sometimes a family member raises an objection to the job or another employer sweet-talks the person into a different job; sometimes the individual himself gets cold feet or finds he does not like the job after starting. Everyone follows a slightly different path when they analyze a career decision, causing them to accept or decline an offer with varying degrees of certainty. The best thing that can happen is for the individual to have a change of heart before they start the new job, but even this turn of events always bothered me. Why could not they have resolved their concerns weeks earlier, saving everyone the ensuing emotion and trouble?

With these unexpected competition and labor problems, my venture was not off to a great start. Nonetheless, instead of dwelling on the setbacks, immediately after the programmer left, I began considering other engineers. It was a familiar list of names, as I had been through it many times before. After weighing the pros and cons of approaching several people, I decided to call Paul Heller.

Paul was more senior than the programmer who had quit on me, having gained excellent experience in personal computer software while working at VisiCorp and Mouse Systems. I had met Paul during the short time he worked at Symantec. I did not talk to him the first time I was looking for a programmer because he did not get along well with the chief program architect at Symantec, and this concerned me even though Paul and I had always worked well together. However, I now called Paul, told him what had happened, and set up a meeting for the next day.

As it turned out, Paul had moonlighted in the past, so he knew what he would be getting into and how to balance it with his day job. I laid out my plans, and then he asked, "How much money do you have?" I explained that I could pay him a few thousand dollars, about one month's salary for an engineer of his caliber. "Well Ken, I can't write the program for $3,000, but here's what I can do...." Paul suggested that he write a collection of building blocks for the user interface as well as software that would allow the program to communicate with disk drives and printers. One building block would draw a rectangle on the screen, another would place a variety of menu options in the rectangle, and so on. Another programmer could take these building blocks to make the user interface that I had designed in my external product specification. Paul suggested that I be that other programmer.

Paul impressed me. I went to him with a problem and he offered me a comprehensive solution, even though it did involve a lot of work on my part. On top of that, Paul's offhand review of the project probably tripled my knowledge of how a program should be architected. Architecting a program is much like architecting a house. The architect drafts a set of plans showing how the many pieces of the project fit together. If he does a good job, the building (or program) is economical to construct, easy to maintain, and provides the desired functionality. In spite of all my market analysis and product design, the plain truth was that I had no idea what a large program should look like under its skin. I did not know how to divide the program into pieces nor how much time the work should require. Yet at the same time, I had just the right amount of knowledge to follow Paul's advice. With any less knowledge, the engineering and programming would have overwhelmed me. With any more knowledge, the enormity of the task and my long odds for success would have terrified me.

I asked Paul to put together a proposal for the project, and in five concise pages he described the following: the categories of building blocks (known as functions or routines), which of us would be responsible for each category, the computers on which the routines would work, how the routines would accomplish the tasks required by my design, documentation of the work, a schedule, and payment terms. Paul explained that his proposed organization of the work put each function in the hands of the person most knowledgeable about how to accomplish it. He was willing to work ten hours per week at about $30 per hour, substantially less than the $35 to $50 he normally charged for contract work.

At that point, it occurred to me that I had been quite fortunate to have the first programmer quit. He did not have the experience to prepare a proposal like Paul's, and I did not even know enough to ask for it. Of course, Paul side-stepped one major piece of the program, the formatter that would actually do the work of laying out an organization chart. Under Paul's plan, I would have to do that piece on my own. Nonetheless, I accepted Paul's proposal, having concluded that I would be able to program and still do all of the other work required to bring Org to market.

So, just a few weeks after losing a junior programmer, I now had a senior programmer, a programming plan, a programming coach, and an even bigger job for myself. I was no longer just founding and managing a software company, but also programming the software. Banner Blue was a bootstrap in the purest sense of the word.

In preparation for managing the project, I had already taught myself how to program in C, making me confident that I could accomplish my portion of the project. However, Paul's proposal should have served as a warning to me: If I had tripled my knowledge of program architecture in the first two hours I spent with him and picked up even more from his brief proposal, I should have realized how much more I had to learn.

I continued to read books on programming and managing programming projects, but they were short on examples in program architecture, which was my main area of weakness. I should have tapped the experience of additional programmers, but I did not, and this would cause problems several years later.

Also due in part to my inexperience, I skimped on one important product development life cycle step—the internal product specification. An internal product specification is a blueprint and description of the programming required to accomplish the functions called for in the external product specification. I had never seen an internal product specification, neither good nor bad; consequently, the one I prepared was mediocre. I should have sought outside advice on the specification, but did not. My programming schedule proved to be somewhat better. I put a poster-sized sheet of paper on my office closet door and attached thirty Post-It® notes to it, each one representing one of the blocks of code I would have to write.

I had already researched and designed the data structure some months ago, so I simply attached a Post-It that said, "Data Structure." The data structure of a program specifies how the computer stores data to represent a real-world problem. For example, a person might randomly jot down commonly used phone numbers on a sheet of paper. Finding a name in that random list becomes very inefficient once there are more than a couple dozen entries. An alternative method would be to keep the phone list in alphabetical order, by name, making the numbers much easier to find. Programmers must make exactly the same choices when writing a computer program.

The most complex piece of the program would be the formatter that took the information in the data structure and turned it into an organization chart. For that, I attached several Post-Its containing the outline of an algorithm—a set of rules like a recipe, giving a sequence of operations to properly locate each box in the chart. Then, emulating Paul, I typed up several pages of notes about how I thought some of these building blocks should work. Collectively, these fragments of thought and Paul's invaluable proposal completed my rudimentary programming plan, so I started programming.

My office was the extra ten-by-ten-foot bedroom in our modest 1,300-square-foot home in Fremont, California. It was adjacent to the room we intended to be Twinkle's nursery. Before Banner Blue, Connie and I had invested many weekends in our home, putting ceramic tile floors in the kitchen and family room, remodeling a bathroom, and effecting a variety of other improvements. It was small, but a quiet and attractive work environment.

My desk was a heavy, Formica-covered door that I mounted on legs intended for a workbench. My chair was from a second-hand office furniture store, reupholstered by Connie. From my computer I looked out on the pretty, mature trees in our front yard. Connie worked during the day at her job as a commercial interior designer. I worked all day and well into the night after she returned home. Once she came up behind me and asked, "Don't you want to do something fun?" to which I replied, "This is fun!"

I programmed the data structure first, since the entire program would insert, remove, or examine the information stored there. By December 15, I had some working code. There was no user interface since Paul was still working on the plan for his coding, but by printing out the contents of my computer's memory I could see that my code was working. I found that one of the joys of programming was the quick, regular feedback about how the work was advancing— every day brought visible progress. I also had fun with the names I assigned some of the variables, something a customer would never see. For example, I identified the topmost person with the term *cheese*, as in "the big cheese."

Next, I started programming the formatter, and by December 23, I had kludged up a way to print out the boxes of a semi-complete organization chart (there were no interconnecting lines yet). The speed of my progress surprised me and the prospect of showing Org to some friends was exciting. The next day, Christmas Eve, was the perfect opportunity, because Connie and I had tickets to a matinee performance of the Nutcracker in San Francisco, and afterwards a number of our friends would be joining us in our home for an open house.

On that same day, Paul completed his specifications for the work he was to do. The result was a twenty-page document, much more comprehensive than his proposal. It described every function he would write, the inputs it required, and the output it would generate. I was on a high, because everything was finally falling into place despite the early setbacks with NorFork Systems and the programmer who quit.

An Unexpected Loss

My memory of events surrounding our efforts to have children are more vivid and detailed than any others during all my years with Banner Blue, each one having played out in my mind over and over again. The desire to have a family was one of the few I never analyzed or prioritized—it just felt deeply important and I left it at that, putting it above everything else. Unfortunately, our goal to become parents continued to be elusive, creating frustration and sorrow.

On Christmas Eve, as I was busy dressing for our trip to San Francisco, I walked by Connie's bathroom and in an anguished voice she said, "Ken, I'm bleeding." This being our first pregnancy, I naively asked "How much?" as if the amount carried some importance. She raised her voice in reply, *"I'm not supposed to be bleeding at all! Please call the doctor."* Our doctor, Gerald Shefren, told us to meet him immediately in the maternity clinic at the Stanford University Medical Center. Connie and I had interviewed several obstetricians before selecting Dr. Shefren, and throughout this Christmastime ordeal, his expertise and understanding reinforced for us many times over that we had made the right decision. We got in the car and headed for Stanford.

Having attended Stanford, I knew the exact location of the Medical Center, but I had no idea where the maternity clinic was. I pulled into the emergency room parking and we went inside to see miles of corridors. Wanting to minimize her walking, I told Connie to wait while I found our destination, and I ran off down the hall. It seemed like an eternity before I found the maternity clinic, but once there, I grabbed a wheelchair and went back to get Connie.

They put her on a bed in an examination room and two nurses we had never met before came in with an ultrasonic stethoscope to listen to the fetal heartbeat. Our own physician had often had difficulty hearing Twinkle's heartbeat with this device, so the inability to hear anything troubled us, but we still had hope. Truthfully, we were not ready to admit that the pregnancy was ending. Then, someone brought in an ultrasound imaging machine, and where there should have been a heart, there was nothing beating. The nurses mumbled to each other and moved the device around with great concern on their faces. Without saying much, they finally left the room and we waited. Shortly thereafter, Dr. Shefren opened the door and quietly shook his head from side to side.

A fetal demise five months into a pregnancy is extremely rare, but that is what we experienced. After discussing the options with us, Dr. Shefren brought in a specialist to remove the lifeless fetus. I called a neighbor and asked her to put a note on the door for our friends who would soon be arriving for the open house. I decided not to call family members, all of whom lived out of state, until later the next day. I did not have the emotional energy to make the calls, there was nothing they could do, and I felt they might as well open their gifts on Christmas morning without our troubles weighing on their minds.

Connie spent the night in the hospital as a precaution. When Dr. Shefren returned at about 9:00 on Christmas morning I asked him if he could identify Twinkle's gender and he told me that it was a boy. I said, "Okay, let us out of here so we can try to celebrate Christmas." We returned home to a refrigerator full of food for the party, but strangely short of some key ingredients for a Christmas dinner. I was able to round up what we needed at a 7-Eleven store that was open 365 days a year. We called our relatives, and they were as sad to hear the news as we were to deliver it. Finally, we opened our gifts, except for one that I have left in its wrapping to this day. I could tell from the outside that it was a small book of names, and the card read as follows: "To Dad from Twink, 'Pick me out a good one.'"

A couple of days later, Connie and I drove to the ocean and placed a single rose in the surf as a memorial to Twinkle.

The ability to see an unborn child develop during a pregnancy causes a bonding, I dare say, more deep than before the advent of ultrasonic imaging. For Connie and me, the difficulty of conceiving in the first place magnified the loss even more. Twinkle had already become a part of our family, and his brief existence made it clear that having a family was in many ways more important to me than business success.

Like many unpleasant things, this unhappy episode ultimately made me a better person and manager. With my own priorities clear and reinforced by experience, I was much more understanding and compassionate about the issues of life, illness, and death faced by friends and employees over the ensuing years.

Org Takes Shape

In the year before founding Banner Blue, I got into a regular exercise routine, jogging about two miles every other day. I was never athletic, but I grew to enjoy rolling out of bed into the quiet morning for a run. As my days got longer and my stress level higher, I found that my regular exercise was an important part of staying healthy. It gave me the physical stamina necessary to build a company. I also learned through experiences like the loss of Twinkle that physical strength aids mental strength. You cannot have one without the other, and the more of both you possess, the better. My morning runs over the next week were a great help in clearing my mind and helping me regain my focus.

Eventually, I had the opportunity to talk with all of the friends I had hoped to see at our canceled party. Most were not very encouraging about Org. Some thought starting any business was risky and because they could not imagine themselves doing it, they had trouble understanding why I would. Others simply thought my product strategy was outlandish—to them the market seemed too small. It is nice when friends offer their approval, but I have always had the confidence to go my own way if necessary. Fortunately, two friends were supportive and a continuing source of positive input throughout the project.

In early January 1985, I reviewed Paul's latest document, which described in detail all of the functions he would write. Paul's specification highlighted many of the bets I was making about personal computer hardware, which continued to be in a state of flux. First, Paul was guaranteeing that his code would run on the IBM personal computer, the IBM PC AT, and the IBM PC, Jr. There were still many computers on the market only partially compatible with the emerging IBM standard, but I felt that they would have no alternative except to fall in line.

Second, although I was building a program to produce graphics, I was making it for computers that could not display graphics on their monitors. The IBM personal computer worked with two different types of monitors, the monochrome monitor that could not display graphics and the color monitor that could. Most entertainment software required the color monitor, so it became popular in home applications even though it displayed text at a very low resolution that was tiring to read for any length of time. Consequently, most businesses opted for the monochrome monitor and that was the one on which I felt Org needed to run. Fortunately, a program written for the monochrome monitor could easily work on the color monitor, it just could not display graphics.

The printer market presented an even more chaotic situation to software developers like myself. There were literally dozens of printer manufacturers, and every printer wanted to talk to the computer using a different language. It would have been impossible for Org to support all printers, so I believed the best choice was to support the most popular printers generally, and those with a strong presence specifically in my target market. Overall, Epson manufactured the most popular printer line.

The Epson dot-matrix printers had either nine or twenty-four metal pins in a print head, depending on the model, that struck a traditional, inked ribbon as the head passed across the page. They were highly reliable, they could print either graphics or textual characters, and they were relatively inexpensive. Unfortunately, the quality of dot-matrix printing was not as good as a manual typewriter, so many image-conscious managers chose a daisy-wheel printer. Daisy-wheel printers were essentially electronic typewriters that created an image on paper by striking a fully formed character against an inked ribbon. They were slow, noisy, and could not print graphics—they were a link back to the pre-computer past. To make an organization chart with a daisy-wheel printer I would have to draw unattractive lines using dashes and slashes, but I could do it.

The newness of the industry made it impossible to predict with certainty the correct printers to support, but I learned over subsequent years that in a fast-evolving market, supporting a link to the past like daisy wheels has many downsides. First, organization charts never looked very good when printed with a daisy-wheel printer because these printers were never meant to handle graphics. Consequently, almost no one with a daisy-wheel printer ever purchased Org. Second, supporting daisy-wheel printers forced me to come up with a "least common denominator" design for the parts of the program that did the printing. In other words, by allowing for the daisy-wheel, I made it more difficult to support the more advanced printers of the day and following years. Finally, because of the daisy-wheel's many limitations, the laser printer eliminated it from the market only several years later. In 1984 at a price of $3495, Hewlett-Packard introduced the first laser printer for IBM personal computers, the LaserJet.

The price dropped quickly and sales rocketed. All in all, supporting daisy-wheels was a bad use of my time. Especially in my early years at Banner Blue, I did a better job of projecting where the market would go than where the technology would go. However, both were important, so I learned to be careful when supporting archaic technology.

By January 1985, Org was able to print out names, boxes, and connecting lines—complete organization charts. I was looking forward to building the user interface with Paul's code. I had revised my schedule, and it called for intensive programming through March. Then I would gradually shift my attention to sales, marketing, and company organizational issues like obtaining the proper licenses and bank accounts. I hoped to ship Org before the end of May.

I always prepared my schedules as simple, one-page Gantt charts because they graphically showed me what tasks I would have to juggle simultaneously. In mid-January I created a revised financial forecast that ran through June 1985. It showed that I would need to borrow $10,000 (about two months' salary) to complete Org without dipping into the cash reserves that I had promised Connie I would not touch. I was happy to see that the required loan amount was approximately what I had predicted in my original forecast—things were progressing right on track.

The next two months of programming were as enjoyable as any two months during my time at Banner Blue. I would jog in the morning, eat a quick breakfast, then shower and start programming. There were none of the business pressures I would later experience, and I had a tremendous sense of accomplishment as each day another piece of the program came to fruition. Early on, I learned to fix all the bugs in my code before quitting for the day because otherwise I would dwell on them during a fitful night of sleep. One night at 3:00 AM I actually bolted upright from a deep sleep and said, "That won't work." The program had been running in my mind and it had come to a point where it could not proceed. The next morning I turned on the computer and verified what I had dreamt the night before. I was a bit concerned about this episode until I read that it was not an uncommon experience for good programmers.

By the middle of March 1985, the program was complete enough to let outsiders begin testing. Several friends and colleagues began to give me excellent feedback, most of it easy to implement. I had a great deal of programming yet to do, but it was also time to turn some of my attention to other business issues. My highest priority was to secure distribution for the program.

Gaining Distribution for Org

Power Up, the software catalog, had just reported selling $1 million of accessory software during their first fifteen months. All of their programs sold for less than $100, meaning they had probably sold several thousand units during February 1985. With this kind of record, I decided they should be my first and highest priority sales target.

In March, I called other companies who were selling or had considered selling through the Power Up catalog. I reached three people who gave me good insight into the terms sought by Power Up, the quantities they were selling, and the nature of the people with whom I would be dealing. The next day I called Pete Sinclair, the general manager of Power Up, and met with a stroke of good luck. First, they were seeking out software developers, so I got right through to him. Second, Power Up had already identified a need to sell an organization chart program, especially one that ran on the IBM monochrome monitor. After a brief discussion, we set up a face-to-face meeting to talk further.

On March 29, I met Pete Sinclair at the Power Up offices in Mountain View, about thirty minutes from my home. After a short meeting with Pete, I spent the remainder of the visit with Chris Penn, the product selection manager. Chris had been with Power Up's parent company, Software Publishing, for eight months before moving over to the catalog operation. Previously, he held a position at IUS, who published one of the first successful word processors for the IBM personal computer. These two or three years in the industry made Chris the most experienced personal computer software marketing manager I had met to date. He was straightforward, earnest, and knowledgeable about the industry and entrepreneurs; we continue to be friends to this day.

In our meeting, Chris provided the details on the Power Up strategy. They were planning three more catalog runs during 1985, for a total of 2.1 million catalogs. They would be deciding the contents of the August catalog by the end of April, so my timing was good. They wanted products where the customer need was perpetual, so sales would increase with the growth of the catalog mailing list.

The best products were selling about 1,000 units per catalog run. Through experimentation, they found that $50 to $100 products sold the best, higher prices did not sell at all, and lower prices did not make up in volume the loss in margin. They were also experimenting with different catalog covers and moving to eliminate pictures of product boxes, replacing them with pictures of the product output. Chris was fuzzy about why they wanted an organization chart program. Evidently, the parent company's chairman, Fred Gibbons, said they should have one. So far, everything sounded good.

Then, however, Chris described their desire to move in the direction of "exclusive," private-labeled products carried only by Power Up. They did not think that in the long run their profit margins would support the distribution of software manufactured by entrepreneurs like me. Instead, they wanted me to write them a custom program. Power Up wanted to create its own brand with common aspects to the user interface, common packaging, copy protection, and online user documentation to save the cost of printing a user guide. Chris told me they did not mind if I also sold the product under a different name at the same time.

All of this was another way of saying they wanted to pay less for what they sold. My royalties for an exclusive product would be about 10 percent of the sales price versus 50 percent for a product distributed under my name. Apparently, Power Up was another pioneering company struggling to find the proper business model among the many being tested. I was not happy about what he was telling me because I was not in business to earn a royalty. What looked ideal for them looked crummy for me.

As a bootstrapper, every step my company took needed to pay for the next one. If I developed a custom program for Power Up, it would delay for months my own version of the program and the resulting revenue. I would be trading what I believed to be a solid income stream from selling my own product for a puny income stream from the royalty alone. Moreover, when I later finished my own version of the program, the royalty stream was unlikely to be enough to fund marketing in additional channels. By definition, a bootstrapper makes a big investment in himself. In essence, Power Up was also asking me to make a big investment in them, and there simply was not enough money to go around. I felt there had to be a middle ground.

I went home and considered my situation. Looking at their catalog, I found twice as many distributed programs as there were exclusive programs. So, even if their plan was to move towards exclusive products, it certainly was not happening very quickly. At the same time, it was clear they wanted Org, so it seemed that I was in a good negotiating position.

On April 9, I met again with Pete and Chris. Pete reiterated that Power Up wanted a royalty deal, and he emphasized that he did not want the catalog to do my advertising for me. I held firm, explaining that I was willing to negotiate the discount for a distributed product, but constructing a custom, exclusive product was a poor use of my resources at that time. I also pointed out that Org would not have wide distribution during their next few catalog runs, so practically speaking, Power Up would have a marketing exclusive. The result of this meeting was a stalemate.

At the next meeting, Chris explained that they wanted to do a deal, so it was time to turn me over to the contract administrator. If Chris was knowledgeable and sensitive to the situation of an entrepreneur, the contract administrator was not. My initial thought—that I had won the argument with Pete after all—quickly evaporated. The administrator presented a contract for an exclusive product that would pay me a royalty in the neighborhood of 12 percent, as I recall. I told her with some anger, "I did not quit my job and work the last six months without income for this." She showed little emotion while presenting the proposal and none after my response. There was no point in reviewing my position with her so we were still at a stalemate.

After the meeting I again looked for common ground. We wanted to do business together, shared a conservative business philosophy, agreed that an organization chart program would be highly successful, and understood the economics. From their perspective, if they did not do business with me, they would be deferring revenue on an organization chart product until they found someone else or built it themselves. So long as they held firm to their position, they had more to lose than I did.

I also put together a *pro forma* income statement for Power Up using the numbers I obtained during our negotiations. The normal distributor discount did create low profits for them. Pete was also correct in saying that the catalog was free advertising for me, a bonus I would not receive with a typical distributor. I decided I was willing to give a substantially larger discount in return for this.

Over the next several weeks I got Pete and Chris to back away from their philosophical position and just talk dollars. We finally agreed that they would act as distributors of the product at a discount of 70 percent. Since my manufacturing cost for each copy of Org was only a few dollars, this was a profitable deal for both of us.

During the ensuing years, I saw many new software companies cave in to the demands of their first distributor. The distributor smells blood because they can see that the company has no revenue and for the very same reason the new company feels that it has to quickly obtain distribution. The reality is that an innovative new product is as valuable to the distributor as it is to the manufacturer. My belief in the value of Org gave me the confidence to stand firm. If one distributor cannot see the importance of a deal that is positive for both parties, another will.

Strangely, during the entire negotiation, Power Up never once questioned whether I would successfully finish the program. Plenty of companies in this new industry failed to complete their software, and I still had a lot of work left to do.

Meanwhile, I decided to stay away from traditional software distributors such as Softsel. Friends advised me that I would be unable to negotiate favorable terms and that the distributors would do little to stimulate sales of my product since they sold only to retailers, not end users. Before talking to traditional distributors, I needed to create demand for the product with vehicles like Power Up and my own direct response advertising.

Final Product Decisions

My bootstrap strategy, combined with my limited savings, forced me into a "do-it-yourself" mode of operation. I was comfortable with that style, having been raised by a father whose favorite saying was, "If you want something done right, you have to do it yourself." But I was now carrying this philosophy to extremes as I juggled innumerable tasks during April, May, and June of 1985. In that time period I was completing the programming, determining a price, deciding whether to copy-protect the program, writing the user guide, designing the product and company logos, designing the packaging, printing a warranty registration card, testing the program, formally organizing the business by obtaining the proper permits and licenses, and writing an advertisement. Finally, during that same time period I also consulted one or two days per week at Symantec, where things had finally taken a turn for the better. The extra income helped me pay for additional marketing.

The pace was sustainable only because I still enjoyed virtually every minute of my very long days. Nonetheless, twice during those months I locked my keys in my car, an act of distraction completely out of character for me. Of course, my lack of assistance meant I was taking longer to complete the product than I might have otherwise, so I was fortunate not to have another competitor appear.

I was choosing a price at the same time I was talking to Power Up. My plan all along had been to price the program in the $50 to $100 range, but now it was time to make a final decision. I reviewed the prices of other programs, considered Power Up's experience, and looked at my costs of doing business, including the cost of direct mail sales. I also estimated the cost savings the program would generate for my customers. At a price of $70, I figured my average customer would pay for the program with the cost savings from making one typical organization chart with Org instead of the old-fashioned way. I wanted the purchase decision to be a no-brainer, so I decided $69.95 was the correct price. At the time, I was not trying to model a specific profit target or cost structure. I was just looking for a reasonable balance between the price to the customer and my costs of developing, manufacturing, and marketing the product.

The detailed market analysis work that I did before I decided to start Banner Blue contrasted sharply with my quick analysis of product pricing. Although my earlier work provided a tremendously valuable framework to keep me pointed in the right direction, my unending forecasts and scenarios gave way to a much more entrepreneurial style. As I juggled dozens of tasks to bring Org to market, I no longer had the luxury of time for such in-depth study. More often than not, my calculations were "back of the envelope," intended to demonstrate plausibility rather than certainty. I knew that small, reversible mistakes were okay, and at that point, survival required speed more than perfection.

Another decision I faced was whether to copy-protect the program, an issue deeply dividing the industry at the time. Manufacturers distributed programs on 5.25-inch floppy diskettes and any computer that could read one could also make an exact duplicate in about two minutes. If the customer made a copy to save in case he damaged the original diskette, that was fine. On the other hand, if the customer gave copies to friends, the software manufacturer was losing revenue.

Copy protection technology altered the information on the original diskette in a way that made it difficult or impossible for the customer to make a copy. Unfortunately, copy protection also made it impossible to make legitimate back-up copies, created problems for installing and using programs on hard disk drives, and sometimes even prevented programs from running on certain computers. Copy protection was a customer nightmare and I had personally experienced every one of the problems with various software programs that I owned. Power Up was a proponent of copy protection, and they even offered me the free use of their copy protection technology. Ultimately, I decided in favor of the customer. If I lost a few sales, so be it—Org was not copy-protected.

As programming neared completion, product packaging became my most time-consuming job. At the time, there was no consensus on what a package should look like. Many programs, especially those trying to project an upscale image, came in expensive, cloth-bound, slipcase binders containing documentation printed with multi-color lithography. Other programs came with photocopied pages in a vinyl binder and still others with a small pamphlet. The cost of the cloth-bound binders was far too high for Org, so I chose the middle course of a soft-cover user guide with a four-color cover and black and white body. I inserted the floppy diskette inside the shrink-wrapped user guide, so my user guide cover also served as the package cover—there was no box. It was always my philosophy that a professional appearance resulted from neatness, attention to detail, and a restrained, classic style of typography and artwork. Expensive materials were nice, but not required. I also avoided trendiness.

I had never produced a user guide before, so the entire process was new to me. On top of that, the printing industry was about to go through a major revolution of its own as computers began replacing old, manual typesetting equipment. I called upon Joan Lasselle at Lasselle-Ramsay to guide me through the process.

Joan and her partner Carol Ramsay had departed from Hewlett-Packard at about the same time I did, and founded a firm for producing technical documentation. I could not afford to have Lasselle-Ramsay actually write the user guide, so I hired Joan as a consultant. First, she explained to me the technical writing process. It was important to begin with a style sheet that enforced consistency in both writing and presentation. We started with a style guide prepared by IBM and added to it information specific to Org. Then, we established a process wherein I wrote the user guide, Joan edited it, and a compositor, Rich Kaneko, typeset the final draft and prepared paste-up boards for the printer. When finished, the user guide turned out to be about sixty pages.

To complete my packaging, I also had to develop a company and product logo, design a user guide cover, design labels to affix to the floppy diskettes, and write a user license agreement. Connie was invaluable with all the graphic design work. Since the Wabash Railroad had been out of business for many decades, we simply appropriated the typography for "Banner Blue." Connie designed a company logo that was suggestive of the aluminum passenger cars that made up the train. In short order, we had designs for everything we needed and Rich turned them into camera-ready artwork for the printer.

I chose the following tag lines for the front cover: "Org Makes Organization Charts. You enter the names. Org automatically formats and draws with perfect spacing." The back contained a product description. I proofread the manual probably a dozen times before it was complete and literally knew it by heart. Connie also helped with proofreading. The final draft of the manual was complete on May 22, 1985, and Rich had it ready to go to the printer a week or two later.

The program itself was essentially complete by that time and in every spare moment, I was testing it. I concocted exhaustive lists to ensure that I tested every possible user input in every possible situation. It was a great advantage to test a program I had written. I knew where to look for problems, but found surprisingly few.

Organizing the Business

As if programming, testing, and writing a user guide were not enough, I also had to formally organize Banner Blue as a company. This included obtaining a city business license, federal and state tax ID numbers for income tax, a Board of Equalization resale number to collect sales tax, fictitious name permission to do business under the name Banner Blue, a post office box, a safe deposit box, and a business phone line. There was also a banking relationship to establish. I needed to secure the loan I had budgeted to pay for the first printing of the user guide, and I had to obtain merchant privileges so that I could accept payment from customers using credit cards. All of these tasks except establishing the banking relationship were fairly simple.

If I had been thinking about it, I would have obtained a line of credit before I quit my job at Symantec. By the time I acted, I had spent much of my savings and was unemployed—it was not the best scenario to present to a banker when asking for money. I also felt the typical banker would be woefully unprepared to evaluate a fledgling software company, so I called a friend in the venture capital business and asked him both to refer me to someone and serve as a reference. The banker I ended up working with asked for a formal business plan, which I readily prepared from the many forecasts I had already generated. I received a line of credit for $14,000, which was equal to about three month's worth of my previous salary. I also received the credit card merchant privileges in late May 1985.

In an effort to reduce credit card fraud, the merchant banking officer had to physically visit my office and examine my signage. They wanted to make sure I really existed. Deed restrictions made it illegal for me to have a business sign on my house, nor did I need one. So, I had a Banner Blue sign on my home for the fifteen minutes during which the merchant banking officer visited. It has been in my file cabinet ever since.

As I was finishing up all of these tasks, it was still two months before Power Up would be mailing out their catalog. Since the software was essentially complete, I did not want to squander two months in which I could be earning revenue, so I decided that running my own advertisement was the best thing I could do. Later, writing advertisements became one of my favorite activities, but this first ad was one more task in a list that was already too long.

Before I wrote the ad I had to decide where I would place it, since that would determine its physical size. Again the newness of the industry made an otherwise simple decision complex. I was not aware of advertisements for any software similar to mine, so I had no clear path to follow. Should I advertise in a business publication because my customers were managers, or in a computer publication because my product was software? Computer manufacturers themselves advertised in both places. I decided to try a business publication first, but to hedge my bet by running a small advertisement. For only $625 I could run a 2.25-by-2.5-inch ad in the *Wall Street Journal* Eastern Edition. The *Wall Street Journal* was running a special software-only advertising section with its own large headline. I checked with a couple of companies who had run similar ads and they reported good, if not spectacular, results. After months of working on Org, I naturally and dangerously concluded my product was better than those of my references and decided my ad would do even better.

At the last minute, I found that I had to apply to the *Wall Street Journal* for the privilege of running a mail order ad. I submitted a financial statement, sample ad, and three business references, and the publication quickly approved my application.

Ship It

The user guide cost $9945 to print and the 3,000 copies took up so much space in my garage that I had to park outside. The software was complete and fully tested and I also had all my fees, licenses, and permits in order. On June 24, 1985, my advertisement ran in the *Wall Street Journal*, and I waited for the phone to ring. After waiting for some time, I waited a bit longer. It occurred to me that many people read the paper at the end of the day, so I continued waiting. Finally, George P. Hresko called from Puerto Rico to order a copy of Org. My voice quivered with excitement. Wanting my company to appear as large as possible, I did not tell him that his was my first order, so I took the order saying only what was necessary. Over the next week I sold—*five copies*—from the *Wall Street Journal* advertisement. I also sold copies to my friend Kevin Schofield and a subordinate from my HP days, Alma Rodoni.

Needless to say I had hoped for a faster start, but I was still very confident of my plan. There was no time for discouragement and I displayed none. If one thing did not work, I tried another.

I made a list of nine additional ways to obtain some orders before the Power Up catalog appeared. One of them involved distributing flyers at the Silicon Valley Computer Society meeting. I was sure that I could get twenty-five orders there and overall it seemed that I should be able to sell fifty copies at a minimum from all the possibilities on my list. Using Microsoft Word, I made a data sheet describing Org and photocopied it on heavy paper. It was unadorned but professional-looking, and I distributed it at the Computer Society meeting.

I also called a list of friends and colleagues at Hewlett-Packard and even some Hewlett-Packard customers. The lack of receptiveness from these people amazed me. Although all of them had a need for Org, they were not comfortable making such a purchasing decision on their own. Their knowledge of me as a person was insufficient to overcome their reluctance to act outside their company's normal channels. Those calls were my first lesson in the differences between the entrepreneur I had become and the corporate executive I had been. Later, when I called one of these people to check the reference of a vendor and someone else to ask about a personnel procedure, I found even more doors closed. It was as if I was trying to learn company secrets. As an entrepreneur I found it both comical and sad. I had entered a new and separate world.

While I tried to jump-start sales, I also looked for someone to do public relations work. I wanted to place product introduction notices in a variety of computer publications and hopefully obtain a product review. However, venture capital money was flooding the software industry, so most public relations firms were looking for large monthly retainers. Fortunately, some friends told me about one firm willing to work on a contract basis. I signed them up.

An associate named Jackie prepared a press release and company backgrounder. We also needed photos, so being an avid photographer, I took some pictures of Org running and of an organization chart being printed.

Jackie's next accomplishment was a surprise. She wangled some free exhibit space for me at INTECH '85, a technology conference and exposition to be held at San Francisco's Moscone Center. INTECH wanted to highlight several creative new software applications. As part of the deal, a half-page article about Org and Banner Blue—with both of the pictures I took—appeared in the August 15, 1985, *MicroTimes*.

The exposition ran for three days in August. Connie helped me prepare my display, including some special organization charts that showed how to use Org in her field of interior design, and took some vacation time so she could help me at my booth. I sold a few copies of Org and made contact with an individual at Pacific Gas & Electric who would later become a large customer. Nonetheless, I decided that the show offered a poor return for the time involved. To my knowledge, the exposition never appeared again, suffering the fate of many ventures in this new industry.

My sales efforts during July and August of 1985 yielded just a handful of orders, nothing close to the fifty orders for which I had hoped. Then Power Up placed a stocking order for fifty units to prepare for the mailing of their catalog, but even that was far below what I hoped to sell through them. Strangely, I do not recall being worried—I just kept trying new things.

I had a few thousand dollars left on my line of credit, and I wanted to use it to run some new advertisements. In late August

1985, I worked on a larger advertisement and studied potential magazines in which to place it. I settled on a half-page, island format. Magazine copy surrounded this ad format, so Org was the only product ad on the page, but the cost was much lower than a full-page ad. Given my poor sales results in the *Wall Street Journal*, I decided to run the ad in a computer publication, *PC Magazine*. I also decided to do an experiment in *Personnel Administrator*, a business publication much more specialized than the *Wall Street Journal*. In some companies the personnel department makes the organization charts, so I thought it was a good bet. These ads would be much more expensive than the *Wall Street Journal* ad, running $2,500 and $1,000 respectively.

Looking back, this was a pretty big bet. I had already beaten the odds once by successfully finishing my product when I had no experience creating anything so complex. Now I was about to invest all my remaining funds in a couple of advertisements when the success of the Power Up channel looked like a big question mark and every one of my other sales ideas had come up empty. As a bootstrap it was not enough for one of these ads to generate a few dollars to allow Banner Blue to survive, I needed enough revenue to finance my next move—whatever that would be. I needed a big win; my company needed a big win.

When you cannot afford your own mistakes, you should learn from others, so I intently studied advertising books by John Caples, David Ogilvy, and other authors. The lessons from these advertising greats completely changed my opinion of what constituted a good advertisement, making me think that I should have done my homework before running that first *Wall Street Journal* ad. I had always liked artistic ads with lots of white space, but the facts showed those ads did not sell. I learned that the headline, the sub-headline, paragraph heads, even the mail-order coupon each played a role in selling the product. As I wrote, I stated the problem, offered the solution, established credibility for my claims and product benefits, then asked for the order. The books told me that the more copy tastefully crammed into the ad, the higher the sales. Statistics even showed which words were superfluous and which words helped pique the reader's interest. So, ads became a game for me—every superfluous word I eliminated helped make room for an additional sales point or product benefit.

The books also taught me a technique called the "split run." A split run involves making two ads and then having the publisher print half of the magazines with one ad and the other half with the other ad. Then the publisher distributes the two versions randomly among the subscribers. By placing a code in the ad coupon, I could tell which ad was generating the most orders. I decided to do a split run, changing only the headline of the advertisement. One ad had the headline "Org makes Organization Charts . . . Quickly," the other ad had the headline "Reorganizing?" Unfortunately, there is a long lead time between writing an ad and seeing it in print. I finished the new ads on August 30, but it would be over a month before the magazines were in customer hands.

During this time when I was concentrating on marketing and sales, new printers continued to flood into the market, so I decided to add a couple more to the list that Org supported. It took about a day to add each new printer, with the time split between programming and testing. I also fixed a minor bug that I found in the program. I incorporated these changes in what the industry calls a "rolling" or "silent" release. I changed the date on the program files, but did not change the version number.

Turning the Corner

Several days after making the programming changes, I received a call from Power Up. The catalog was in customer hands and they had sold out their stocking order of fifty in just three days. They ordered 700 more units! I was ecstatic. My confidence had remained unshaken during all that happened in getting Org to market. I had also kept my perspective during all the ups and downs. But now, for the first time since I had quit my job to found Banner Blue, I felt successful.

That night I was up until 2:00 AM, one by one copying 700 floppy diskettes in my personal computer. As I shuffled diskettes in and out of the machine, I would occasionally forget whether I had already copied one or not. Then back into the machine it would go, just in case. The next day, Connie helped me apply the diskette labels. I do not remember complaining for a second about this mind-numbing work; nonetheless, I quickly found a vendor to perform disk duplication and started making plans to hire help.

At least until I relocated to an office, I needed an employee that I could trust to give a key to my house. Fortunately, a close friend was looking for work because her children were both in school. Connie and I had met Annie McMinn and her husband Chuck when he and I were in business school together. They had also moved to California after school and eventually found themselves in Fremont. My hiring Annie was a great way for her to re-enter the workforce, and Connie was comfortable with her having the run of the house. So by the end of September I had my first employee, and it was not any too soon. She dove into work answering the phone, shipping product, and doing basic bookkeeping, leaving me more time for marketing and product improvement.

A few days later, I was driving to Palo Alto for a meeting with someone about Org. I pulled up to the toll booth of the Dumbarton Bridge, reached into my pocket for my wallet, and found it empty! I looked sheepishly at the toll collector and asked if it was possible to write a check. A check to cross a toll bridge—I could not believe it! He directed me to pull my car over to the administration building, where I could indeed write a check. At the counter, I opened my checkbook and realized that I had never written a check for less than one dollar (the toll was seventy-five cents). Should I write "Zero and 75/100" or "Got none and 75/100" dollars? Fortunately, I looked up and saw a giant poster on the wall describing the procedure: "75 cents only," was what the bridge authorities wanted me to write. As I drove away, a single thought repeated itself over and over in my mind, "I don't have enough money in my wallet to cross the bridge. It's time for Org to pay back." The next day, with immense satisfaction, I wrote myself my first paycheck. It was a pleasant surprise to Connie that things were working out, and she liked the idea that we had two incomes again.

At the same time we were both disappointed that we did not have children. There was never a conclusive answer as to why we had lost Twinkle, in spite of a number of tests. We had returned to the infertility specialist, this time with dimmer hopes. As time went on the procedures became increasingly intolerable. Eventually we stopped the process and Connie began investigating adoption agencies.

The First Program Update

The sales through Power Up were starting to generate a number of technical support calls every day. I would find myself telling a customer how to connect their printer while at the same time filling out

address labels for the day's shipments. Much of the work was poor
use of my time, so it was important to obtain more help. On the other
hand, the technical support calls gave me invaluable, first-hand
knowledge about Org's strengths and weaknesses.

My strategy had been to ship a program with the essential features, listen to what customers said, then quickly fix the deficiencies
found in actual use. I had completed the first element of that strategy; now I had to implement the second and third. Customers who
called indicated that Org was extremely reliable in the field, and I had
almost no bug reports. Instead, many calls involved helping users set
up their printers. Often, Org was the first graphics program a user
owned, so their printer might work correctly with their word processor, but fail to print graphics because of incorrect installation. Other
calls indicated that I had some design problems to address.

I quickly found that users wanted their charts to print on one
page, no matter how many people were in the organization. If it was
not possible to print on one page, they wanted to avoid pasting pages
together at all costs. I had already provided Org with a method for
keeping the chart from becoming too large—shorter name fields that
printed an abbreviated name if the chart became too wide—but this
was not acceptable to customers. The typical customer was also unwilling to break the chart into smaller pieces, something I had made
very easy to accomplish. They wanted it all.

A limitation of dot-matrix printers exacerbated the "one-page"
issue: they could only print text in portrait mode across the narrow
eight-and-a-half-inch width of a standard sheet of paper, not landscape. Unfortunately, organization charts tend to be wider than they
are tall, so this posed quite a problem. However, another inexpensive
program called Sideways enabled these printers to rotate the text
ninety degrees so that extremely wide documents like financial
spreadsheets could print "sideways" across the long length of the
page. If the user had continuous-form paper (each page connected to
the next), Sideways even printed across the perforations from one
page to the next. Customers suggested that I modify Org to allow its
use with Sideways. Doing so would not squeeze large charts onto
one page, but at least it would spare the user the difficulty of taping
pages together.

In early November, I shipped Org version 1A, which now included support for Sideways, allowed charts of unlimited width, provided more control of chart formatting, and added support for several
new printers. I announced this upgrade in a mailing to current users

and offered them the improved version of the program for only twenty dollars. I was able to continue using the existing user guides by printing a single-page, new feature update. As I recall, more than a third of my registered users ordered the upgrade, and I received no complaints about the price.

Although I had originally planned for a quick upgrade to the program, the nature of the problems that I fixed in this upgrade were surprising to me. My experience at Hewlett-Packard taught me that the major design flaws of a program are obvious after talking to only five or six people. Yet I did not uncover the "one-page" problem before shipping, even though I had tested the program with at least that many people. Clearly, customers were using the program differently than were my testers—they were making larger charts.

After I identified the problem, it seemed obvious that people making large organization charts would be the most likely buyers of a product that automated their production. Yet, finding testers who would use a new program or feature in the same way as the ultimate customer was to be an ongoing problem throughout my years at Banner Blue. We selected testers according to our own imperfect hunches about actual usage, while customers self-selected themselves through their own decision process. What the customer wanted was often surprising to us, but of course the customer was always right and the problems they uncovered seemed obvious in hindsight.

The customer feedback also confirmed to me that I was correct to include only the most essential features in the first release, incorporating additional features only after hearing from users. If I had written a more elaborate program, I would have invested resources in the wrong product features and delayed the delivery of a product that gave customers what they wanted. The customers who purchased the program at this early stage of development turned out to be willing participants in the process, freely and cheerfully giving me their valuable advice. They enjoyed being on the leading edge of change.

The sales process turned out to be analogous. I had poor results with the customers whom I had thought would be ideal, such as my colleagues at Hewlett-Packard, but had an excellent response from mass advertising, where the customers chose themselves. The *PC Magazine* and *Personnel Administrator* ads generated an increasing stream of direct orders, climbing to 135 during November. Each ad returned at least twice as much money as it cost, so I quickly looked for additional publications to try. December direct sales jumped to 361 units with help from an ad in *Lotus Magazine,* a publication that combined the two characteristics of my target user, a manager and computer user.

Of course while programming version 1A, I was wearing many other hats. I developed a more professional product brochure with a first-class graphic artist, negotiated a site license with Pacific Gas & Electric, rejuvenated Banner Blue's public relations effort, and incorporated the business so that it became Banner Blue Software Incorporated. The sales volume increased enough to get United Parcel Service to pick up packages directly from my home, eliminating the daily trip to their local drop-off site. However, as we eliminated our trips to United Parcel Service, our trips to the bank became more frequent. I kidded a friend who thought Org was a bad idea that I now had to put my deposits in two envelopes because a single envelope had become so fat it would no longer fit in the night deposit slot.

The site license I negotiated with Pacific Gas & Electric was the only one Banner Blue signed for a number of years. It allowed them to make as many copies of Org as they desired for $5,300 up front and an annual maintenance fee of $530. This outwardly arbitrary fee was actually all they had left in their budget, and I was glad to take it. Although it was good money and it helped validate Org in conversations with others, I decided the extended negotiations from October through December 1985 were a marginal use of time for the return involved.

Closing Out the Year

Nineteen eighty-five closed with strong momentum. From May through the end of the year, Banner Blue sold 2,240 units of Org, generating sales of $95,037 and a profit of $22,124. December 1985 was also a productive month for public relations, with announcements for Org appearing in *Infoworld* and the *San Francisco Chronicle* and an article with pictures appearing in *PC Week*. Fortunately, my competitor was not having the same success. In the end, the announcement I had seen in *PC Magazine* was one of only two times I ever saw mention of PC-OrgChart. So, with all signs positive, I started looking for an office.

Reflecting on Banner Blue's first year, I saw that I had made many correct decisions—enough to be successful. Yet, any successful business strategy generates habits that are difficult to break when they are no longer needed, and my bootstrap strategy was no exception. Some aspects of my "do it and pay for it yourself" approach generated positive returns indefinitely. I learned every aspect of the business inside and out, making me a more effective manager, certainly a manager hard to bluff. Yet, Banner Blue was quickly coming out of its bootstrap phase as it generated more and more cash from operations. I learned that although I might do a job better, this did not mean it was a job I should be doing. Occasionally, I was to forget that Banner Blue's success came from the big decisions like choosing to participate in the personal computer software industry, selecting the right product, specifying the product objectives and requirements, establishing an effective product development life cycle, and choosing the proper distribution.

3

Defining the Banner Blue Culture

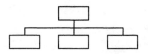

Although our industry continued to change as fast as ever, many of the new things I addressed over the next three years revolved around learning how to run a company. Teaching myself as I went, I defined a successful business philosophy; but being a first-time entrepreneur, I spent a disproportionate amount of time doing so. Amidst everything involved with building a company and a number of surprises at Banner Blue and at home, I would find myself neglecting the market analysis that had been so important to Banner Blue's successful beginning.

Putting the Books in Order

My highest priorities at this time were to develop an organization to support Org's success and to continue enhancing the product. Developing the organization meant that I needed new accounting and management systems, as well as additional employees. Until that time, I had been using my computer to maintain an invoice database, so I was recording revenues in an acceptable fashion. But, with Org's quick growth from $0 to approximately $65,000 in sales for January 1986, circumstances caught me using "shoe box" accounting for my expenses—I was just throwing every receipt into a box. I figured it was more important to ship the orders than to account for the expenses.

To help find an acceptable solution to this new problem, I called Monty Allen, a friend from business school who had worked for one of the larger accounting firms. I figured he would be able to tell me about correct accounting procedures and how to select a tax accountant.

Monty gave me some guidelines that allowed me to straighten out my accounting system in short order and he also had good, simple advice for selecting a tax accountant. He said I would receive better tax advice from a large firm that had a specialized staff. On the other hand, a large firm would assign my account to a junior employee who would turn over as often as once a year. I would receive better continuity with a small local or regional firm where I would be able to work with the same individual, probably the principal, for an extended period of time. Theoretically, the reduced turnover would result in lower costs and more accurate returns. I have always been a believer in long-term relationships, so I decided to search for a local firm and called a number of friends with small businesses to obtain some referrals. I finally chose Curt Revak, who was a partner in a small firm in Pleasanton.

I also wanted to hire an operations manager to be responsible for order processing, shipping, inventory, product assembly, and technical support. With someone to fulfill these duties, I would be able to concentrate on marketing, product development, and finance. On February 5, I hired Anne Cooke for the operations manager position. I had known Anne at Symantec, where she had worked for only several months before being laid off. Anne had a lot of common sense, and that was just what I wanted in an operations manager.

Around that same time, *PC Magazine* ran the first product review of Org—other publications had printed product announcements without any editorial commentary. Glenn Hart, the reviewer, said, "Org does only one thing, but it does it exceedingly well . . . It is difficult to conceive how producing an organization chart could be made any simpler. Given the tortuous procedures required by other software to produce organization charts, Org is highly recommended for the next time you're confronted with producing organizational graphics." Over the history of the product, reviewers rarely stated the marketing philosophy for Org with such clarity. I was happy to find that this review substantially increased our sales from the ads in *PC Magazine*.

Planning Version 2.0

In February, I began summarizing over 500 technical support calls to help me determine which new features should go into the next version of Org. I had been recording the nature of all technical support calls since the very beginning, but when Anne came on board, we also established systems to monitor how long calls took. The customer had to pay for the initial call, but our objective was to answer his question with a wait of no more than several minutes. If it was longer than that, we would call back at our expense. Sharing the expense of technical support with the customer in this way helped make both parties efficient. The customers tended not to make frivolous calls because they were paying for the initial call. In turn, we had an incentive to provide well-trained support personnel who could answer the calls quickly, thus avoiding a return call, and an incentive to improve the product to eliminate the need for a call in the first place. Summarizing the nature of these calls was the first step in a process I was to repeat with every new version of the program.

Using a spreadsheet, I categorized the technical support calls into eight or ten groups, such as user interface problems, desirable formatting enhancements, and printer support issues. For each individual problem or enhancement request, I tallied the frequency of the problem in one column and in another column I made special note of those items mentioned by someone who reviewed the program for a magazine. Often reviewer comments were substantially different from those of users, and sometimes completely off base. Nonetheless, reviewers influenced new purchasers and I could not ignore them. In later releases of the program, I would also incorporate data from user surveys.

These three pieces of data, combined with my own thoughts about the direction in which I wanted the program to grow, summarized the "demand" for new product development. In additional columns on the spreadsheet, I recorded my estimates of the "cost" for each item, measured in time and difficulty rather than dollars. Could I fix the item or add it to the program? What impact did the prospective change have on the user interface? Did an algorithm exist, or could I modify the existing data structure to support the change? If the work was possible, how long would it take and who would do it? I enjoyed mulling over these spreadsheets, weighing the demands against the cost to arrive at a package of improvements. The spreadsheet represented my product requirements document.

As a cross-check on my results, I would often write a draft advertisement or upgrade letter to make sure the product would sell. Ultimately, we would have to ask the customer for money and I wanted our pitch to make a good story. Over the years, there were times when my draft marketing document did not sizzle and we determined that we needed more features to make a successful upgrade or product. Other times we concluded that the features were too unrelated to one another to make a good pitch—for those occasions we looked for a different collection of features to make the new product successful.

In the case of Org 1A, there was demand for four major improvements: more flexible chart layouts, smaller chart size, increased capacity, and support for Hewlett-Packard pen plotters as an output device. My spreadsheet broke the first two improvements into dozens of specific requests. Fortunately, these demands had a reasonable cost and I decided to address every one of them in the new version. I was lucky, because my lack of experience when I architected Org had made some areas of the program difficult to modify. Later this became a problem, but not for version 2.0. By the end of February 1986, I had chosen the new features, divided coding between Paul Heller and myself, and started design work.

Formulating an Organizational Philosophy

As I finished mapping out my plans for the next version of Org, I realized that this same process would have taken many months when I was at Hewlett-Packard. A marketing engineer would have spent a couple of months deciding what he wanted and additional time getting his managers to agree. Then he would have thrown the demands over the wall to the engineering department, which would have told him that he could only have 25 percent of what he asked for in the available time. This would start a long process of negotiation and gamesmanship with neither side fully understanding the other. At Banner Blue, I had the advantage of possessing both the market knowledge and the technical knowledge. I was able to balance one against the other without any interdepartmental games, and the result was a tremendous productivity improvement.

I could not do every job at Banner Blue myself, but it occurred to me that a flat organization (one without layers and layers of hierarchy) staffed with well-rounded, multi-talented people could replicate the productivity improvement I experienced doing both marketing and engineering. As I surveyed the situation at Banner Blue, I also found a practical reason to organize the company in this way. At our small size, most tasks did not constitute a full-time job for someone. If I were to keep people busy, they needed to be capable of doing more than one job. Banner Blue's future needs were highly uncertain as well, so a flat organization without lots of specialized people and departments would offer flexibility as our needs changed. I also thought that the flat organization would dovetail nicely with the profit discipline I had learned at Hewlett-Packard.

While I worked at Hewlett-Packard, their focus on making a profit, even when opening a new market, sometimes frustrated me. This emphasis forced them to abandon some promising new opportunities. Then, my time at Symantec showed me the danger of ignoring profitability to chase market opportunity. I concluded that requiring a good level of profitability created organizational discipline as much as anything else. It was a discipline that prevented Hewlett-Packard from making big mistakes even if it cost them a few opportunities, and whether I liked it or not, it was a discipline inherently required of a bootstrap like Banner Blue.

I saw no reason why I could not combine my ideas for a flat, productive organizational structure with Hewlett-Packard's profit discipline to get the best of both philosophies: a company that could go after new market opportunities while maintaining a reasonable profit. Profitable software companies had revenues of about $200,000 for each full-time employee and I set that as my target, even though most small software companies came nowhere near that level of productivity. I would only hire someone if my revenues already justified it. This philosophy also fit nicely with my strong desire to offer permanent employment opportunities without fear of layoffs.

The flip side of this philosophy was that it required people to work harder than average. If I only hired people after the workload and revenue level justified it, then existing employees would have to make up the difference until that time. Balancing the equation required strong employee incentives, so I copied Hewlett-Packard's profit-sharing plan to help accomplish this. Hewlett-Packard set aside a certain percentage of pre-tax profit to distribute among its employees. Typically, it was an amount equal to four or five weeks of salary on an annual basis. I budgeted the Banner Blue profit-sharing plan to pay a bit more if we met our targets. I was also more generous with discretionary bonuses than my former employers had been. Later, key employees would receive stock.

Our philosophy took further shape as Banner Blue grew over the years. Our salaries were competitive with other companies, and every employee had an annual (sometimes semi-annual) performance evaluation and salary review—another policy I copied from Hewlett-Packard. These performance evaluations were thorough, summarizing the employee's performance against his objectives, reinforcing his strengths, offering constructive suggestions for performance improvement, and suggesting options for career development. They generally were two to five pages long and it was the job of the manager to tailor each one to the employee receiving it—there were no standard forms. It was also the job of the manager to communicate this same information on an ongoing basis. By the time of evaluation, we wanted every employee to know what her manager was going to say.

We obtained detailed salary surveys from industry associations and local universities to ensure that we paid everyone a fair market wage based on merit and results, not cost of living or seniority. If an employee was performing at the 75th percentile for his position, then it was our objective to pay him at the 75th percentile of salaries for comparable positions in our industry. To ensure consistency among managers, I approved every performance and salary evaluation.

Of course, every employee also received employer-paid health care. Although we did not have dental coverage during our first couple of years, I soon decided to add this benefit. Surprisingly, I found the policy rates were equal to about one-third of the maximum payout, and the policies had a large deductible as well. They seemed like a bad deal for both the company and my employees. I stepped back from the problem and decided there was a better approach: we could simply reimburse our employees for 100 percent of their dental expenses up to the same maximum offered by the insurance companies. I figured that at the worst we would be out a few hundred dollars per employee, and the employee enjoyed no deductible and minimal paperwork. It worked like a charm. Over time, our dental expenses were less than the cost of equivalent insurance.

The philosophy "there's no such thing as a free lunch" reigned at Banner Blue, because employees did have to work hard, but they shared in the benefits. This balanced approach gave Banner Blue good acceptance rates when we made a job offer, good retention rates over time, and excellent productivity.

Interviewing Prospective Employees

Our landlord still had not completed the build-out for the new office, but Anne needed help with operations, so I determined that we could fit at least one more employee in the two ten-by-ten foot bedrooms I had taken over in my home. Anne posted a job description at Ohlone College and we received several promising resumes. One of the first people we interviewed was Corinne Speer. I was self-conscious about interviewing Corinne in my living room with my wife's dog, Pooh Bear, quietly resting in the next room, so I made a point of talking about our new office. In addition to traditional interview questions, I also asked Corinne to solve a number of math problems.

While I was at Hewlett-Packard, I became a firm believer in giving job-related tests to help judge a candidate's knowledge. I will never forget the experience that introduced me to the simplest form of this technique. During an interview, I was driving to dinner with a candidate and another Hewlett-Packard manager, John Sien. The candidate had an MBA with an undergraduate degree in electrical engineering, both from the University of Michigan. We had high regard for the school, and the candidate's grades were excellent.

As we drove, John said to the candidate, "If you don't mind, I like to ask everyone a few simple questions." The candidate said, "Sure." John asked, "Define a milli-, micro-, and a mega-." John's ridiculously simple question to such an obviously qualified candidate embarrassed and absolutely flabbergasted me. The candidate's response surprised me even more; he correctly defined only one of the three terms. Then John said, "Define a transistor for me." By this time I realized I was learning something highly useful. I was attentive and no longer embarrassed. The increasingly nervous candidate asked, "What do you mean?" John replied that there were many ways to define a transistor using physics, an electronic circuit, or even the schematic diagram used to represent a transistor in a circuit. "Pick one," John said. The candidate was unable to answer.

Afterwards, John explained that he asked every candidate the same questions to get a feel for their technical knowledge, regardless of their background. He told me that our experience in the car was not unusual for him. Never again did it embarrass me to give little tests, no matter what the candidate's degree or experience. I only once had someone refuse to take a test, but many times the person could not answer.

Some people have argued with me that giving tests during an interview creates too much pressure on the candidate. In a less stressful setting, some candidates who answer incorrectly during an interview might answer the same question just fine. I agree completely! I want an employee who gives the correct answer under the stress of an interview, because a start-up harbors exactly the same kinds of tension day after day. We never used our little tests as an exclusive measure of a candidate's knowledge. We still asked the routine questions about strengths, weaknesses, accomplishments, and goals, but we considered the tests to be a valuable part of the evaluation process.

Corinne handled the math questions with aplomb and on March 20, she reported to work for Anne doing customer service, shipping, and technical support. Several weeks later, we finally moved into our office, over two months behind schedule. It was in an attractive, new building in Newark, California, that looked more like a large house than an office building. We started out by renting about 1,000 square feet, and there was plenty of empty space in the building for our future growth. Connie had done all of the interior design work. I wanted the office to convey a feeling of openness, so the only enclosed office was my own, and even it had sidelights at the door, allowing anyone to see what was going on inside. We ordered quality office furniture to complete the setting. With the additional space we also hired Tina Nomura for a position identical to Corinne's. Both new employees were just out of high school and full of energy.

Competition Changes the Landscape

In a different arena, makers of the presentation graphics program Harvard Graphics announced that they had added an organization chart module to their program. Typically, the emphasis of presentation graphics programs had been the production of pretty bar charts, pie charts, and bulleted text charts for making presentations to a group of people, so adding an organization chart module was an innovation that I did not like.

Because the price of Harvard Graphics was almost ten times as much as Org and it had limited organization chart capabilities compared to Org, there was no immediate threat. However, when I checked out the program at a computer store I found that they had copied many aspects of my user interface—both good and bad features. I felt ripped off rather than flattered. I decided to apply for a patent for Org with the thought of forcing them to change their design. (Unfortunately, by the time I obtained the patent two years later, the issue was moot—a common occurrence in fast-changing, high-technology markets.)

Occupied with building the company and programming the new version of Org, what I did not do during 1986 was analyze how the Harvard Graphics innovation affected Org's market position. Would Harvard Graphics limit Org's growth potential? Would most individuals want their organization chart capability integrated with another general-purpose program? These were questions I did not ask.

Instead, coding for the new version of Org was accelerating, and that's when I got a lesson in the difference between managing and programming. When I was working on my own during 1985, I was able to program for weeks at a time with very few unplanned interruptions. For that first version of Org, most of the programming was complete by the time I had to start juggling dozens of tasks to get the company organized. Now, I had to juggle dozens of responsibilities with programming, and having other employees around meant I had much less control over interruptions.

These circumstances highlighted the unique mindset required to create software. Programming is a very linear and narrow task. Eyes focused on the monitor and ignoring everything in my peripheral vision, I would write a chain of logical steps that eventually became the code for Org. This was a 180-degree turnaround from the big-picture thinking I tried to achieve when focusing on marketing. And when I was managing people, I wanted eyes in the back of my head. I found that I could not mix the programming and managing, so I prepared a special location at home where I could program and everyone had instructions not to interrupt me. Even so, on days when I programmed at home in the morning and managed at the office in the afternoon, it sometimes took an hour or two for me to become sociable again.

We wanted to ship Org version 2.0 during August, and I was so confident of the schedule that I agreed with Connie that she could schedule a one-week vacation in Hawaii starting August 15. The ship date was important because we would run out of version 1A manuals at that time and it was clear that sales were off substantially during June and July—version 1A no longer satisfied customers. Unfortunately, by July it was also clear that the schedule was in trouble and I needed to look for features that I could cut. I went through a process similar to the one in February when I first selected the features to include. This time, however, I also looked for features that I did not need to document in the user guide. It would be easy to add those features in a rolling release after the new version first shipped, taking pressure off the schedule. I also looked for features that accomplished an objective which the user could obtain in some other way, features with a "workaround." After making some adjustments to the original plans, we were back on track.

Bucks for Bugs

The new version of Org required substantially more testing than the original program, and I had to train the entire staff to use and support the new version. I thought I should be able to combine the two activities, using the testing process itself as training; however, testing is a tedious process if done thoroughly, going well beyond the needs of a training exercise. The challenge was to keep people interested and focused.

As an answer to this problem, Anne suggested a technique used by a previous employer; they called it "Bucks for Bugs." I liked the idea, so in July, we started our own Bucks for Bugs plan that paid people a bonus for every bug they found. We set the amounts at $1 for finding a typo on a screen, $10 for a regular bug, $50 for a control flow problem (something appearing on screen out of sequence), and $100 for crashing the program (where it ceases to accept input or abnormally terminates). $100 was equal to about a day's pay for a clerical employee, so it was an enticing incentive.

I was coordinating the testing and continuing to program, but I also had many marketing tasks to accomplish during the summer, most important among them the production of a new advertisement. We had been advertising regularly in *PC Magazine*, *Lotus Magazine*, *Personnel Administrator*, and *Personnel Journal*. We had also tested *PC Week* and *PC World*. Through May 1986, our ad results continued to be extremely cost-effective, with revenues of several times ad costs. I decided that I should increase the size of the advertisement to a full page and expand the selection of magazines carrying the ad. The marketing manager for another new accessory program, an address list manager called *The Little Black Book*, had told me he was having excellent results with the airline seat-pocket magazines distributed free to airline passengers. I wanted those magazines to be my next experiment and I also thought I should try the *Harvard Business Review*.

I designed the new advertisement exactly in the David Ogilvy style. A photograph of several organization charts occupied the top third of the page. Beneath that was a brief caption, and then came the bold, easy-to-read headline: "The quick, professional way to show who's boss." There was also a sub-headline, lots of copy, crossheads, and an ordering coupon. We called it "The Boss" ad. I had constructed many mock-ups of the ad and asked friends for feedback.

I also studied and re-studied every word to make sure each one helped sell the product. I felt Banner Blue had been picking the low-hanging fruit with the half-page island ad because the results were good even though the ad was very basic—we were getting the customers who were desperately looking for an organization chart solution. I wanted this advertisement to be a couple of notches up in professional appearance and effectiveness so that it would entice customers with a lesser need. I was happy with the results of my work, but when I submitted the ad to magazines during the first week of August, it would be four weeks before I would know what customers thought.

The program now required 256 KB of memory and had a capacity of up to 350 employees. It had six new chart styles, several new box styles, support for Hewlett-Packard pen plotters, and support for the Hewlett-Packard LaserJet in landscape orientation.

I decided to change the program's name to Org Plus version 2.0. "Org" was so short that many people thought it was an acronym and others pronounced it with a soft "g" ("ordge") instead of a hard "g" as intended. Over the phone, I always had to spell it out for the person on the other end to understand. Adding the word "plus" was my lame attempt to fix these annoying problems, and strangely enough it helped.

With all of us working long hours, we finally completed version 2.0 on August 14. I left the office well after midnight, and Connie and I got on an early-morning flight for Hawaii the next day. I had a splitting tension headache by the time we arrived, but soon relaxed and had an enjoyable break from Banner Blue.

When I returned there was plenty of work to do, but we also celebrated the shipment of our new version. The winner of the first Bucks for Bugs contest was Corinne, who earned $360. With no technical training, straight out of high school, Corinne was a born software tester. She could crash any program she set her mind to and typically earned twice as much in each Bucks for Bugs contest as the second-place finisher. During her years at Banner Blue, she earned $8,000 in Bucks for Bugs bonuses.

Bucks for Bugs was a complete success and we used it on every significant program release while I was at Banner Blue, paying out $100,000 over ten years. Not only was the bonus itself an incentive, employees got extremely competitive in trying to find more bugs than anyone else. I reinforced the competitiveness by holding an awards ceremony after each program shipped. Starting with the person receiving the smallest bonus and proceeding in order to the winner, I paid the bonuses in cash. I had read that a cash bonus was much more memorable than one added to a regular paycheck, and I certainly found that to be the case. The entire company counted out the bills as I placed them one by one into the outstretched palms of the recipients, who loved every minute of it. I also paid people's taxes on the awards, so the cash was something they could truly spend. It was great money for our employees and a bargain for the company relative to any other method of testing.

While I was getting back in the groove at work, Connie went to the doctor because she had not felt very well during our vacation in Hawaii. To our surprise, we learned she was pregnant with a due date in April 1987. It seemed that the emotional roller coaster of our efforts to have children continued, and we were at the highest part of the track one more time. I joked that we should have stopped infertility treatments a couple of years earlier. Yet, with all that had happened to us, we showed restraint in what we told other people, partly to keep our own expectations in check. We hoped for the best, but were all too aware of what could happen. I do not believe we told anyone that Connie was pregnant, even our parents, until a number of weeks later.

Version 2.0 Starts Shipping

I sent an upgrade announcement letter to our list of 5,000 users. Several thousand ordered the new version at a price of twenty dollars, which was an exceptionally high response rate. The surge of upgrade orders could have easily disrupted technical support and the shipment of regular orders, so I asked people to come in on Saturdays just to ship upgrades. Banner Blue bought breakfast for everyone at a nearby restaurant and then we all went to work clearing out the backlog.

This surfeit of orders showed how important it was to hire outside vendors for certain tasks. I wanted to contract out things that we could do more cheaply on the outside, that were outside my management expertise or style, or that had a very uneven demand for labor. For example, Anne Cooke arranged for the disk duplicator who had done the work at a previous employer, DisCopyLabs, to duplicate our diskettes and assemble our product. This was work that we could do more cheaply on the outside. Norm Tu at DisCopyLabs was an entrepreneur like myself and we had a long, mutually beneficial relationship.

Norm was fond of telling me that I was his pickiest customer and he had a collection of stories about me to bolster his claim. I remember one occasion when we had received some defective manuals from the printer that we did not discover until they showed up in our finished goods inventory. Our operations people were busy shipping orders, so I personally went to DisCopyLabs to dig through the boxes of manuals, pulling out the bad ones. Norm wandered by while I perched myself on top of a pallet, cutting open the boxes. He *never* forgot that I personally sorted through those manuals, often kidding me that he had never seen another executive do anything of the sort— *nor* did he forget that I was serious about quality. Sometimes a small example goes a long way.

Upgrade fulfillment certainly fit the category of uneven demand for labor and we found that Norm was glad to process those orders for us in the future. Banner Blue people worked hard enough as it was without shipping orders on Saturday. Over time, I also contracted with print brokers for our printing needs, graphic artists for the production of marketing materials, and a variety of temporary workers for other tasks. However, I never contracted out activities that I believed were critical to our success.

"The Boss" ad was doing fantastically, as were the airline seat-pocket magazines. We were receiving almost 300 orders with each ad placement. During this time period, Banner Blue also obtained new distributors for Org Plus at an increasingly fast pace. Egghead Software was one of the first successful software-only chains, and they quickly became one of our best customers.

Number Two in Command

With version 2.0 out the door, upgrade orders fulfilled, and the new ad appearing in magazines, I surveyed our employee situation and decided that I still had far too many tasks on my plate. I needed another experienced manager to be responsible for marketing and finance. The first person I thought of was Alma Rodoni. Alma was a junior marketing engineer at Hewlett-Packard, just out of business school when I transferred to the software division. Her manager reported to me. Alma was the most energetic, results-oriented, successful marketing engineer in the group. She got things done and did so without alienating people in the process.

Alma had left Hewlett-Packard to join another former manager at General Electric Information Services in Maryland, where she managed a marketing group working with personal computer software. We still kept in touch; in fact, she had bought one of the first copies of Org. I gave her a call, and in a coincidence that was almost too good to be true, Alma explained that she was getting married and wanted to move back to the West Coast. Joining a smaller company interested her, so she was open to exploring the opportunities at Banner Blue.

After visiting the office and discussing the position, Alma wanted the job. This was an extremely important, senior position, so I compensated Alma accordingly. We agreed on a package that included our standard profit sharing and other benefits plus a bonus tied to her objectives and a series of stock grants that represented several percent of the shares outstanding. She started on December 1.

Nineteen eighty-six closed with all indications positive. Sales had grown to $884,829, representing growth of almost 1,000 percent over 1985. Pre-tax, pre-bonus profits were $341,000. *PC Magazine* gave Org Plus its "Best of '86" award as one of the best new programs of the year. My five dedicated employees and I celebrated the holidays with dinner for ourselves and guests at Chez TJ, one of the finest restaurants in Silicon Valley. I looked forward to an even better year during 1987.

Amber

Connie's pregnancy was going well. She had several normal ultra-
sounds and an amniocentesis. This time we decided we wanted to
know the gender and found that we were going to have a girl, so the
debate about names began. I suggested Amber, my great-grand-
mother's name, but later favored Victoria. At the same time, Connie
grew attached to the name Amber. We both agreed that she would
have Connie's maiden name, Irish, for her middle name.

Unfortunately, more difficulties lay ahead. Like those of losing
Twinkle, my memories of this time are as vivid and detailed as if it
were yesterday, making my recollections of Banner Blue seem fuzzy
and unimportant by comparison.

On Friday afternoon, February 6, 1987, an ultrasound showed
that the fetal growth had stopped and the volume of amniotic fluid
was extremely low. A non-stress test showed the fetal heart had poor
variability. It was racing rather than speeding up and slowing down
according to need. Dr. Shefren recommended aggressive treatment,
asking that Connie check into the hospital immediately. He wanted
to perform some additional tests to evaluate whether to deliver the
baby, as she would die soon if we did nothing. It took a moment for
all this to sink in. Connie went into the state of disbelief that occurs
when the mind is both surprised and overwhelmed by its input. Neither of us were experts, but we knew that a baby delivered ten weeks
prematurely was at the very limit of survivability for medicine at that
time.

At Stanford University Medical Center there were some additional tests, then they wrapped a primitive fetal heart sensor around
Connie's womb. This device was straight from hell. Physically
painless, it was mental torture. Every time Connie or the unborn
baby moved, the heartbeat stopped. The only way we knew whether
the device had momentarily lost contact or the baby had died was to
wait to see if the heartbeat returned one or two minutes later.

Dr. Shefren quickly decided it was necessary to deliver the baby.
This was the prognosis: girls had better survival rates than boys in
similar situations. The fetus was the size of a twenty-five-week-old,
but it was approximately twenty-nine to thirty weeks old. This was
also good because of a self-fulfilling Darwinian effect: any fetus
tough enough to survive such stress does better after the doctor re-
moves the stress when compared to those babies randomly born at the
same size.

Dr. Shefren wanted to increase the baby's odds for survival even more by giving Connie an experimental drug, betamethasone, to help reduce the surface tension in the baby's lungs. An unborn baby's lung tissue does not make enough surfactant for efficient breathing until approximately the thirty-fifth week of gestation. Without surfactant, the tiny air sacs in the lungs collapse, breathing becomes labored, and the body suffers from a lack of oxygen. The synthetic steroid betamethasone accelerates production of surfactant, especially in girls. The catch was that we had to delay delivery long enough to allow the drug to take effect—forty-eight hours was desirable. Dr. Shefren tried to be encouraging.

I stayed at the hospital that night with Connie. The nurses were kind enough to find us a room that had an unused bed, so I was able to get a little sleep. Most of the time, however, I stared at the Hewlett-Packard 8040A fetal monitor. Steady at 150 to 160 beats per minute, the heart beat away with extremely low variability. Then suddenly it would fall off to 80 whenever Connie had a contraction, often disappearing to zero for thirty seconds before returning. My heart seemed to stop in synchrony.

Saturday morning, as I was driving home to shower and pick up some things for Connie, I started crying for the first time. After a short while, the continued sobbing made me angry with myself. I needed to call our parents when I got home, and I did not want to sound like a blubbering imbecile. I also knew that I would be much more comfortable making the calls if I could keep them as unemotional as possible—I wanted to project confidence and optimism. Then as my anger increased I realized it had caused me to stop crying. The one emotion had replaced the other. I wondered if this would work again.

Sure enough I started crying before calling each parent, the emotions welling up as I thought about what I was going to say. So, I slammed my fist hard on the countertop, dialed the phone number, explained what had happened and the planned course of action, hung up the phone, then started crying again. I also left a message on Alma's answering machine telling her that I was going to become a father ahead of schedule and that I would be back in the office . . . sometime. If nothing else, I had learned something about controlling my emotions.

After returning to the hospital, I saw that the situation remained stable, so I went to the medical center bookstore and bought several books on premature babies. I had to satisfy my innate need to understand our situation. After being out for a while it was hard for me to readjust to the unnerving fetal heart monitor. Later, I visited the neonatal intensive care ward and had the nurse show me the babies that would be the size of our own—less than two pounds. Out of fifteen or twenty babies, there was only one that small; her name was Lauren.

I started reading the books. Depending on the baby's exact birth weight, its chance of survival was fifty-fifty at best. Many surviving babies of this size have permanent disabilities or long-term health problems such as mental retardation or cerebral palsy. I started preparing myself for what that would be like. I also reviewed what I had read with Connie, but mostly we just tried to pass the time.

The unborn baby clung to life while the betamethasone took effect and finally Sunday arrived. Connie and I had decided we were not going to have another baby without a name. She still liked the name Amber and I still liked Victoria. Connie suggested Amber Victoria Irish Hess as a lengthy, but fair compromise given that we only had a few minutes to discuss it in private. My initial and unstated thought was that it was a waste of two good names. The baby's chances were not good and I knew that Connie would never consider using the names again should this baby die. But that thought passed in a second. This was no time for pragmatism and the only thing I said to Connie was, "Okay."

A nurse told me during my tour of the intensive care nursery about the importance and soothing effect of a parent's voice even for an extremely premature infant, so I leaned over Connie's womb and gave Amber a pep talk. Soon they wheeled Connie off to prepare her for the operation. Dr. Shefren had decided to deliver using a Cesarean section because he did not think the baby would survive a vaginal delivery.

After having to wait two days for the betamethasone to take effect, we then had to wait even longer. The operating rooms were behind schedule, then someone was slow bringing the blood from the blood bank. Connie had asked not to receive any blood because of her concern about contracting the HIV virus, but Dr. Shefren insisted that blood be available in case of emergency. He also reassured her that the Stanford Hospital screened its blood for the virus. (As I recall, that was not the case for all hospitals at the time.)

I paced circles around Dr. Shefren and expressed my desire to "get this show on the road." With great understatement Dr. Shefren commented that I "didn't wait well." As an entrepreneur, my impatience was a valuable asset—in situations like this, it was a liability.

Finally we got our turn. There were about a dozen people in the operating room, four to work on Connie and six or seven waiting for the baby. I sat beside Connie's head, holding her hand. I had to stand up to see anything because of a towel hung across Connie's chest to screen her view. The thickness of the abdominal wall and womb was much greater than I imagined. It took over thirty minutes to open up the womb.

Then all of a sudden, Dr. Shefren quickly pulled Amber from Connie's womb, snipped the umbilical cord, and passed her to the awaiting team. In the brief second I could see her she looked limp, gray, and totally lifeless. Dr. Shefren looked at me and said simply, "She's very sick." In the previous days, the neonatal intensive care unit had prepared us for what would happen. As they worked on Amber all I could make out was the phrase, "bag her," which I knew meant they would use a small device to resuscitate her.

Doctors use the Apgar score to categorize the health of a newborn infant on a scale of zero to ten. Amber was born with an Apgar of zero: she had no activity or muscle tone, no pulse, no grimace or reflex irritability, blue-gray skin color, and no respiration. They had to give her chest compressions to start her heart. After several minutes, the six or seven specialists, still crowded around the small, wheeled cart with Amber on top, shuffled her out of the room without saying a word. We knew this was a good sign—if they had been unable to resuscitate her, they would have left without her. Yet two days of emergency procedures had drained my emotions, and I was not optimistic. No one who saw that baby could be.

The room was quiet as they sutured Connie's incision. I was despondent and so was everyone else. One of the nurses asked the baby's name. Then a half hour after the birth, someone from the neonatal group walked briskly into the operating room and handed me two Polaroid photographs, saying, "Here are some pictures of your daughter, she's doing great." I was of no further use to Connie in her drugged state, so in disbelief I raced across the hospital to see Amber.

To enter the intensive care nursery, I had to wash my hands and arms with disinfectant and put on a special gown. Amber was lying on what I called the "French fry warmer," a padded surface heated by an infrared lamp. The nurse had bathed her with a sponge and she said it was okay to touch her. I held out the little finger of my left hand and Amber grasped it. Grasp is a relative term. Amber's fingers were only long enough to reach halfway around my finger. Nonetheless, the emotional extremes of this weekend exceeded any of my previous experience, and her touch swung the pendulum to euphoria.

Amber was twelve and a half inches long, the size of a Barbie® doll except for a head the size of a large plum. She weighed one pound seven ounces. My wedding band would have easily slid over her hand. Her features were more proportional to their adult size than was common for a "preemie" of this weight, so much so that the doctors thought it might be a problem. Her skin was translucent, giving her a beet-red color. She was on a respirator, but appeared to be alert. Her rib cage was more cartilage than bone, so that with each breath her sternum sunk halfway to her spinal cord. Yet there she was, thriving after being released from a troubled womb. I silently vowed that I would never underestimate this child again.

Amber began what a number of the doctors told me was an "amazing" recovery. While many babies in her situation require a respirator for a month or more, Amber was on room air and CPAP (a device that keeps the lungs inflated, but does not do the breathing like a respirator) within a day.

Connie got to go home on February 12, but like many mothers of preemies in the intensive care nursery, she was having trouble bonding with Amber because of the plastic isolette that Amber had to stay in. It meant that Connie could not hold her baby. We quickly learned that the nurses were the humanitarians in the intensive care nursery. On February 13, one nurse told us to come back that night after the doctors were gone. When we returned, the nurse scooted a portable infrared light beside the isolette to keep Amber warm, and I moved a rocking chair into position. With tears in her eyes, Connie finally got to hold Amber outside the isolette. It was just for a minute, but it was enough. I took a quick turn as well, and then Amber was back in the isolette.

The intensive care nursery was a cold, noisy, mechanical, inhuman substitute for a womb. Yet in spite of this oppressive environment, each tiny premature baby expressed its personality in a way to which anyone else could relate. And each personality was different—they were individuals, human beings. Amber was more alert than other babies in the intensive care nursery, sometimes sleeping with one eye cracked open. She was often active, other times cranky like myself. Another baby looked to be a future couch potato, for it was always asleep.

One doctor told me my daughter's mental processes were immature and extremely limited, incapable of reasoning or connecting any cause or action with an effect. I had read that only several years earlier, some of these same doctors thought that a baby born ten weeks early was incapable of sensing pain because of these same, limited mental powers. Just what was it they were looking at? While Amber was still in the womb I saw the ultrasonic image of her jumping to avoid a needle, and now I saw her scream when a technician withdrew blood for a test. Most importantly, she was tough enough to survive whatever killed our first child—she was unique and clearly human in her actions. Perhaps the error was in the doctor's perspective on what it is to be human. If Amber's mental processes were indeed immature, then I had to conclude that much of what it is to be human is more basic than symbolic thinking. We are not just intellect.

Clearly, many elements of Amber's personality were pre-wired before birth—they were deeply instinctive, genetic and biochemical rather than rational. This lesson gave me pause about ever again asking something of an individual that contravened their basic, natural personality. Some things are so deep that they never change. It is better to enjoy and capitalize on someone's personality than to make a futile attempt to change it.

I had only talked to Alma once during the week, so for me, it was time to return to the office. There had been no preparation or planning for my unexpected absence, yet when I returned, I found that Alma had done an excellent job keeping everything running. I had good people. This episode should have been a lesson to me that my primary value was not dealing with Banner Blue's day-to-day problems, but I did not even think about the issue.

I began a routine that was to last for several months: Every day Connie drove to the hospital while I was at Banner Blue. Then she returned home for dinner and we both drove over to visit in the evening. I would soon find out whether I was able to balance the demands of Banner Blue with those of parenthood. Without such a balance, I would feel hard-pressed to lay claim to the right to create a culture for Banner Blue.

Version 3.0

By March 1987, I had set the course for version 3.0 of Org Plus. I analyzed the technical support data as before and found that the desire for smaller, more dense charts was the dominant request far above all others. Unfortunately, I could only think of several minor improvements that would reduce chart sizes. So to maintain our growth rate, I decided to open new market segments for Org Plus in engineering, statistics, project management, architecture, and interior design by adding features suited to these new areas. Many of the charts in these applications would not contain people; instead, they might contain the components of an airliner or the tasks in a project. Although they would have the same shape, the resulting charts would be tree diagrams rather than organization charts.

I briefly considered the possibility of Banner Blue adding products to produce other structured graphics like flow charts, a product area where some new competitors were emerging. A flow chart program could make organization charts, albeit not as easily as Org Plus, but Org Plus could not make flow charts. At the time, however, we did not have the resources to pursue that direction, so I quickly moved on to other work.

As before with Harvard Graphics, I never considered how these new, indirect competitors affected the Org Plus market position. I looked inwards, thinking about the direction in which I wanted Org Plus to evolve instead of looking outwards, analyzing how the playing field was changing. I envisioned the ultimate organization chart maker and planned how I could migrate Org Plus in a direction that would provide advanced graphics capability while interacting with personnel systems, databases, and planning systems—whether the market wanted it or not.

My version 3.0 product strategy was to use advertising and marketing to teach people why they should start using tree diagrams. We also decided to set a fast pace for new ad development; one or two new advertisements per month. The first new advertisements would be modifications of "The Boss" ad, but when version 3.0 shipped, the ads would shift emphasis from why Org Plus was the best way to make organization charts to why people needed to make charts in the first place. We also planned to do advertisements specifically targeted to the new markets and to prepare application notes showing how to use Org Plus for engineering and accounting tasks. We tracked ad response in detail, including the position of each ad in the magazine, so we could measure and compare the effectiveness of advertisements and publications.

As I started programming, my workload reached its absolute limit. Yet, as long as Amber was having a good day at the hospital and I was able to express my creativity at work, I was happy. It would have been easy for me to justify some slack during this difficult time, but I actually performed some of my most creative programming. I remember one design problem that gave me special satisfaction, and I recount it for that reason. Version 3.0 was to have a feature that would produce a tabular report, like a phone book, of all the names and facts in an organization chart. I knew that users would want to alphabetize this report by last name, even though the names in the organization chart were most commonly first-name-first. Most software solved this problem by putting the first name and the last name in different data-entry fields, something I could have implemented in minutes. Unfortunately, that would have required all my existing users to re-enter their organization charts.

Instead of making users go to all of that work, I surmised that I should be able develop a means for the computer to pick out the last name. This was not as straightforward as one might think. Some last names contain two or three words (e.g., Van Buren), a suffix followed many last names (e.g., Jr.), and some of my users had already entered names last-name-first. So, I could not just take the last word and assume that it was the last name because I would have been wrong quite often. This was the perfect project to work on while I was in the car with Connie making the one-hour round trip to the hospital every night. Relying on the standard and very regular punctuation for a name, I was able to come up with a set of rules that was correct most of the time. Then I had exception dictionaries for last names and suffixes that did not obey the rules. The program would use these dictionaries when it knew the algorithm would fail. During several drives to the hospital, I read the Fremont phone book to build my exception dictionary and ensure that I was able to extract every last name. The feature worked so well that once we shipped it, I do not recall a single complaint from an end user. This feature required lots of work from me when time was extremely precious, but it saved even more time for our thousands of customers.

We visited Amber every day, except for one Sunday when Connie and I practically collapsed from emotional exhaustion. Although Amber's progress was positive, there were many ups and downs caused by occasional setbacks and frightening days. Then finally, on April 15, 1987, Amber came home. She weighed three pounds ten ounces. There was speculation that Amber might be the lightest baby ever allowed to leave the hospital, but a hernia operation delayed her discharge and she ended up a few ounces heavier than the previous record holder. We stopped at the office to show her off through the car window and then headed home to Fremont.

Our excitement was even greater, I think, than parents bringing home a first child after a normal birth, and more cautious as well. Every time I awoke during the night, I would walk to her bedroom, lean over, and listen to make sure that she was still breathing. Then at 5:00 AM I got up to give Amber her first feeding of the day. In spite of this schedule, my many responsibilities became more manageable with Amber at home, and just in time.

A new "tree math" feature was proving difficult to design and implement. This feature would let users in our new target markets calculate budgets, revenues, project hours, or any other quantity, position by position up the branches of the chart. When a user rearranged the chart, Org Plus would automatically recalculate the totals. There was no other program that did the kind of tree math that I was implementing. Spreadsheets, for example, operated on tables of numbers, not branches. Unfortunately, our customers were of very limited assistance because this unprecedented feature was outside their experience—I learned that people can only extrapolate a small distance from what is familiar and common. So, I again found myself in the role of pathfinder. I drew analogies with other programs wherever possible, and one by one I worked through all the problems. In the end I was happy with everything except one minor aspect of the design.

In spite of the difficulties, programming progressed on schedule and we shipped version 3.0 on August 31. Absent significant competition, we raised the suggested retail price to $79.95 at the same time.

Over the next months I did several rolling releases to clean up minor problems and we learned that *PC Magazine* nominated Org Plus for their Technical Excellence Award. For the second year in a row, Org Plus also won *PC Magazine's* Best of '87 award as one of the best personal computer programs of the year.

Changes in Customer Behavior

Upgrade sales alone reached $210,000 during 1987, but elsewhere I uncovered a disturbing trend. In spite of the increased energy our advertising received during 1987, direct response sales to customers from our advertisements were falling from 35 to 25 percent of total sales. On November 23, I prepared a matrix with the possible reasons for the direct response sales decline in one column, a possible test for each reason in a second column, and the solution for each problem in a third column. There were several possibilities: we had overworked the publications where we advertised, readers no longer noticed our advertisements, we had saturated our primary market, or the direct response channel was simply drying up.

To take our advertisements to the next higher level, we retained an advertising agency. They did a good job of preparing two ads for us, but in split-run tests they had the same response as our existing ads (one of which, I was proud to say, an author selected to appear in a management textbook). Comparing the agency to in-house advertising, we were spending more on ad development, production, and placement; consuming the same amount of management time; yet obtaining the same results. It did not seem like a good deal.

The most important trade-off was between spending time with the agency to communicate the product benefits versus simply writing the ad copy ourselves. I enjoyed writing copy, and I also thought it was valuable for management to be deeply involved in communicating with customers. Writing ad copy forced me to isolate the most critical "why to buys" of the product and state them in the most concise form possible. I saw it as a very good use of my time, because I could leverage what I learned writing an ad in my communications with everyone both inside and outside the company. In my mind, working with the agency became a losing proposition. In the end, we decided we could improve the polish on new ads ourselves and so bought ourselves out of the contract.

There is an important lesson here. Most companies never consider creating their own advertisements. As a bootstrapper I had no choice—I had to come up with our first ads because I did not have the money to hire anyone else. In the end, I developed an important skill that paid lasting dividends.

Over several months, we tested each hypothesis for the decline in direct response sales and concluded that the direct response channel was simply drying up. As software stores like Egghead became popular, customers came to prefer buying in person and at a discount from the retail price. This shift in customer behavior drove dramatic changes in the channels through which Org Plus reached our customers.

Indeed, during late 1987 and early 1988, we added many new wholesale distributors for Org Plus, including Kenfil, Micro-D, and Softsel. Egghead also became a distributor to government accounts, Power Up started selling Org Plus in the United Kingdom, and J.B. Marketing picked up the program to distribute in Canada. Asais also began translating a version for the French market. Since we had a proven, successful product, the distributors initiated contact with us in almost every case and we received excellent terms.

Our approach with the wholesale distributors reflected our belief that they were order takers and warehouses, not a sales force actually generating a higher level of sales. They constantly sought "co-op" money, funds based on a percentage of the sales of our product. Ostensibly, these funds were for marketing, but often they simply added to distributor profits. We authorized co-op dollars only for specific marketing projects that would help our product and only on a case-by-case basis. For example, we sometimes authorized co-op spending in return for the level of stocking we wanted. When we did not want to authorize the spending it was easy to say, "We're small and don't have the budget" or just, "No." We did some limited telemarketing promotions with distributors, but we stayed away from ads in distributor catalogs and any other expenditures that we felt did more for the distributor's bottom line than for our sales. We also insisted on timely payment from distributors, and we were willing to hold new shipments if an account was overdue.

What we strived for was a relationship of mutual respect with our wholesale distributors. We kept them informed about new products and we shipped when we said we would. If a distributor requested extended payment terms in advance, we often obliged. For example, we sometimes accepted extended terms during the holiday season when it was in everyone's interest to have well-stocked shelves. Later, when we dealt directly with many large retailers, we followed much the same set of principles.

Total sales during 1987 were running at twice the rate of 1986 in both units and dollars. I was proud of us as a company because we had successfully completed our largest program update since the beginning, and we had even done it during a time when my personal life was under tremendous stress.

Yet, without thinking about it, I had strayed from several precepts that made Banner Blue successful in the first place. Instead of manufacturing a productivity tool for a job that people performed in spite of the job's difficulty, with version 3.0 I was trying to persuade people to do something they had never done before. I also neglected to follow the minimalist product strategy I used with the first version, where in entering a new market segment I programmed only the essential features, shipped quickly, then revised based on user feedback. Instead, the tree math functionality was extremely robust, as if Org Plus was competing with spreadsheet products when I really had no idea what math functionality my customers wanted. To my recollection, I did not even think about these important principles. It should have been no surprise to me that over the next year our efforts to open the new market segments had limited success and most of the tree math functionality had limited usage. I learned the hard way that the product criteria I used when I founded Banner Blue retained their value.

During 1988, we repeated the upgrade cycle once again. For the new version I wanted to meet the needs of our existing customers, who I had neglected in my enhancements of the previous year. So, I mailed a survey to 500 users to verify the features sought by our customers. This enabled me to ask about potential new features that customers would never mention in a technical support call. Thirty-seven percent of the users returned the survey and overall they were extremely happy with Org Plus. Reduced chart size still remained the number one request and we also found that over five percent used the program to make family trees for their genealogy hobby. To raise our average selling price without pricing ourselves out of the market we decided to split our product line, offering a low-priced and a high-priced version. We left version 3.0 on the market at $79.95 and shipped the new version, called Org Plus Advanced version 4.0, at a suggested retail price of $129.95.

The Importance of Employee Communications

During the first ten months that Org shipped, there was no need to think about how to communicate to employees. I was either alone or jammed together with up to three employees in 200 square feet of space. After moving into our office, we were still small in number and all located in one large space. There were no secrets; everyone knew everything.

By the end of 1988, Banner Blue had a dozen employees located in our Newark facility, where we had more than doubled the space we were renting to about 3,000 square feet. In addition, I was spending about one-third of my time at home programming.

As we spread out physically, there was a need for more formal communications to ensure that everyone was aware of the many regular and important developments, so I decided to hold company meetings every month. Because running a meeting like this was boring relative to many other things I was doing at the time, I assigned a manager working for Alma the task of preparing an agenda and running the meetings. We held the meetings at a local pizza parlor to foster a relaxed atmosphere. Unfortunately, this communication scheme was not enough.

We had recently lost a well-liked accounting clerk, JoEllen Thornton. To become a certified public accountant, JoEllen had to work under another certified public accountant, forcing her to resign. She left a void at the company. Of the thousands of job applications I have read, JoEllen's was one of two I remember. She began by stating, "I love numbers," and she certainly did. She could even recite her husband's drivers license number. Yet, as much as we liked JoEllen, we had another new employee who seemed to be working out well.

Then, Alma and I were surprised to realize that this new employee was acting as what I can only call a "counter-management" force. The issues were generally trivial. Two that I recall were her constant demands for a photocopier with an automatic sorter and a hot-water spigot for the water cooler. Ever since my Symantec days, I believed that spending energy on such trivial issues distracted the organization from the real work that would make the company successful. We could farm out big photocopy jobs to local copy shops and there was a microwave oven to heat water. When the equipment broke or demand rose to a point requiring a second machine anyway, that was the time that the organization should consider upgrading the equipment. That was my philosophy, period.

Unfortunately, while I talked to employees one-on-one about their individual performance and used the monthly company meetings to talk about overall company direction (and through another employee at that), the new employee personally worked the back rooms to talk about her issues. Alma and I never bothered to address them.

She found that her strongest case was to argue that Alma and I did not know what we were doing. She could *prove* that it cost less money to buy a big copier than it did to use a local copy shop for big jobs. Obviously, Alma and I were incompetent. With a variety of equally trivial issues, this had been going on for some time before I realized it. She was elevating items of minor substance to issues of symbolic importance and she was very good at it, acquiring some converts to her way of thinking. Suddenly, what amounted to a cancer had invaded our cozy, singularly directed organization. People were expending invaluable energy on issues of no importance to our survival.

When I suddenly recognized what was happening, I was *scared*—more so than at any other time during my years at Banner Blue. I felt as if I was losing the confidence of my people because of this pied piper, and it was even worse that I was not sure of the problem's extent. Banner Blue was nothing without its people and they worked at Banner Blue only because of their trust in me. I had visions of losing everything.

I also felt stupid, for it was my own detachment that had let this situation develop in the first place. Only one person could lead Banner Blue and it was not the new employee.

Alma and I talked with each other and with the employees to whom we were closest. After several agonizing discussions we decided that the new employee had to go.

Fortuitously, and only days after I became aware of the problem, the employee decided to resign of her own accord. We immediately showed her the door, and also asked an otherwise excellent employee that had fallen under her spell to resign. This was quite different from normal circumstances. We often asked an employee to stay as long as possible before leaving, giving us time to find a replacement.

Keep in mind that there were only ten of us at the time. I had just shown the door to 20 percent of Banner Blue's employees, and I knew that others were sympathetic to their complaints.

With a knot in my stomach, I called everyone together to describe what had just happened. I spoke with some difficulty and I remember getting no feedback from anyone in the room—none. It was days before I was sure that everything was going to be fine. We had stopped the cancer before it spread.

Alma and I learned the hard way that Banner Blue's growth had made effective communications one of our most important tasks. We had to talk about what employees thought was important in addition to what we thought was important. As Banner Blue grew, my role needed to change. I had to actively sell my philosophy to prevent losing it.

Spurred into action, I took over the monthly meetings and devoted a substantial amount of time to making them interesting in my own unique style, using humor, hand-drawn slides, and even an occasional costume or funny hat to hold people's attention. In meetings, in conversations, in the employee handbook, and during interviews of prospective employees, I repeatedly described Banner Blue's philosophy. Of course, we were also on the lookout for bad hires, hoping to terminate them before they created a problem.

Defining the Banner Blue Employee

Another thing we discovered were the differences among employee education, job experience, aptitude, and the ever-hard-to-pin-down "fit" with the organization. Quite simply, we had another less-than-perfect employee who certainly did not look like one. He was a manager who worked sixty hours per week, always displayed enthusiasm, expressed complete loyalty, cared about people, showed initiative, and stuck with a problem when it arose. He had the finest education available and previous experience at a well-managed company. His ethics were unquestionable, his bearing always professional, and everyone liked him, including me. We thought we were lucky to hire him. How could this person fail?

His performance evaluation said this: ". . . we measure the success of individuals and the company by the *results* achieved. Effort, sometimes extreme effort, may be required to achieve results. But effort without results is effort wasted."

The management process is a never-ending cycle that consists of defining objectives, assigning tasks and responsibilities, measuring results, then correcting the process when someone does not meet the original objectives. As a manager, this individual rarely measured the results of his staff or corrected their actions, because he hated confrontation and wanted to please everyone. Consequently, his people were often out of sync with the goals of the organization, and he did not get results.

As an individual contributor, he was a self-starter, but not a self-teacher. As the company grew and the industry changed he could not adapt quickly enough to keep pace. Overall, he had almost as much

experience as Alma, but carried a fraction of her workload and gar-
nered even fewer tangible results. In short, he was not pulling his
weight. He responded that poor communications and events beyond
his control caused these problems. He thought that with more
coaching, the problems would disappear. However, Banner Blue was
a start-up, not a school. For the proper individual it was a great place
to learn, but no one had time to teach. In my opinion, he just could
not see the big picture.

The old adage for someone who cannot see the big picture is that
he cannot see the forest for the trees. Yet, this aphorism somehow
misses the mark, because it is easy to correct anyone who sees trees
only as individual trees. Tell them that a group of trees make up a
forest and they immediately understand. The person who cannot see
the big picture never understands, because seeing the big picture involves understanding more complex relationships than does seeing a
forest. Their perception of a situation does not generate the same
abstract concepts that allow someone else to understand important
relationships and take action. The situation is more akin to a class-
room experience wherein a student does not understand the teacher's
explanation of a key concept. Not understanding the underlying concept, he cannot do the homework no matter how hard he tries. He
just does not "get it." We have all had this experience at one time or
another. For the individual at Banner Blue, the lack of understanding
occurred in those very areas for which we had hired him.

This person belonged in a more stable, structured environment.
There was absolutely nothing wrong with him and nothing wrong
with us. He simply did not fit Banner Blue's needs or personality.
He deserved to succeed, so we asked him to leave the company. He
never understood or agreed with our analysis, but in my mind he verified it before he found another position. We asked him to manage
our move into larger facilities in the neighboring town of Fremont,
California, where I resided. It was a structured project and he understood every required task from day one. The result was the smoothest
move in which I ever participated. Unfortunately, we had almost no
other tasks like this one, so his resignation was in the interest of everyone. He was a wonderful employee and human being, but suited
for a much different company.

This episode caused Alma and me to spend many hours trying to
define the ideal characteristics for a Banner Blue manager by comparing those individuals who were succeeding with those who were
not. We wanted to hire people whom we knew would fit, rather than

finding out after they were already on the job. We came up with several characteristics of the type of person we thought would succeed:

1. The ideal person had a driven personality; was hungry to succeed; was results-oriented; had clear, specific, aggressive career goals; and had high self-awareness and self-confidence.

2. The ideal person was comfortable handling uncertainty and possessed an ability to identify, analyze, and solve problems not seen before.

3. The ideal person worked hard and was hands-on, tackling any job that needed doing without worrying about whether it was part of the job description. He or she spent company dollars as if they were his or her own and always wanted to do every job correctly.

4. The ideal person was able to balance many projects at once as the situation required.

5. The ideal person had depth in his functional specialty and the industry.

In practice, we found it hard to reliably identify these characteristics during the interview process. Most people will not tell you they can only do one project at a time. For every individual, some characteristics stood out and some remained cloudy. In the long run, it remained easier to look back at the interview notes for someone not succeeding and see the warning signs of their failure than it was to identify the subtle clues in advance. Nonetheless these difficulties did not keep us from trying and improving over time; fortunately, our hiring decisions were correct much more often than not.

Little Things Are Important, Too

Many little things also defined the Banner Blue culture, reinforcing the value we placed on every individual and emphasizing the need to work as a team. Soft drinks and popcorn were always free and readily available, but we considered it bad form for someone to take the last drinks without restocking the refrigerator. Every Friday morning we selected a different employee to provide or cook breakfast for the entire company. When it was my turn, everyone knew what to expect, a balanced meal of donuts and fruit! Fortunately, others put on a much more elaborate spread, including such treats as crêpes and omelets. We also carried on an otherwise dying tradition, the gift of a holiday turkey to every employee.

As we grew, promotions became more frequent, and I was very particular about how we announced each one. I had never forgotten the devastation suffered by a manager of mine at Hewlett-Packard. The division general manager passed over him for a promotion in favor of a colleague. My boss did not find out until I did, when the general manager made an announcement in a large meeting of about one hundred people. It was one of the few times I ever saw such a lack of class at Hewlett-Packard. At Banner Blue, we confidentially pre-announced promotions to every employee who might have been in the running—I wanted no surprises. Then at the general announcement to the entire company, we carefully listed the reasons for the promotion. People did not have to agree with our thinking, but I wanted them to know exactly what it was. Of course, we still occasionally had hurt feelings and jealousy, but I think we kept it to a minimum.

Individually, none of these little things had much significance. In the bigger picture, they were all symbols that showed we cared about each other, and in the long run, I think they all made for a much happier work environment.

Taking Stock

At the close of 1988, I was successfully balancing the responsibilities of fatherhood with those of Banner Blue. Although to be fair, I must point out that Connie was a full-time mom, so the demands on me were not great during Amber's first eighteen months. Connie and Amber went to a variety of classes together and did some traveling as well. I would soon find that the balance between work and home becomes more difficult as a toddler grows up to be a young girl.

To our great relief, Amber suffered no ill effects from her early birth. She ran everywhere, walking only when she was dragging mommy or daddy along. Fortunately, she was a very gentle little girl and household damage was minimal. Cute as a button, she gradually caught up in size with other babies her age. One of her favorite playmates was Maggie Cooke, the daughter of my second employee, Anne Cooke.

Amber had very little hair during her first two years. This was always good for jokes, "Like father, like daughter." Of course, we knew her hair would fill out, while unfortunately mine only fell out.

Amber's favorite pastime with me was playing with her Duplo® blocks. At first she liked to take apart what I had put together, but towards the end of the year she built some fantastic "things." Only she knew what they were! Joint Amber and Daddy projects included castles, a bridge, and several trees (our contribution to new Duplo art). Some of these projects were quite elaborate, and engineer that I am, I always tried to teach good design principles. Indeed, it is amazing what you can build with a simple set of blocks.

Amber also enjoyed playing on the computer with me. I believe it was on Christmas Day 1987 that I wrote a program for Amber that put a colored block on the screen every time she pressed a key. This continued until the screen filled, then every press of a key took one block away. I tried another program that displayed the letter on each key, but that was less interesting. Like most dads, I was trying to interest her in the things I liked most, namely computers and building things. To my great satisfaction I had some modest success.

As Christmas 1988 approached, Amber talked about "Danta" (Santa Claus) all the time, but like many children, she did not want anything to do with him in person. That large man with a strange beard and bright red suit was just too scary.

Banner Blue's sales for 1988 exceeded $2 million. Alma and I had developed a company culture that reinforced our values with conservative, selective hiring practices, rewards for hard work, and open communications. We had maintained our flexibility with a flat organization and improved our product development life cycle with customer surveys. We had been responsive to our customers and our changing distribution channels. Overall, the discipline fostered by our bootstrap origins allowed us to earn profits in situations where many companies would not.

On the other hand, our market understanding was running on borrowed time. While I had focused on our narrow market niche and internal company problems, indirect competitors like Harvard Graphics and flow chart programs were changing the geography of the larger market in which we participated. As a result, our sales growth was decelerating faster than we realized. I needed to look outward once again, reaching beyond the internal problems that intrinsically *demanded* attention to those external problems that *needed* attention.

TABLE 1

BANNER BLUE SOFTWARE SUMMARY 1984-1988

Year	Net Sales	Sales Growth	Profit Before Tax[1]	People[2]	New Programs	Total Releases[3]
1984	$0			1		
1985	$92,820		23.8%	1	Org	4
1986	$884,829	853.3%	38.5%	5		6
1987	$1,814,917	105.1%	36.9%	8		7
1988	$2,044,275	12.6%	32.5%	10	Org Plus Advanced	14

[1] As a percentage of net sales.

[2] This count of full-time employees represents an average number for the year. It includes temporary employees, full-time contractors, and summer hires.

[3] Total product releases include new programs, upgrades, and rolling releases during the year.

4

Family Tree Maker and Diversification

With pre-tax profits exceeding 30 percent of sales, Banner Blue was very profitable, but the rate of sales growth had slowed substantially to about 13 percent for 1988. Because our efforts to increase primary demand for Org Plus were not successful, I decided that Banner Blue needed additional products to reinvigorate growth. It was a big decision made with much less thought than it deserved. Nonetheless, for the next four years we vigorously pursued the goal of creating a diversified product line. Ultimately, the results of our diversification efforts were nothing like what we had envisioned.

Selecting a Second Product—Family Tree Maker

I wanted any new product to meet essentially the same criteria as Org Plus, with some minor adjustments based on our experience over the past years:

1. Be first in its market niche

2. Solve a single, well-known productivity problem

3. Make good use of the computer with high performance

4. Leverage existing sales channels

5. Be buildable in one or two person-years

6. Have low support costs

I knew that about 5 percent of Org Plus owners used the program to make family trees, so that was a logical market to examine. Family trees are predominately of two types: ancestor (pedigree) charts and descendant trees. Ancestor charts show an individual's parents, grandparents, and so on into the past. At the time, genealogy hobbyists typically prepared these trees by hand, using preprinted forms showing four or five generations per page. Descendant trees show an individual's children, grandchildren, and other descendants. They look forward from a vantage point in the past. Hobbyists rarely made descendent trees because each individual had a varying number of children, ruling out the use of preprinted forms. Org Plus was unable to make ancestor charts, but it made a passable descendant tree. This meant that, were we to produce a family tree program, we could borrow code from Org Plus, reducing development time.

Unfortunately, our family tree program would not have been first in its niche. Upon investigation, I found approximately twenty-five genealogical software programs that did some kind of family tree diagram. About five of them were serious competitors, with the most important four being Roots II, Roots III, Family Ties, and Personal Ancestral File (PAF). With all of this competition, I wondered why people were using Org Plus to print trees. When I tried using the existing software, I found out why.

Generally, these genealogy programs had the look, feel, and features of a database. Most of them had limited flexibility and produced printed ancestor charts of very low quality. Data entry was confusing and the programs were difficult to learn and use. In addition, only one program produced any kind of graphical descendant tree. Thus, even with its limitations, Org Plus offered unique advantages.

My mother was our family genealogist, so I decided to have her verify my impressions. Mom also knew virtually nothing about computers, which I thought would be true of most users of a family tree program. When she visited early in 1989, I set up the leading programs for her to try one by one. Even with my coaching, she found them unusable. She also told me that few of her friends in the gene-alogy hobby were using software at the time.

Separately, I found that no potential competitor had wide distri-bution. Typically, manufacturers distributed these programs as shareware or sold them through genealogical publications, genealogy stores, bulletin boards, and consultants. The Church of Jesus Christ of Latter-day Saints (the Mormon church) had developed Personal Ancestral File and sold it through the church. All in all, a customer had to look hard to find one of these programs. And, given the lim-ited sales channels and unsophisticated user interfaces, competitors sold their programs almost exclusively to the serious genealogist. In spite of this situation, I estimated from manufacturers' claims and anecdotal evidence that all competitors combined sold approximately 20,000 units of software per year.

By February of 1989, I had decided that none of the twenty-five existing genealogy programs qualified as effective competition. I felt that our distribution channels represented a considerable advantage, and that we would make this class of software available to the general public for the first time, significantly expanding the market. I also thought that attempting to market a family tree program could edu-cate Banner Blue about the potentially huge hobby and education market.

Ineffective competition was as good as no competition, so I de-cided to proceed. We called the program Family Tree Maker, and I set the following design objectives for it:

1. Family Tree Maker will have the prettiest, most-flexible, most-complete family tree diagrams in the industry—abso-lutely without exception.

2. Family Tree Maker will have the best user interface in the industry—absolutely without exception.

3. Family Tree Maker will maximize use of existing Org Plus code, enabling shipment in time for the 1989 Christmas sea-son.

Although I considered the competition ineffective for the mass market Banner Blue would target, I wanted to flank them just in case I was wrong. My strategy was to sell Family Tree Maker to existing users of genealogy software as a supplemental program for producing attractive family trees. I would not try to convert them; indeed, Family Tree Maker would lack some key features that existing users valued. I just wanted my competitors and their users to underestimate the potential for Family Tree Maker while I built an impregnable lead in the mass market. If they thought of Family Tree Maker as a useful accessory program, they would never imagine that it could obtain the largest share of the overall market, nor would they bad-mouth the program's limitations.

Later, Banner Blue could add features to make Family Tree Maker more attractive as a primary program to the advanced genealogists, but my inclination was to let the existing competitors keep that market. As a measure of the lengths to which Banner Blue carried out this strategy, I directed that the package and ads for Family Tree Maker would not even contain the word *genealogy*. Family Tree Maker was to be a program for printing heirloom-quality family trees—nothing that should concern existing competitors.

I wanted potential customers in the general market to see Family Tree Maker as a fun, rewarding program in order to capitalize on impulse and gift purchases. Family Tree Maker's standard-setting graphics and ease of use also opened the possibility of giving the family trees themselves as gifts. We decided we could encourage this use by bundling some parchment-like printer paper in each package.

A Plan for Diversification

Also during this time, I began work on a general plan to diversify our product line with a wide family of products beyond Org Plus and Family Tree Maker. To carry out such a plan I would need an engineering manager, because I would not be able to handle the workload myself. It happened that a colleague from my days at Symantec, now their vice president of research and development, was ready for a change. He had a liberal arts degree and no training in engineering, an unusual background for a development manager, but we had worked well together when I was at Symantec and his development work had won awards. He wanted to explore the possibilities at Banner Blue.

The downside was that he wanted an extremely lucrative package to join Banner Blue, including stock options and a royalty based on product revenue for each product he developed. It was a lot to ask for. To justify the package he would have to deliver extraordinary product output; however, I agreed to it after constructing a back-of-the-envelope business model that showed how he could do it.

The model required the VP to develop and maintain two new products per year, each with a twelve-month development cycle. I felt I could easily accomplish that myself if I did not have all the other responsibilities of running the company. It also required the resulting products to be, on average, about half as successful as Org Plus. That, too, seemed like a conservative assumption. If we met these conditions, then each product would cost about $200,000 to develop. If cost of goods sold (the materials cost of the program) ran 15 percent of revenue, sales and marketing 20 percent of revenue, and overhead 10 percent of revenue, then each product would pay back the initial investment plus a surplus of over 30 percent of revenue after one year on the market.

The VP was not sure about my numbers. In particular, the cost of hiring good programmers concerned him. However, he validated my model by talking to several friends who were active software developers and in the end he agreed with me. On February 20, 1989, he became Banner Blue's first vice president of engineering and we immediately began exploring which two programs he should investigate.

The first program was an easy choice. The DOS operating system running on IBM personal computers and compatible computers had owned the market since 1983, but in 1989 Microsoft's Windows operating environment and Apple Computer's Macintosh were both making inroads. It appeared that DOS, Windows, and the Macintosh would co-exist for at least a few years. If Org Plus ran only on DOS, we would be missing a sizable fraction of the market and perhaps open up an opportunity for competitors. Since there were some similarities between Windows and the Macintosh, we thought it would be cheaper to develop a program first for one environment and then later for the second. We chose to do the Macintosh program first.

Selecting a second program for the VP to work on was more difficult. About 7 percent of our users created phone directories using the table and report feature we had added to the last version of Org Plus. I liked the concept of a phone book maker, a program that would format professional-looking phone books for clubs, associations, schools, and companies. Such a program would offer much more flexibility than the limited functionality in Org Plus and higher-quality printing than the address book programs already on the market. The VP would have to do some market research to verify the idea, but we tentatively decided the phone book maker should be his second product.

Building Family Tree Maker

Meanwhile, I was managing the Family Tree Maker project and the team was well into the product development life cycle. I completed the product requirements document in April 1989 and the internal and external product specifications in May. We hired Hugo Paz to do much of the programming, although the plan was for me to program the parts that we salvaged from Org Plus since I knew that code so well. Hugo showed his entrepreneurial streak on the first day we interviewed him. There was some work going on in the office, so I moved a couple of chairs under a carport in the driveway and interviewed him there. Unfazed, he accepted our offer.

As I found common, especially in the first version of a new program or feature, the external design of Family Tree Maker required substantial iteration based on user feedback. Hugo built three working data-entry screens before I felt we had the proper approach. I never found a way around this trial-and-error prototyping; it seemed the only alternative was to ship a poor design. After a busy summer of programming, manual writing, testing, package design, and advertising development, we shipped Family Tree Maker on September 28.

We had taken a unique approach with the user guide. A photograph and description of a team member or one of his ancestors introduced each chapter. Our objective was to create a warm and fuzzy, personal feeling among our users, and it worked. Customers commented positively about it almost every week.

To sell Family Tree Maker, Alma actively opened new distribution channels, since a number of likely outlets for the program were not carrying Org Plus at the time. We shipped 6,630 units of Family Tree Maker before the end of the year, almost exactly the same quantity as Org Plus. It was a great start.

Competition for Org Plus

On the same day that we completed Family Tree Maker, we had an unpleasant surprise and our first lesson that while working on one product we could not take our others for granted. I was visiting the president of Power Up, Ed Lauing, when he told me that they had developed their own organization chart program, Company Ladder. They were severing all ties with Banner Blue, including distribution in the United Kingdom. Ed explained that he had to have revenue from the retail channel, not just the catalog. After years of a mutually beneficial relationship, Ed summed up his decision by saying, "It's just business." Well, it was not the way I did business—I thought that Ed's decision was extremely shortsighted. Power Up was a much smaller part of our business at that time than it was when I started the company, but they were still a large account. What made me angrier than the lost sales was Ed's cavalier attitude about the value of a business relationship.

Company Ladder was not nearly as sophisticated as Org Plus, but we did not want to take any chances. We decided to stop offering our low-end product, Org Plus 3.1. We would now only sell Org Plus Advanced, and at the reduced price of $99.95. This made our comparative advantage even stronger and represented a great value for the customer.

We then received a second surprise in October 1989 when Power Up sent a letter to their customers offering to upgrade them from Org Plus to Company Ladder. They had a shockingly low opinion of their own customers. They offered to "upgrade" customers to a program that was less sophisticated and unable to read the files they had already prepared with Org Plus, acting all the while as if they produced both programs. We sent a letter of our own, including a testimonial from a manager who had tried Company Ladder and then purchased fifty copies of Org Plus. I felt vindicated as we pummeled Power Up in the marketplace. I am sure that Ed made more money selling Org Plus than he ever did with his own program.

Software Publishing Calls

During December of 1989, Steve Cullen of Software Publishing contacted me. Software Publishing had set up several operating divisions, and Steve represented the PFS Division that had a charter to market to the needs of first-time or casual computer users. In addition to their low-end integrated product called First Choice and a desktop publishing program called First Publisher, they wanted to offer a collection of accessory products targeted to small businesses and corporations, such as form makers, flow charting programs, contact managers, and organization chart makers. The division had a product development group, but they also wanted to acquire some of the products. Steve wanted me to think about the possibility of Software Publishing buying Banner Blue.

I loved what I was doing, thoroughly enjoying my role as an entrepreneur. I quite literally thought I would run Banner Blue forever and had never considered selling the company. It also seemed that Software Publishing did not want to pay more than one times annual revenues, which was not a great price. So, I did not express much interest. However, Steve did not give up easily. He played amateur psychologist, trying to probe the personal reasons why I did not want to sell, and I gave him some financial information under nondisclosure. Steve was successful in getting me to admit that there might be circumstances under which I would sell, but they did not exist in 1989. I was having too much fun.

After more organizational turmoil at Software Publishing, they soon sold the PFS Division. I had other challenges to deal with and the issue of selling Banner Blue did not come up again for a number of years.

Sales and Profits Decline: Am I Doing Something Wrong?

While Banner Blue was dealing with these peculiar problems, changes, and opportunities, the market was undergoing many changes of its own. As computer hardware became more of a replacement market, hardware sales slowed, which also slowed the growth rate of software sales. Additionally, distributors and retailers were extremely cautious during the first months of 1990 because Microsoft was planning to introduce a new version of Windows—version 3.0. Resellers did not want to stock up on DOS programs, only to find out that their customers really wanted Windows programs. During the first quarter, our sales actually decreased relative to the previous year even with the additional revenue from Family Tree Maker. It was a new and unwelcome experience.

Costs were also increasing. One reason was that the rise of software stores and computer superstores changed the way we sold our products. To encourage sales of our products from store shelves, we now needed expensive packaging where a shrink-wrapped manual had been sufficient before. Inside the package, most products now

shipped with both 5.25- and 3.5-inch diskettes to accommodate different vintages of IBM personal computers, an additional expense
created because stores did not want to stock a different package for
each disk size.

Marketing costs were also climbing because there were almost
no direct-to-consumer sales anymore, so advertisements no longer
paid for themselves. Instead, we often did promotions such as paying
the retailer a fee in return for locating our product in a prominent,
visible location on the store shelf or temporarily reducing our wholesale price so that the retailer could offer a promotional discount to the
customer. These marketing programs were expensive and often did
little more than break even. Our before-tax profit fell to 21 percent in
1989 and 19 percent in 1990, down from over 30 percent in the period from 1986 to 1988.

The demands placed on me had grown tremendously. As president, I had to maintain the strategies for multiple product lines instead of one, manage new distribution channels, develop tactics for
fighting new competitors, evaluate inquiries about purchasing the
company, and now, deal with a decline in sales and profits. At the
time, I was confident that I had adjusted for the mistakes I made
when choosing features for Org Plus version 3.0, features that did not
meet the criteria that were so successful for the first version of the
program. Indeed, I had good reason to be confident. I gave the new
product selection criteria a great deal of attention before deciding to
develop Family Tree Maker, and it had become a successful program.

Nonetheless, I had an extremely full plate. Was I truly paying
attention to what made me successful in the first place? Or was I
succumbing to the "heat of battle" syndrome, wherein the deluge of
day-to-day demands overwhelmed any thoughts about the big picture? I do not believe I even considered the question at the time. Instead, my plan to solve our many challenges was almost reflexive:
quickly develop product upgrades to stem falling sales in the short
term, improve our management control system so we could handle
the increasing number of tasks facing us, and develop more new
products to continue expanding the company. Regrettably, Banner
Blue was about to enter a very unsettling period.

Upgrading Family Tree Maker and Org Plus

In spite of the market conditions, Family Tree Maker continued to do well. Nonetheless, as with every first release of a program, our initial user feedback contained a number of surprises for which we wanted quick solutions. Users wanted more capacity and the ability to handle marriages between cousins, and they were absolutely irate about the way we handled adopted children. On the other hand, our features for tracking medical information were essentially unused, because people had enough trouble finding someone's birth date, let alone the detailed information required for a medical profile.

So, in response to this feedback, we doubled our capacity to a thousand individuals (which still was not enough) and documented a workaround for people who wanted to record marriages between cousins (something much more common than we expected). The adoption issue was especially interesting and reflected our success in selling the program into the mass market.

We had handled adoptions in exactly the same way as every other genealogy program. Genealogists trace blood lines and do not pay much attention to who raised an individual. Consequently, if someone entered an adopted child, we did not print that individual in the tree under the person who raised them. We suggested that people instead place an adopted child under their birth parents. That was completely unacceptable to our mass-market customers who in some cases had quite different needs than a genealogist. They wanted adopted children to print just like any other child and did not want to hear anything about blood lines and birth parents. So, we gave them the option to print the child anywhere they wanted. Later, as the popularity of the program grew, we would face similar issues revolving around same-sex marriages.

The new Family Tree Maker 1.01 that incorporated these changes shipped on April 12, 1990. However, since our installed base for Family Tree Maker was so small at the time, there were no significant upgrade sales and no revenue boost. I responded to the revenue shortfall by accelerating our schedule for the upgrade of Org Plus Advanced. Instead of shipping version 5.0 late in 1990, I wanted to release a new version just a couple of months later in May. The upgrade revenue from our large installed base of existing Org Plus users would stem our sales decline.

Fortunately, market changes played in our favor with Org Plus. The percentage of our users with laser printers had continued to climb and was now in the majority. I became aware of some extremely small laser printer fonts that we could ship with our program. The new fonts would enable users to put as much as four times more information on each page. Finally, I had a solution to the problem of fitting a chart on one page. We shipped on our revised schedule and had one of our most successful upgrade programs ever. Retail sales rebounded at the same time, so we were back in growth mode, albeit at a slower rate of growth than our historical average.

To celebrate our modest turnaround, I treated the entire company to a first-class dinner in Palo Alto. We dined in the loft of MacArthur Park restaurant, off to the side, but still visible to the other guests. I was passing out the Bucks for Bugs awards, and following tradition, we started with the small awards and progressed to the big ones. The Banner Blue employees counted out the amounts as I placed them into the outstretched palms of the winner, "$50, $100, $150, $200 . . . $700!" All of a sudden, I realized that most of the 200 people in the restaurant were staring at us. As our software and company grew, so had the size of the awards—I had not considered the danger of publicly passing out several thousand dollars in cash, and here we were gleefully shouting the amounts to make sure we had the attention of everyone! Visions of my best employees being mugged raced through my head. I stuffed an extra fifty into the pocket of the waiter on the way out of the restaurant, hoping to make him a friend. I also insisted that everyone walk to their cars in a group. From then on we passed out the awards at the office.

Our response to the increasing costs required more creativity and discipline, but every time one of our expenses ballooned beyond our control we looked for another expense that we could cut to help balance it out. Nonetheless, at this time we did little more than stabilize our profit situation.

On May 22, 1990, just after we shipped Family Tree Maker 1.01 and Org Plus Advanced 5.0, Microsoft finally shipped Windows 3.0. Even though it placed heavy demands on the computer hardware, Windows took off like a rocket, changing the entire platform situation. At the time, most home users had insufficient computer power to upgrade to Windows, creating a great deal of uncertainty about when we should make a Windows version of Family Tree Maker. If we developed a Windows version too early, our sales would be poor. On the other hand, Windows penetrated the business market segment almost immediately, requiring us to finish Org Plus for Macintosh as quickly as possible so we could begin work on a Windows version.

Management by Objective

As the market tested Banner Blue with the need for cost containment and rapid product development, our success relied on the execution of our plans by larger and larger groups of people. To meet this need, I refined my process for establishing and monitoring objectives. Over a period of time, I refined a system that worked quite successfully—both the company and the average employee were meeting 80 to 90 percent of their objectives on a regular basis.

The process began with annual objectives for the company. I personally studied my vision of where I wanted the company to be two to three years in the future, and from that I extracted the key activities for the coming year. This draft contained objectives for sales, financial results, product introductions, management system improvements, hiring, and training. I tried to keep it on a single page, but occasionally it spilled over onto a second. Next, I shared the objectives with my senior managers to obtain their comments. Typically, the draft would circulate several times before we came to agreement. Then each manager, including myself, prepared his own annual objectives based on those of the company. This step usually involved several more rounds of iteration before I granted my approval. Many companies stop the process at this point, but at Banner Blue we had barely begun.

Every month we each carved out monthly objectives comprised of key items from our annual objectives and other tasks that came up as the year moved ahead. Occasionally I also approved changes to the annual objectives to allow for changing market conditions. And, every Friday I asked my direct subordinates to turn in a quick, fifteen-minute summary of their progress towards their monthly objectives.

This last step improved performance against objectives more than anything else I tried, because it forced everyone to take a moment from their busy day to actually look at their objectives and consider what they needed to do to meet them. During certain periods of time, I used my weekly staff meeting as a forum for each subordinate to review progress towards objectives. I thought peer pressure would improve performance towards objectives even more, but my conclusion was that it did not. The weekly report was superior in this respect.

To further infuse our organization with the importance of meeting objectives, we reviewed the key ones at monthly, all-employee meetings. Then in every performance evaluation, we reviewed the individual's performance versus his own objectives. I wanted every employee in the company to know whether the company was meeting targets for sales, profits, and product development, and I wanted every employee to know whether he was doing his part.

Although it took a great deal of effort to manage, I eventually tied a bonus equal to about 20 percent of salary to each senior manager's performance against objectives. This required the additional step of assigning a weight to each objective, because some were much easier to accomplish than others. Nonetheless, for most managers this carrot rewarding individual accountability and performance increased results one more notch. Of course, profit sharing was already in place as part of our culture to reward group performance.

Our system of management by objective was exceptionally powerful, giving us a unique focus on results. It ensured that every employee was working towards the same ends with the correct priority—that every employee was doing the right things. If we met our objectives, but failed in the marketplace, I had to look no farther than the mirror to identify the source of the problem.

Brochure Maker

Around this same time, we began investigating a completely new program, Brochure Maker. This program was unusual for three reasons: the idea originated with another company, the software itself was part of a larger service, and we were to develop the product as part of a joint venture. Heath Printers in Seattle came up with the idea for Brochure Maker. Their president, Terry Page, had tried to sell the idea to Scott Cook at Intuit (makers of Quicken®), but it was outside the product focus of Scott's company, so he suggested that I talk to Terry.

Brochure Maker was a concept for a program that would create low-cost, hassle-free, high-quality four-color brochures. It would have a number of standard brochure, or data sheet, layouts. The user would look at actual samples of these standard layouts in the user manual. After selecting one, the user would type the text for the brochure into the program and the program would make sure that everything fit on the printed brochure. There would be no need for a graphic artist or typesetter because the program would take care of these functions. After completing his brochure, the user would then mail a copy of his data diskette and photographs to Heath Printers in a mailer that came with the software. Forty-eight hours after Heath received the information, they would send a full-color proof to the user via Federal Express. Four days after the user approved the proof, Heath would ship printed brochures. Satisfaction was 100 percent guaranteed or the user paid nothing.

We decided to pursue Brochure Maker because it took advantage of a number of powerful market forces. First, digital electronics were remaking the world of high-quality, four-color printing, and this project was taking advantage of that. Also, desktop publishing programs had moved the design and layout of printed material into the consumer's hands (albeit a skilled consumer). Brochure Maker reinforced these two trends by simplifying design and layout and integrating the four-color printing process itself. At the same time, new full-color photocopiers were creating an awareness of the impact of color, but Brochure Maker offered both higher-quality and lower-cost color. Finally, society continued to want things faster and faster (Federal Express delivery, fax, fast food, sixty-minute lubes, and sixty-minute photos, to name a few). Brochure Maker cut the turnaround time for high-quality, four-color printing by about two-thirds. Brochure Maker also met our new product criteria fairly well. There was, however, a requirement to use a limited number of standard layouts, which resulted from limitations with the printing equipment. This resulted in a lack of brochure design flexibility, but interviews with potential customers made us feel that the limitations would be acceptable.

After a number of meetings during the summer of 1990, we agreed to jointly develop Brochure Maker with Heath Printers. Banner Blue would be responsible for the software, software sales, and software customer support. Heath Printers would be responsible for printing and printing customer support. Our agreement called for a 10 percent cross-royalty: we paid 10 percent of software revenue to Heath and they paid 10 percent of print revenue to us.

Problems with the Diversification Model

As 1990 moved on, some cracks started appearing in my diversification model. By this time, we should have been starting an additional program, but instead we were having trouble with the existing projects. Org Plus for Macintosh was becoming very expensive, although it was on schedule. The VP had done additional investigation of the phone book maker and it was sufficiently positive for us to proceed, but now it was also over budget and I had concerns about whether the programmer would be able to complete the program in an acceptable time frame. Surprises were too common, wherein we found we were not able to accomplish some items called for in the product specifications. The VP did the most complete external product specifications imaginable, but because he was not an engineer, he had the programmers do the internal product specifications with minimal supervision, and our results were spotty.

On June 12, the VP proposed a revised development model. He was having trouble recruiting programmers at all, let alone at the price we budgeted. His other responsibilities were also taking longer than expected. He proposed a higher salary and budget to obtain programmers more senior than we had planned and a development cycle averaging twenty months instead of the original twelve.

This proposal would have raised the average development cost to over $330,000 compared to our original target of $200,000. Of course, the problem with the proposed revisions was that the cost side of the equation was going up and the revenue side was not. Ultimately, Org Plus for Macintosh was to cost $450,000 to develop and the phone book maker $261,000 before being canceled. As the phone book maker looked more and more troubled, I remember asking my dad what they did at his employer, Packard Electric Division of General Motors, when a development project got into trouble. He replied that they would sometimes run a second development team in parallel with the first. Well, that was not going to work in my situation, so I pulled the trigger, wishing I had killed the phone book maker earlier. Unfortunately, that did not solve the overall problem with the development model.

The VP and I spent a great deal of time during the balance of the year trying to work out the problems in our development model. We agreed that the internal product specification document needed to be more complete and that he should be using available code building blocks. There were also a number of areas where we did not agree. The VP wanted to do less complex products. He also felt I was asking him to accomplish too much on his own, so he suggested hiring project leaders, additional product marketing engineers, and a QA manager and QA engineers. Combined with his earlier request to use senior engineers, all of these additional people would have increased our development cost substantially. Making matters worse, I was still managing Org Plus and Family Tree Maker, so I did not have time to study our new product ideas or formulate company strategy. I was disincented from turning management of these programs over to the VP, because with his royalty arrangement it was like free money for him, whether we resolved the difficulties in our development model or not.

I slowly realized that our problem and my mistake was that I was trying to get the VP to operate like me. That was inappropriate because the VP, although extremely intelligent and capable, differed from me in training, experience, and temperament. The VP was a designer, not an engineer or an engineering manager. At Symantec he always had an engineering manager to assist him.

My Model of a Project Manager—Resourceful and On Time

I was learning the hard way how different people added value to a project. Take me as an example. Through a combination of my natural interests, experience, and often plain luck, I came to possess a collection of skills and knowledge that allowed me to look at development projects in a very holistic fashion. I had the technical skills to make important judgments at an early, efficient stage. I was also familiar with our markets, and I had my finger on the overall pulse of the business, so I always knew the financial impact of my decisions. I created value when I combined my skills and knowledge to obtain the most functionality and best product out of a constraining schedule and budget. Ironically, I was using senior programmers quite cost-effectively because I was using them only in key areas, not for the whole project. I will elaborate on my methods because they contain several useful lessons.

First, the ability to communicate in engineering terms enabled me to obtain and judge technical input from proven, world-class engineers. This gave me the means to understand the already existing building blocks, and as a first priority I designed the product to take advantage of them as much as possible. Consequently, the product was easy to construct. For example, I was already familiar with the building blocks for Org Plus, and I used them extensively as I designed Family Tree Maker. In contrast, the specification of new custom components built from scratch is time consuming, expensive, and often risky—the custom components might not even work.

Second, knowing enough about the technology to have a feel for what was easy and what was hard enabled me to create a rough schedule before designing a product. Then I regularly updated the schedule as the design progressed. In so doing, I was not only making estimates of work but implicitly giving the schedule priority over the design. Where my estimate was wrong, I would change the product in a way consistent with my understanding of customer needs to make it fit the time and budget allowed. In contrast, other companies facing a similar situation often just extend the schedule. Regrettably, a longer schedule has two negative effects: it reduces future revenue because some customers defect to alternate solutions, and it increases costs because the development team works longer.

In other words, my personal development philosophy was to subordinate the design to the available materials and to subordinate the product feature set to the schedule—I focused on being *resourceful* and *on time*. This philosophy helped me obtain the greatest possible functionality at the lowest possible cost. It was a method I had developed when I was scrounging for parts to build my childhood projects, and I refined it while bootstrapping Org Plus and Family Tree Maker—over the next several years I would use it successfully time and time again.

I wish I could say my development philosophy resulted from a tremendous insight, but the truth is I often desired something that I could afford through no other means—I had to be inventive. I could not have built most of my childhood projects in any other way. The initial version of Org had to ship on time or I would have run out of money. At the risk of comparing apples and oranges, my desire exceeded my funds, and I took great satisfaction using the creative process to overcome the dilemma. Unfortunately, I had not developed an organization that could always work in the same manner.

For example, the VP needed to design the product in detail, then ask an engineer to give him a schedule. Worsening the situation, he held the design as something sacred because that was his specialty and where he put so much of his energy. While the VP agreed with the need to use building blocks, when actually designing a product he felt too constrained by them. Building blocks never quite looked or performed the way he wanted, so he specified new code. The VP's development style had worked well for him at Symantec, a larger company working on a much different class of product, but at Banner Blue it just was not feasible.

In retrospect, these differences between the VP and me seem clear, yet it took months for us to work our way to an understanding. We had successfully worked together in the Symantec environment years before and that had veiled our evaluation of how the VP could implement Banner Blue's diversification strategy. Ultimately, the VP and my diversification strategy for Banner Blue were incompatible because the only way for the strategy to succeed was for him to operate like me and he could not. When I operated through others, I needed a strategy that was compatible with their strengths and weaknesses. At all times, a strategy must be consistent with its constituent parts and with the resources available to implement it.

I wanted to keep the VP because he was an extremely talented individual, so I decided to tone down the aggressiveness of our diversification strategy. We would attempt to build fewer new products and I would stay involved in product development to help with some of them. Since our costs on some of these products were going to be higher than I preferred, we would have to be more selective, choosing only those ideas where we expected a higher return. I was not happy about this new plan, but at the time I did not see any better alternatives.

Some months later, I adjusted the VP's compensation scheme to make it more traditional and more compatible with the revised strategy. Lesson number one of exceedingly lucrative employment contracts is that when things do not work out as planned, the contract itself becomes a source of friction. Adjusting the VP's compensation was not a pleasant experience for either of us and to me it was one more indication of why I should avoid such compensation schemes in the first place. It is overwhelmingly preferable to increase an individual's compensation if and when he succeeds at meeting his objectives.

Anticipating Organizational Stress

As we looked ahead, 1991 seemed to be shaping up as our most challenging year to date. To address our slowing growth, we wanted to upgrade both Org Plus Advanced and Family Tree Maker. We shipped Org Plus for Macintosh on October 17, 1990, and we thought it was extremely important to ship a Windows version of Org Plus before someone took advantage of our absence and entered our market. Additionally, we wanted to complete Brochure Maker and I hoped to develop an undetermined companion product to Family Tree Maker. I wanted to accomplish these product introductions while increasing profits to 25 percent of revenues. So, to help us determine where to direct our profit improvement efforts, I also set an objective to implement cost accounting on a product line basis. Overall, it represented an extremely full plate for a staff of twenty-five people.

I wanted to meet these aggressive objectives even though the stressful effect on our people concerned me enough to institute some preventative measures. I organized product teams so that almost no one was a team member for consecutive projects. That way each person would have a break between the crunch of shipping a new product and starting the next project. I also revised some of our benefit plans.

The average employee (including myself before becoming self-employed) had a "what have you done for me lately" attitude about employee benefits. This comment is not a criticism; the employee response simply reflects human nature. Consequently, I tried to make annual improvements to the benefit package, even if they were small. We had recently implemented a new benefit called the "computer purchase plan." This plan reimbursed our employees up to $500 per year for personal expenditures on computer equipment. It was unique and very popular among employees. If the benefit was new, I purposely started it small so I could improve it later. At all costs, I tried to avoid reducing any of the benefits.

I also found that how I communicated a benefit was as important as the benefit itself. Everyone liked profit sharing, but no employee, including myself, knew how much the profit sharing plan would pay until the close of the year. I saw this as a serious defect. I wanted to make profits more visible so every employee would adjust his day-to-day actions accordingly.

After examining profit sharing at other companies, I chose the following plan: for every percentage point of pre-tax profit measured as a percentage of sales, every employee would receive one day of pay. Part-time employees received a pro rata share. We would report cumulative profits every month at our company meeting so that each and every employee in the company, regardless of education or background, could see whether our performance would result in a check large enough for a nice dinner or a trip to Hawaii. This plan worked wonderfully. Employees' mindfulness of profit sharing increased dramatically and I often heard individuals express how one thing or another was good or bad for profit sharing.

Shortly thereafter, I also began an annual process of reporting to employees the total, itemized cost of employee benefits, including vacation time. It was a large amount of money and I could not expect employees to be appreciative if they were not aware of our spending. We also experimented with individual reports showing employees what Banner Blue spent on their own personal benefits.

At each company meeting I selected a topic related to our aggressive objectives. At one meeting I talked about how growth brought job changes, new responsibilities, and new procedures. At other meetings, I compared the fast pace of the personal computer software industry to other industries, job-related stress and how to deal with it, and the importance of meeting schedules. For reviewing schedules, I developed an analogy with a number of trains (different products) on a single track (our small company). Each train must stay on schedule or we would have a train wreck as they collided into one another. For example, we only had resources to write one user guide at a time. If a project got off schedule, requiring two user guides simultaneously, we would have a big problem.

The train analogy proved to be an effective communication tool, so I decided to expand the concept into a special session at each company meeting called "Train Time"—a cute play on the origins of Banner Blue's name. I donned a railroad engineer's cap and blew a train whistle before reviewing the status of each project. I would often make hand-drawn overhead slides using caricatures to depict the actions key individuals needed to accomplish. Whenever I drew myself, I made sure to poke fun at myself in some way that everyone would notice. Sometimes a little corniness is just what it takes to hold people's attention.

The Banner Blue Movie Guide

Early in 1991, I decided to develop a totally new program called the Banner Blue Movie Guide, instead of a companion product to Family Tree Maker. By this time, we were surveying our customers to ask which among a variety of program ideas they would actually purchase. The Movie Guide did not test well relative to many of our other ideas, but I rationalized the results by explaining it was because the Family Tree Maker customer represented the wrong market. Instead of doing additional market research, I simply convinced myself that the idea could not fail, and besides, every friend I talked to loved the idea.

The Movie Guide was to be a database of information on 10,000 movies, including the cast, plot, a critic's opinion, awards, and much more. I brought Jeff Levinsky, a computer scientist whom I had met at Hewlett-Packard, on board to design and build the search engine and compression scheme for all of this data. I personally designed an extremely straightforward user interface for the program that I estimated would take only about a week to create, once again specifying as many of our existing building blocks as possible.

None of our engineers would buy into my time estimate, so I accepted the challenge and for the first time in two years did some programming myself. I packed up a computer and sequestered myself at a vacation home Connie and I had purchased two years earlier in Carmel, California. I had found that getting away a few weekends every month helped maintain my energy, even though I always took work along with me. Of course, this trip was 100 percent work. I returned a week later with a functioning user interface, although Jeff disputed whether I had left too many things out to have won the challenge. Nonetheless, our disagreement was all in good fun, and I considered my work to be a good example of my *resourceful* and *on time* development philosophy. I had another engineer finish up the user interface.

One by one, we completed all of the 1991 projects on schedule except Brochure Maker. The Banner Blue Movie Guide had excellent sell-in to our resellers. Banner Blue's sales growth climbed to over 36 percent and profits before taxes recovered to 23 percent. We had tackled gargantuan objectives for the year and largely succeeded. At the same time we had some clear problems to address during 1992. Our product line cost accounting showed that Family Tree Maker was not contributing as much to profits as it should, and of course, we had to get Brochure Maker on track.

Brochure Maker Sputters

Brochure Maker had turned into one of those projects where nothing went right. We had personnel problems with an engineer who did not work out, design problems revolving around whether to develop for DOS or Windows, and a whole set of additional new issues brought about because the project was a joint venture. Slowly, we worked through the personnel and technical issues, but we never got our hands around the problems stemming from the joint venture.

I had learned at Symantec how valuable control was to my happiness. Since then I had built a company around me and it shared my personality. Now we were trying to share decision making with another party and we did not have the temperament, people skills, or appropriate product development life cycle to do a good job. Nonetheless, we continued to stumble through the process and eventually completed the software.

During this time we also refined a canvassing technique for evaluating packaging materials. One of our product managers, Courtney Kermeen (now Courtney Corda), went to a local software store with a bag of cookies. Collaring shoppers, she asked for feedback on package mock-ups in return for a cookie. Although people would not read anything of length, the technique was effective for finding out what a prospective product name implied to the shopper and for evaluating the effectiveness of a tag line in communicating the key product benefits.

Typically, the first canvassing of thirty or forty users showed that our ideas were totally off base. Words that meant one thing to people who had worked on the project for months often meant something entirely different to a shopper whose first introduction to the program was when they saw the packaging. I immediately thought of all the meetings I had attended at Hewlett-Packard to determine product names and slogans—how misguided they now seemed. It was another example of the importance of talking to customers rather than colleagues. After applying the feedback from the first group of shoppers, we prepared a new set of packaging materials and tried again and often again. Usually, the third try was the charm. Canvassing was invaluable in helping us write marketing materials that communicated the concept of Brochure Maker.

Because of concerns about how fast we could ramp up the printing service and continuing doubts about the viability of the product concept, we decided to introduce Brochure Maker into a limited test market. We felt it was less expensive and more reliable to do an experiment than it was to do additional market research. The test market would give us an opportunity to debug the printing service at low volumes and limit our expenses if our worst fears about the product concept were true. Starting in September of 1992, sixteen months after the originally intended ship date, we ran ads in a single national software catalog and Heath advertised the program locally in Seattle.

Sales were very poor during our tests. New, easy-to-use desktop publishing programs had come to market while we developed Brochure Maker, negating one of our projected advantages. At the same time, high-quality paper stock with multi-color, pre-printed designs became widely available from companies like Paper Direct. This paper stock made for very professional brochures at a far lower cost than we could offer, albeit without photographs, and these brochures were instantly available from the customer's own laser printer. Thus, we learned that integrating a variety of technologies into one product before the technologies stabilize was very problematic. Competitors were improving every step of the brochure-making process while we froze two-year-old solutions into our product. Unfortunately, our fears about the lack of flexibility when designing a brochure also proved to be accurate. Almost no one who purchased the program ordered brochures—the inflexible templates did not meet customer needs. We eventually discontinued the program.

Uncle Sam's Budget Balancer

Brochure Maker was a stressful project. Fortunately, the 1992 U.S. presidential campaign provided some unexpected diversion when the large federal budget deficits during this period became a prominent campaign issue. I generally made it a practice to keep politics out of the office. At the same time, it occurred to me that if I did not tell employees how much money the company paid in taxes, they would have no way of knowing, and the lack of knowledge might lead them to make incorrect voting decisions (at least from the standpoint of taxation).

For this reason, I estimated the federal and state income taxes and social security taxes paid by both the employees and Banner Blue. I also estimated the federal unemployment tax, state unemployment tax, local business license fees, sales taxes, and county property taxes paid by Banner Blue. Finally, I estimated the sales taxes paid by our customers when they purchased our products. The total came to almost $1 million, or $34,314 per employee! The amount was roughly equal to the average employee's salary, and they all wondered just where this staggering amount of money was going.

Having opened Pandora's box, I could not stop. As a public service and for no other reason, I decided to build a program called Uncle Sam's Budget Balancer with the following objectives:

1. Educate people about the budget and the magnitude of the budget problem by bringing it into the user's personal perspective. (The average person cannot discern the differences among a million, billion, or trillion dollars.)

2. Raise the level of political discussion about the budget by empowering the average well-educated, computer-owning person to speak about it on an even plane with "experts." In other words, provide easy-to-use but powerful tools of analysis so it is more difficult for politicians to obfuscate and grandstand.

3. Serve as a test of whether this kind of public issue can be addressed using the appropriate personal computer software.

I designed the program to use our existing building blocks, then hired a student intern to write it and assigned Jeff Levinsky as his coach. My plan was to keep development costs below $20,000, then place the program in the public domain for anyone to use free of charge. Uncle Sam's Budget Balancer empowered users to modify the federal government's budget with hundreds of deficit reduction options researched and documented by the Congressional Budget Office. And, they could instantly switch between different views of the same information, for instance, choosing to look at the foreign aid budget in per capita amounts instead of billions of dollars.

We shipped the program several weeks before the election, and by our standards received enormous publicity in newspapers, magazines such as *Business Week*, and even on CNN. Given our small investment, I felt we met our objectives because thousands of people used the program. However, the several hours someone needed to spend with the program in order to learn something about the budget was more than most people were willing to give up. I also learned that interest in a program like this was fleeting. After the election we continued to update it for a couple of years, but received scant attention except from several educators who incorporated it into their curriculum.

Diversification Fizzles Out

During our attempted diversification over the previous four years, we had investigated developing programs to plan vacations, print checks, remove errors from database files, print GANTT charts, track employee attendance, and many other tasks. We had actually shipped Family Tree Maker, the Banner Blue Movie Guide, Brochure Maker, Uncle Sam's Budget Balancer, Org Plus for Macintosh, Org Plus for Windows, and sixteen product upgrades (not counting rolling releases). Yet we had not met our original diversification objectives, and among the new programs, only Family Tree Maker had proved itself to be a winner. After a strong sell-in to our retailers, the Banner Blue Movie Guide quickly fizzled, proving that my positive gut feelings about the market were a poor basis for action. Brochure Maker was also a flop, as I have already described. At this point, I was beginning to realize how very difficult it was to duplicate a valuable, successful product franchise like Org Plus or Family Tree Maker.

To compare prospective product ideas and improve our success rate we had developed what we called the product prospectus. In this prospectus, we first measured the idea against our new product criteria. Then, our prospectus included an environmental impact statement that described any special demands of the program on our existing functions, such as contracts, project management, quality assurance, documentation and packaging, distribution channels, marketing, manufacturing and fulfillment, technical support, general management, or finance. Finally, the prospectus included a market analysis, sales forecast, technical analysis, and investment analysis. We only proceeded if a product passed this rigorous examination and overall scored higher than any of our other ideas. Obviously, however, our new product criteria were insufficient to guarantee success, even when augmented by the additional research contained in the prospectus.

Our two most successful product lines, Org Plus and Family Tree Maker, simply grew out of my own personal experience. I had created Org Plus based on the needs that I had encountered at Hewlett-Packard, and Family Tree Maker on the behavior of Org Plus customers. There is a lesson here: it is extraordinarily difficult to analyze a truly new idea. Prospective customers can only extrapolate very small distances from their current experience, making surveys a weak tool for testing innovative products. Given the limited data, it is easy to concoct a theory about why a new product should succeed and easy to fool oneself into thinking that the theory is actually valid. In reality, proceeding on this basis represents a roll of the dice. On the other hand, personal experience with prospective customers actively seeking a solution to a problem creates tangible knowledge that forms a good basis for action. Such knowledge greatly increases the odds of success.

Although Banner Blue nominally retained its strategy of diversification, the reality of 1993 was that our work to make Org Plus and Family Tree Maker successful on the Windows platform consumed virtually all of our limited resources. There was little management time or engineering talent left over for new products—we did not have much choice in the matter. Was this a blessing in disguise? I had no way of knowing.

Amber Grows Up

At least on the home front I could be sure that things were going well. I was experiencing the rewards and increasing demands of fatherhood as Amber was growing up to be a delightful young girl. Although I am sure many parents spend more time with their families than my business permitted me, I was in no way an absentee father. What worked for me was to make as much family time as possible a matter of routine that my family could count on. I almost always came home for dinner, the one time of day we were all together as a family. Even if I brought work home, Amber and I would play together for a half an hour or so after dinner. She and I still loved to build with Duplo and Lego® blocks. I also attended every school event, even if it occurred during working hours.

These activities took more discipline than time and I look back on them with a great deal of fondness. I know there were evenings after a stressful day at work when I really did not want to play, but I am now very glad that on most occasions I did. I think the extra time I spent with her as a child went a long way to building the good relationship we now have.

Fortunately I did not travel much, but when I did, Connie and Amber sometimes came along. I especially remember a business trip to San Diego. While I was in meetings, Connie and Amber visited the San Diego Zoo and the Wild Animal Park. Then all of us drove up to Disneyland, where Amber loved seeing the familiar Disney characters in person. The following year business again called me to Southern California, so we made it a family trip once more.

It helped immensely that Connie was always there for Amber. She found motherhood very fulfilling and the two of them would often travel alone to visit our parents during the summer when I just could not get away. She also enrolled Amber in a wide variety of mother-daughter activities, including swimming and gymnastic classes.

In addition to being a mom, Connie remained active in the interior design field. She studied for and passed a new State of California certification test and did interior design work for Banner Blue. The mayor even appointed her to the City of Fremont's Art Review Board, an organization responsible for recommending art for all city buildings.

In September of 1992, Amber entered kindergarten at Mission San Jose Elementary and took dance classes after school. Somehow, "The Star-Spangled Banner" became one of her favorite bedtime songs for me to sing, so it did not surprise me when she sang it at an audition for the school talent show. She made the cut and sang our national anthem solo for the entire student body and their parents. I hung on every word as she sang, fearful for her that she would make a mistake and be disappointed. Fortunately I had nothing to worry about, as she sang beautifully.

In October 1992, with Connie's help, five-year-old Amber prepared a flip-chart presentation of all the reasons why I should let her have two pet mice. She knew her dad well enough to know that the only way to win him over was to lay out the advantages of her case in an orderly and concise presentation. Simple whining or begging was not the way to get things done in the Hess household. To Amber, thinking through a problem and reaching a creative solution was becoming a way of life at a very young age. It was also hard to resist that kind of initiative, so two white mice, Rainy Day and Wild Sunflower, came to live at our home.

At the office, however, some new feelings were just beginning to surface. I was finding some aspects of being president tiring and lonely. I always sought perfection and had spread myself thin as a result. Often like the boy trying to stick his fingers in the leaking dike, I personally tried to close any important gap in our efforts—and there were always gaps. My situation was partly a reflection of our hiring strategy. Growing and developing our many young managers took a lot of extra time and effort, and I had to step in to help much more often than I would have with more experienced employees. Also, in spite of our fast-changing environment, I was a little bored. Although the specifics changed, I had been doing much the same thing for almost nine years, and boredom increased my fatigue.

The feelings of loneliness did not result from a lack of people contact—I had plenty. Rather, it was a matter of what I could communicate with my employees. There are often issues that the president cannot discuss with anyone else at the company. For example, I couldn't talk about my sense of fatigue. This would have been unsettling to people, which would have made things even worse. Although I discussed almost everything with Alma, even that relationship had limits of what was professionally appropriate.

These feelings of fatigue and loneliness were occasional and mild at first, but grew in frequency. While I did not yet want to trade Banner Blue for anything else, I came to the realization that I would not want to run the company forever. So, while I had no idea what I wanted to do after Banner Blue, it was time to start planning my exit.

Working with Microsoft

Unfortunately, while Banner Blue had attempted to diversify and I directed my strategic thoughts towards new products, Org Plus became boxed in from a marketing perspective. On one side were general-purpose drawing and flow-charting programs that could also make organization charts, albeit inefficiently. On the other side were presentation graphics programs like Harvard Graphics and Persuasion that could also make organization charts, albeit only simple ones. If we added capabilities to move the program in either direction we would quickly run into the entrenched competition that I had ignored since the programs were first introduced many years earlier.

User surveys made it clear that Org Plus sold primarily to *production* organization chart makers, those individuals creating a number of often complex charts. *Casual* organization chart makers, those individuals producing an occasional chart, did not use Org Plus, but one of the other two options instead. We concluded that somehow reaching casual organization chart makers was the way to grow Org Plus sales, and new technology from Microsoft provided an intriguing means to accomplish this objective.

Windows 3.0 contained a new technology called object linking and embedding (OLE). Essentially, object linking and embedding enabled one program to insert or embed a document in that of another. So, for example, a presentation graphics program could use Org Plus to produce an organization chart to appear on an overhead slide or a word processor could use Org Plus to insert an organization chart as an illustration in a document. Microsoft and Claris had both called us two years earlier in 1991 suggesting this idea. The conversations with Claris had not gone anywhere, but those with Microsoft had.

In 1991, PowerPoint, Microsoft's presentation graphics program, did not have an organization chart maker and it was suffering for this weakness in comparative reviews against Harvard Graphics and Persuasion. Microsoft thought they could trump the competition by using object linking and embedding to connect PowerPoint to Org Plus, an organization chart maker far superior to the ones in Harvard Graphics or Persuasion. They suggested that we remove some features from Org Plus, creating a special version that was smaller, simpler, and even easier to learn. If we also added the object linking and embedding technology to this new program, they would be able to bundle the product with PowerPoint and Word, their word processor.

My primary contact at the time was Connie Clark, a product manager with Microsoft's Graphics Business Unit in Menlo Park, California. At a meeting in February 1991, I asked Connie how much Microsoft was willing to pay us. She replied, "Some companies think the additional exposure of having Microsoft include their product brochure in each package is sufficient compensation for their software." It was all I could do to keep from breaking out in laughter, yet I knew that what Connie said was true—the exposure did satisfy some companies. I explained to Connie that we were not one of those companies—we were in business to make money. She said they did not like royalties. They preferred one-time payments, but could do annual payments justified as a programming charge for changes and updates. I told her I would prepare a proposal.

As we reviewed the situation, some factors argued for a higher price:

1. Banner Blue's expertise, and the fact that Org Plus was a well-known, highly regarded product.

2. Microsoft's desire for an exclusive agreement.

3. The risk of cannibalization (building sales of the special Microsoft version at the expense of Org Plus). We believed this risk was low for something like PowerPoint, higher for Word, and potentially dangerous if every word processor manufacturer felt they needed this capability.

4. The lack of competition. We were the only company with a product on both the Windows and Macintosh platforms, something that was essential for PowerPoint.

At the same time, other factors tended to keep a lid on the proposed price:

1. The value to Banner Blue of this relationship with Microsoft.

2. The cost of Microsoft building its own organization chart capability. If we bid too high, they would just write it themselves.

Since there was no competition, we concluded that we should try to obtain a price close to the cost of programming Org Plus from scratch. We were willing to settle for less if Microsoft only bundled Org Plus with PowerPoint, greatly reducing our risk of cannibalization. When we suggested a number in the hundreds of thousands of dollars, negotiations quickly moved up the chain of command. Darrell Boyle, the director of marketing, became the key contact for Microsoft.

Microsoft had acquired the Graphics Business Unit, so there were still a few entrepreneurs on staff and Darrell was one of them. His internal dealings reached as high as Mike Maples, one of the top three Microsoft executives at the time, who said Microsoft must bundle Org Plus with both PowerPoint and Word or nothing. Since I was not about to cave on price, negotiations broke off and that is where things remained for almost two years.

Then in December of 1992 Darrell called me and said he wanted to talk. The way he described their project budgeting process, scarce developer resources always ran out before they could commit to building their own automated organization chart maker. Since PowerPoint did allow users to draw organization charts in a tedious manual fashion, other things that the program could not do at all received a higher priority. Popular wisdom holds that Microsoft is omnipotent and can do anything it wants to do, but even Microsoft cannot do everything at once. Consequently, they still did not have an organization chart maker, they were suffering even more competitively, and this time they were willing to pay us what we were asking.

Microsoft was still against paying us a royalty because they did not want a company like Banner Blue to receive a windfall if PowerPoint were successful for reasons we had nothing to do with, but Darrell suggested an alternative. Typically, outsiders wrote code for Microsoft products on a contract development basis, meaning that the code belonged to Microsoft, they marketed it under the Microsoft name, and the price paid was fairly low. However, Darrell thought that since Org Plus was the leading product in its market, it was an advantage to include it in PowerPoint and advertise it as such. Consequently, he could justify paying us more than usual. He also suggested the possibility of creating this new version of PowerPoint so that users could upgrade from the reduced to the full version of Org Plus, and still have the two programs work together seamlessly.

Remembering how negotiations had broken down before, I wanted to make sure Banner Blue was proposing an agreement that had a high probability of approval. Negotiations like these were very time-consuming and I did not want to go through them only to come up empty-handed. So, while Darrell and I continued our discussions, I called executives I knew at two other companies who had concluded large deals with Microsoft.

The first executive commented, "Gates got rich on royalties for DOS [the original IBM personal computer operating system] and now he wants to make sure that no one else does. That's the religion. Other Microsoft executives are starting to pay homage to the religion, but you should look for creative ways around it." He thought that maintenance fees per copy shipped, annual support fees, and bonus payments based on volume shipped were all possible. He also suggested that we restrict the bundle to Microsoft products that had a high selling price, minimizing cannibalization. The other executive commented that they got almost nothing for their deal because they had competition for the business. Then the changes required in their program were much more extensive than they expected. Microsoft just kept coming back for more. The executives gave me two very different and valuable perspectives, both consistent with what Darrell was telling me.

Darrell's approach was unique within Microsoft, as well as controversial. Over a period of several weeks he and I roughed out a

feature set for a Microsoft program based on Org Plus. Then Darrell
began a complex internal approval process. To help move things
along, he asked me to prepare a comparison of the superior organization charting capabilities of a slimmed-down Org Plus versus
PowerPoint's competitors. We sent the analysis and copies of Org
Plus to Pete Higgins, Microsoft's Vice President of Applications
Software. In Darrell's conversations with Pete, he stressed that including a brand-name product like Org Plus in PowerPoint was worth
a premium over the cost of pure contract development work. Eventually Darrell convinced Pete, and Bill Gates approved the project as
well.

We signed a letter of intent on March 16, 1993, and a contract
on May 17. During the contract negotiations I made sure that we addressed some of the problems that my colleagues had encountered
when haggling with Microsoft. When the deal was done, Microsoft
named the program Microsoft Organization Chart and work began
immediately.

For the first time in several years, I felt good about our Org Plus
strategy because we were finally reaching beyond the production organization chart makers. We made an attempt to sell a similar
slimmed-down Org Plus to several other presentation graphics software manufacturers, but not much came of it.

Corel called with an interest in purchasing non-exclusive rights
to the full Org Plus for Windows. For that, we wanted far more than
Corel was willing to pay, so those talks were brief. My many negotiations while working at Hewlett-Packard had taught me the value of
killing an unfavorable deal early. There is no sense negotiating if it
will come to nothing in the end. At Banner Blue I learned the additional lesson that most deals consummated to make a few incremental
dollars end up being a distraction at their best and a time sink at their
worst. Consequently, when someone called with a proposal as had
Corel, I was not shy about quickly presenting an aggressive price to
see if there was anything to discuss. More often than not, the other
party was bargain-hunting—it was not our kind of business.

Broadening the Market—Family Tree Maker for Windows

Simultaneously with our development of Microsoft Organization
Chart, Banner Blue also began work on a Windows version of Family
Tree Maker. Windows was pushing the Macintosh to the margins of

the market and fast becoming the dominant personal computer platform.   Although DOS programs could run under Windows, most
Windows users wanted a native Windows version and we saw development of a Windows version of Family Tree Maker as an important
defensive move against potential competitors. It was also an offen-
sive strike into a broader market. Reinforcing our decision to move
ahead with a Windows project was the fact that Intuit successfully
introduced the Windows version of Quicken, a very popular home
finance program, for the 1992 Christmas season.

At that point in time, Family Tree Maker commanded the lion's
share of the retail genealogy market, something on the order of 70
percent of the dollar value, and we wanted to keep it that way. So
far, our strategy of befriending the pre-existing genealogy competitors had worked like a charm. We had even done joint mailings to
the installed base of two of the competitors, positioning Family Tree
Maker to their users as an accessory program. At the same time we
completely dominated the retail marketplace, selling approximately
50,000 units per year. Now we wanted to increase the size of the
market faster than it was already growing.

As usual, we surveyed our existing customers to understand the
improvements they wanted to see. One of the highest requests was
capacity for an even greater number of individuals in each file. By
this time, we had marginally increased the capacity of Family Tree
Maker on at least three occasions, so the demand for greater capacity
was something I did not want to ever hear again—I just wanted the
program to hold any conceivable family tree. As we debated how
much capacity would be insatiable, Jeff Levinsky suggested that we
simply design the program to handle the earth's entire population,
which we guessed to be about four billion at the time (actually our
estimate was low by over a billion).

We all agreed that four billion certainly qualified as insatiable.
Jeff sold his suggestion with the intriguing idea that we set up a
clearinghouse for our customers' trees. They would submit their own
tree, then if we found other customers working on the same family
lines we would send the trees to everyone with a match. Conceiva-
bly, merged trees could become very large and anyway, the incremental costs of designing for the entire population of the earth were
not large. We decided four billion was the number, although we ta-
bled Jeff's idea of a clearinghouse for customer trees.

While it was what customers said they wanted, adding greater
capacity was not a new idea, so it seemed that surveying our existing

customers was not going to provide the information we needed to accelerate our growth. I thought we had one of the best teams of people at any software company and I was tired of growing at roughly the same speed as the market. Although we had been successful by almost any measure, satisfaction is always relative to one's current level of achievement. I wanted to do better. I resolved to apply everything we had learned during the eight years of Banner Blue's existence, and a few new things as well, to achieve my goal.

Courtney, now the product marketing manager for Family Tree Maker, helped develop our concept of market broadening as an adjunct to our product development life cycle. With Org Plus, we had repeatedly surveyed existing users of the program, making it better and better for a smaller and smaller market. Eventually competitors had boxed in the product line. Courtney emphasized the need to find out why people were *not* using Family Tree Maker instead. By adding features and positioning the program in a way that appealed to non-users, we would broaden the program's market.

This concept of market broadening was subtly and importantly different from my earlier and unsuccessful effort to create primary demand for Org Plus. First, we wanted to tap into existing demand rather than create it. Second, we based our effort on thorough market research. Utilizing mailing lists from friends at other software companies, we surveyed thousands of people who were not using Family Tree Maker to determine their interest in family history and to discover what encouraged them or prevented them from studying it. The marketing department did not complete these surveys until after Family Tree Maker for Windows shipped; however, the results provided vital information for our subsequent product plans.

As we discussed what features to include and what features might be better in an additional product, I developed the concept of why a *rich* product was better than a *lean* product. I argued that the feature set was not a matter of manufacturing cost (more features required more diskettes and a larger manual) nor of product design (more features can make a product hard to use, although there are solutions to this problem). Rather, the feature set was a matter of marketing in the following sense: If we could effectively communicate the breadth of features in our product, then a rich feature set created higher entry barriers for potential competitors, offered better value to customers, consumed less shelf space (which was again becoming tight in stores), and ultimately resulted in higher sales volumes because the product would appeal to a broader cross-section of customers.

A product's sales volume is like a rolling snowball. As the snowball tumbles along, it just keeps getting bigger and bigger. In a similar fashion, having a higher sales volume at one retailer makes it all that much easier to obtain distribution at yet another retailer, further increasing total sales. Higher volumes also make it more cost-effective to do sales promotions, which in turn increase sales. A collection of products would not have this snowball effect, but one single, strong product would. The first release of Family Tree Maker for Windows would not embody the rich-product concept, because that would take too long to develop, but I wanted a robust foundation in place. Then we could enrich the product as needed over time.

From then on, I was careful to contrast this rich-product concept with the idea of leanness when entering a new market area or developing a new product feature. In that way, I still held to my earlier philosophies. In other words, I believed that a truly new product or feature not before seen in the marketplace should contain only the essential elements. Only after obtaining user feedback should the feature be enriched. A Windows version of Family Tree Maker was different; we had several years of market experience, and we could anticipate the directions that the product might take over time.

Program Architecture

We had done a poor job of this anticipation with most of our products, Org Plus for Windows in particular. Although Org Plus for Windows was a highly successful program, it had a limited architecture that made many desired changes extremely difficult to implement. We had not been forward-looking when we designed the program. I learned from this that the program architecture was a key leverage point deserving of senior management attention, even as Banner Blue grew in size. For a businessman, good architecture was a matter of product development cost-effectiveness; for an engineer, it was a matter of pride.

I will describe the details of a key architectural decision for Family Tree Maker for Windows because it shows the interaction between new technology, customer need, implementation, and marketing communication. At different points in the process, an entre-

preneur must look at technical minutiae, the big picture, and everything between the two.

I spent a great deal of time examining technology trends that we
might capitalize on with Family Tree Maker for Windows, because
these would have a deep impact on the architecture. I had been experimenting with some new, inexpensive hand-operated scanners that
transferred an image to the computer as you dragged the device
across the page. The quality of scanned photographs and the ability
of new printers to reproduce the resulting images impressed me. It
was clear that this technology would continue to improve. After
toying with the idea of a program dedicated to organizing these images, I concluded that a large percentage of the photographs people
take are of family members. What better place to organize such
photographs than in a family tree–making program? It was a concept
that our users readily understood, and user surveys indicated a strong
interest in this capability.

At the time, programs that worked with images were not easy to
use. Typically, a user would scan a photograph with specialized
hardware and software, then crop or adjust the image with another
piece of software, compress the image file so it did not take so much
space on the disk drive, then finally paste it into the intended document. I saw every reason to believe we could integrate and automate
all these functions into Family Tree Maker, making it a one- or two-
step process requiring no additional software. We decided to incorporate this capability within Family Tree Maker for Windows.

As we discussed the high-level requirements of the program, implementing technologies began to recommend themselves. Wherever
possible, we wanted to use industry-standard technologies or technologies we felt would become standards. This was a new consideration on our part, an extension of my philosophy of resourcefulness
that was important for two reasons. First, programs were becoming
increasingly complex, and utilizing standards would allow us to occasionally use code written by third parties. Of course, such usage required a good deal of prudence and caution since we would be relying on the quality assurance of another organization.

Just as important, we wanted to ride every little wavelet passing
through the market that we could. When organizations developed
standards they also promoted them, and we would be able to piggy-
back on their efforts when we recruited employees and when we sold
our product. Microsoft provided a perfect example for us. They
were extending the object linking and embedding technology men-

tioned earlier to the file structure of Windows programs. At the time, Microsoft called this aspect of object linking and embedding a docfile.

Jeff campaigned strongly for utilizing docfiles to simplify the storage and retrieval of photographic images. There was also a side benefit: docfiles would allow us to store documents, audio clips, and video segments as well. The risks of being an early adopter of this technology concerned me; I did not want us to be doing quality assurance for Microsoft. Rather than debate my concerns, Jeff ran some tests on early docfile code to verify performance and reliability.

Jeff was an expert at putting together little test programs or mock-ups to validate a technical issue. By minimizing the user interface and sticking to the issue at hand, he could typically assemble a test program in a matter of hours. It is a far-underutilized technique, and most people fall into the trap of letting opinions rather than facts make technical decisions. In this case, Jeff's test results were positive and we decided docfiles were a good gamble. We also took advantage of emerging standards for image compression (the JPEG format) and for the preferred means of obtaining a digital image from our users' photographic film (Kodak Photo-CD). Family Tree Maker for Windows would have a robust architecture indeed.

As I have mentioned, I like to write some draft advertising copy early in the design process to see if it sizzles. In the case of Family Tree Maker for Windows, management quickly coalesced around a high-level theme tying directly into the product architecture: the program would store and manage any quantity of any kind of information, including text, images, audio, and video. Ultimately, we employed this theme in some of our marketing materials.

A Beehive of Activity

Banner Blue was always a beehive of activity, and early 1993 was no exception. The engineering VP had resigned to start his own company at the end of 1992, so we were looking for a replacement. That meant that in addition to my high-level work on Family Tree Maker for Windows, I had to step in to design the user interface for the program. While work progressed on Family Tree Maker for Windows and Microsoft Organization Chart, we were also creating a companion program for the Family Tree Maker line called Biography Maker, which shipped on February 19, 1993, and an upgrade for the DOS version of Family Tree Maker which shipped on June 13, 1993.

Biography Maker did just what the name implies—it helped the user organize and write a biography. It was an interesting project because the manager and programmer was a young liberal arts graduate with no prior programming experience, Dan Handalian. Dan started with us as a technical support representative. Consistent with my philosophy of a flat organizational structure with low barriers between departments, a technical support representative typically spent half his time answering customer questions on the phone and half his time doing a variety of other projects. For example, our technical support representatives often played key roles testing new products as part of our quality assurance process. By structuring the job in this way we attracted higher-quality applicants, there was less burnout from the stressful telephone work of listening to people's problems, and we created a pool of employees to whom we were able to offer increasingly responsible work. It was an excellent entry-level position.

After a period of time, the exposure to our product development process led Dan to decide that he wanted to become involved in product design and project management. Reflecting on the difficulties faced by our first engineering VP, I suggested to Dan that he first learn to program. Dan accepted my advice and took a programming class (we reimbursed him as one of our normal personnel policies). Dan did well in the class, so we assigned him this small project.

Dan's success was a testament to both his tenacity and to the product development life cycle we had evolved. With some good coaching by Jeff and Dan's awesome work ethic, our techniques and tools allowed an employee with a non-technical background to complete a product—a task at which people with much more technical training had sometimes failed. Biography Maker served as an example to me of the leverage to be gained from my work on the procedures that constituted our product development life cycle. Instead of managing every project myself, I had tuned our procedures sufficiently so that at long last, others could take my place with successful results. I was also learning how to staff a project team that had the highest odds of succeeding. Ultimately, our rich-product strategy led us to fold Biography Maker into another product, but that does not take away from Dan's accomplishment.

Nineteen ninety-three also saw many efforts to reduce our costs. For example, as packaging became more expensive we found ways to reduce the printing costs of our user guides. Probably our biggest cost improvement resulted from the absence of any albatross-like development projects such as the phone book maker or Brochure Maker. Engineering shipped everything it worked on in 1993, generating substantial revenue.

Meanwhile, the work on Family Tree Maker for Windows accelerated. It was the biggest project we had ever attempted. I may have been the only one with this opinion, but I thought it was proceeding with exceptional smoothness given its complexity. As summer rolled around, it was clear that if we were to ship in time for the Christmas selling season, when sales were twice their normal level, we would have to cut the product feature set back. Conforming with my on-time philosophy, we decided to postpone photographic image management capabilities until the second release.

On Halloween, we finished the program, after several engineers had slept in the conference room during the final days before completing the project. Although I did not spend the night at the office, I made it a point to be around for extreme hours myself whenever the team was working this hard. Often I would be working on something else, but I considered this moral support to be exceptionally important when I was asking so much of others.

Microsoft Wants to Change Our Agreement

Microsoft Organization Chart shipped to customers several weeks later during November of 1993, and I happened to meet Pete Higgins and Mike Maples at a conference shortly thereafter. Mike suggested what a good idea it would be for Microsoft to sell embedded applications like Microsoft Organization Chart as standalone products or in a bundle of embedded applications. Yes, it would have been good for Microsoft, but it also would have killed the Org Plus product line.

I was glad I had talked to others who had previously made deals with Microsoft, because those conversations had led me to insist on restrictions on how Microsoft could distribute the program, and fortunately, the contract prohibited what Mike suggested. Microsoft executives were smart, savvy, and exceptionally aggressive. Indeed, I liked and respected almost all whom I met. I am sure they did not see every partnership as an opportunity to take advantage of people, but it was important to think two steps ahead so that was not the end result. Other people at Microsoft occasionally tried to nickel-and-dime the agreement, but Darrell proved himself to be totally honorable and Microsoft lived up to both the letter and spirit of our contract.

Later, when we billed Microsoft for the contract's annual renewal, Darrell called to say that the business unit manager, under cost pressure from the corporate offices, thought they were paying Banner Blue too much. The interval between versions of PowerPoint had increased, so an upgrade was no longer an annual event, and the Microsoft team had not intended to pay us so much unless we upgraded the program during the renewal term. I trusted Darrell's integrity and his explanation even though I considered this episode unfortunate. Darrell had already told his managers that he was leaving Microsoft and he soon told me. He felt it would be best to reach some kind of compromise before he departed, so we did. Another colleague at Microsoft summed it up for me as something of an organizational imperative, "Gates is cheap and Higgins is cheaper. To show he is worthy, the business unit manager tries to be the cheapest of all."

In the end, was our deal with Microsoft a good one? As much as I like to measure results, it was hard to draw a firm conclusion about our Microsoft partnership because it generated neither a big win nor a big loss. We experimented with ways to upgrade PowerPoint and Word users to the full version of Org Plus, but none of the experiments covered their costs. This was not terribly surprising, since we were attempting to reach the casual user who had little need for the full product. Conversely, we found no evidence that Microsoft Organization Chart cannibalized sales of Org Plus. Another up side was that we occasionally obtained help with product development issues through the contacts we had made at Microsoft, and I suspect that the aura of our relationship helped in our recruiting of personnel. I also made a good friend in Darrell, something one should never overlook. Since Microsoft paid us fairly for the goods we provided, I would have to say it was a good deal. There certainly was an intangible satisfaction to working with the leading company in the industry, knowing that they distributed tens of millions of copies of our program.

A Quota and Commission-Based Sales Organization

Alma and I closed out 1993 working on some important organizational changes. Almost two years earlier, Alma had told me that she and her husband were ready to start their family and they wanted to move to a town near Point Reyes, California, where she herself was born and raised. Point Reyes is about an hour and a half from Fremont. She hoped we could work out a way for her to stay involved with Banner Blue, but she could not commute that far and for that reason was telling me about this far in advance of their expected relocation date.

On hearing this news, I decided that there was no way I was going to lose my right hand. As the number-two person in the company, Alma had played a huge role in our success. She was my sounding board and the one person I could always count on when I needed her. Her departure would create a hole that would be extremely difficult to fill, the likely result being an even heavier load on me. My philosophy was to take care of my top performers and not to worry about or get rid of those not performing. Over time, we decided the best course of action would be to have Alma reduce her role somewhat to become senior vice president of sales. That job would not require her to be in the office every day, since most of her contacts would be with people outside the office rather than within.

Working at home was something many more people wanted to do than I was willing to allow. In the three times we had tried it, two employees were successful and one was not and I did not want to open the floodgates to something that required careful control. Although I had learned that it was dangerous to hire a new employee with special considerations that cultivated jealousy, I decided this was different because Alma already had the respect of the company and no one wanted to lose her. I was willing to offer the same flexibility to anyone when they reached Alma's level of accomplishment. The new organization would become effective on January 1, 1994.

At the same time, we decided to move to a quota and commission-based compensation plan for Alma and her sales subordinate, Julie Rice. Having begun with a direct response distribution scheme, Banner Blue had a tradition of using its advertising to do the selling, which meant that the sales organization concentrated on coordinating promotions and taking orders. As more and more sales moved into mass-market distributors such as WalMart and Sam's Club, we had to change our way of selling. We needed to be out there aggressively asking for the order because our competitors already were. I wanted an appropriate and healthy incentive in place, so a sales commission seemed the way to go. We established a split of 60 percent salary and 40 percent commission at the sales target. The commission did not have a cap, providing an unlimited incentive to exceed the sales target. Julie was apprehensive, but Alma convinced her they were in the same boat and would row together. During December 1993, the three of us busily negotiated an appropriate sales target.

Summing Up an Unsettled Time

Our lean organization came through several difficult years with bottom-line numbers that many organizations would envy. Some might question what I complained about, but I felt we could do much better. I knew that we obtained the results we did because we were lean, had excellent discipline, and possessed a strong company culture, not because I had made the best product decisions. If we had been sloppy and over-staffed, we might have perished. Finally, our performance during 1993 began to realize the potential of which Banner Blue was capable.

As the last orders left our building, we had shipped almost 20,000 copies of Family Tree Maker for Windows before the end of 1993. These sales results clearly supported my earlier decision to cut features so we could ship on time. Overall, sales growth exceeded 25 percent and pre-tax profits topped the 30 percent mark for the first time since 1988. We had continued a nice reversal of our downward trends in revenue and profit growth. Nineteen ninety-three also marked a transition between our earlier attempts to diversify and what lay ahead.

The efforts to diversify certainly had not worked out in the way I had anticipated—excluding Family Tree Maker, the other new products combined never exceeded 5 percent of our total revenue. I had looked outside our organization and original market niche, but in an over-reaching way that allowed insufficient time to analyze each additional, fast-changing market in the depth that was necessary for success. In the heat of battle, I focused almost exclusively on our new product criteria when evaluating the deployment of resources, not recognizing that the quantity and quality of our resources were far too meager for the number of markets we tackled.

I was not looking at a big-enough picture. We were trying to build unique new products, not clones; consequently, there was almost no management leverage from one product to another. Knowing all there was to know about Brochure Maker told us almost nothing about the market for the Banner Blue Movie Guide. Such a strategy takes immense amounts of senior management time, and we did not have enough to go around. The market forces that caused us to concentrate our resources on Org Plus and Family Tree Maker were indeed a blessing in disguise—they helped lead us out of our unsettled period.

Instead of emerging with a broad product line, we were largely refocused on a single market (albeit a different one than where we started), for most of the company was now working on Family Tree Maker. We had excellent people across the entire company, a proven product development life cycle, outstanding organizational discipline, and two successful product lines. Family Tree Maker for Windows was a world-class product with a solid foundation to grow on because we had successfully avoided many of the development and marketing mistakes made with Org Plus. Soon we would have the largest opportunity of my professional career and we had everything we needed to exploit it. It was our time.

TABLE 2
BANNER BLUE SOFTWARE SUMMARY 1984-1993

Year	Net Sales	Sales Growth	Profit Before Tax[1]	People[2]	New Programs	Total Releases[3]
1984	$0			1		
1985	$92,820		23.8%	1	Org	4
1986	$884,829	853.3%	38.5%	5		6
1987	$1,814,917	105.1%	36.9%	8		7
1988	$2,044,275	12.6%	32.5%	10	Org Plus Advanced	14
1989	$2,757,579	34.9%	21.0%	16	Family Tree Maker	10
1990	$3,410,661	23.7%	18.6%	19	Org Plus for Macintosh Data Exchange Utility[4] Laser Fonts Disk[4]	19
1991	$4,660,481	36.6%	23.2%	25	Org Plus for Windows Banner Blue Movie Guide Family Ties[5]	27
1992	$5,674,820	21.8%	27.9%	35	Brochure Maker Uncle Sam's Budget Balancer	10
1993	$7,113,215	25.3%	30.4%	42	Family Tree Maker for Windows Microsoft Organization Chart Biography Maker Direct Elect[6] Exercise in Hard Choices[7]	20

[1] As a percentage of net sales.
[2] This count of full-time employees represents an average number for the year. It includes temporary employees, full-time contractors, and summer hires.
[3] Total product releases include new programs, upgrades, and rolling releases during the year.
[4] Accessory program for Family Tree Maker.
[5] This program was manufactured for sale by another company.
[6] A version of Brochure Maker designed for candidates for political office.
[7] A special version of Uncle Sam's Budget Balancer for the Committee for a Responsible Federal Budget.

5

Riding Waves of Change

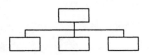

After reviewing our product development life cycle from top to bottom, we had just introduced our best product ever. Now I wanted to repeat the same process of analysis for Banner Blue's entire strategy.

I sought a happy medium. We had spent too much time on internal problems while shipping just one product, then we had overcorrected by trying to analyze too many new and different markets at the same time. I wanted us to balance our time correctly between the internal and external issues facing the company while we also focused on the optimum number of markets. To find this sweet spot I studied the needs of potential customers, evaluated trends in technology, looked at the strategies of other companies, and re-evaluated our selection process for new products. I also added a new constraint to our strategy: Because I continued to tire of running Banner Blue, I wanted to put an exit plan in place.

I began by analyzing Banner Blue's product focus. By default, we were concentrating on a single market more than we had in many years just because a sophisticated program like Family Tree Maker for Windows consumed such a large proportion of our resources—was that good? Further, was Family Tree Maker the best object of our focus? I reserved a large chunk of my time during January and February 1994 to address these issues.

As part of my analysis, I scheduled a great deal more networking meetings with people outside the company than I had for quite some time. I had always considered looking outside oneself to be a necessary and key ingredient to any successful strategy, but in the heat of battle I had unintentionally neglected this important executive responsibility. Fortunately, my work on the Family Tree Maker for Windows strategy served as a wake-up call, reminding me of the actions I needed to take at a corporate level.

The Broadening Survey

Courtney, our product marketing manager, had just summarized the results of our survey of people who did not use Family Tree Maker: our potential customers. Because we offered a free copy of the Banner Blue Movie Guide to each person who replied, we had obtained a high response rate to this survey—over 25 percent—and the information was staggering. Over 90 percent of the respondents wanted to learn more about their family history, yet fewer than 20 percent had purchased genealogy software of any kind. The potential market was even further from saturation when we considered that the penetration of personal computers into homes was still low, albeit growing very quickly.

These potential customers told us that an important reason they did not pursue their interest in family history was a lack of time. They also thought family research was too difficult or they did not even know how to start. A large number of respondents wanted the software to trace relatives for them. Fewer wanted software that organized the information and printed it out in pretty trees. In other words, fewer people wanted what Family Tree Maker did.

As I reflected on the survey results, I considered how many times I had had the following conversation in the past four years. I would meet someone, and they would casually ask about Banner Blue's products. After I mentioned Family Tree Maker, they would say something like, "Oh, does that help you research your ancestors?" I would reply that it did not, thinking to myself that most people certainly were not very perceptive and wishing that we had invented our canvassing techniques before selecting the product name. To me it seemed obvious from the program name that it printed family trees, but not to everyone else—they thought it helped find them. Now I realized that it was I who lacked perception. All along those people were telling me that I was solving the wrong problem.

The survey also reinforced our decision to add image-handling capabilities to Family Tree Maker and confirmed our knowledge that the average Family Tree Maker user was older than the average computer user. Young adults with a busy career and heavy family demands had less time to work on genealogy.

This analysis pointed out another fact: Biography Maker had been a step in the wrong direction. It simplified a task so time-consuming, writing a biography, that only a tiny number of people ever considered the project in the first place. It deepened our product offering instead of broadening it.

The numbers in what we came to call the "broadening survey" were the highest we had ever seen among the dozen or so surveys we had done in the past. Exceptionally large proportions of the respondents were telling us that researching one's family was a classic productivity problem awaiting a solution. People wanted to learn about their family, they just did not have time. Family Tree Maker was improving their productivity, but for only a small portion of the overall task. If we could dramatically reduce the time it took to research the customer's family, we would broaden the market far beyond its current size. We needed to expand the scope of the problem we addressed. The rule of thumb that I applied in cases like this was that we needed to achieve a tenfold productivity improvement for people, because smaller improvements were insufficient to cause them to change their behavior.

We were aware that CD-ROMs containing genealogical source material such as compilations of pedigree charts, marriage records, and the like, were beginning to appear in the market. As a first step to see how we might improve the productivity of research, we immediately assigned an assistant product manager to survey all genealogical information available in any electronic form. She found that there was already more available than we had imagined.

I was so enthusiastic about the possibilities for a CD-ROM–based product that I quickly summarized my thoughts about it in what I called a "starter kit" and assigned a small team to answer my many questions and flesh out my ideas in a product prospectus. Of course, this would include evaluating the product against our new product criteria. I envisioned a program that had several possible components: "how-to" information telling a user what steps were required to research his family, archival data with intelligent means to search it, and a research management function that would help prepare letters for obtaining information from a variety of sources. I wanted to know what information was most valuable to researchers and what it would cost Banner Blue to obtain it. The rich-product concept also applied as I envisioned these new data components being added to the existing Family Tree Maker product.

I did not want a possible CD-ROM product to slow the schedule for the new version of Family Tree Maker for Windows, so this new team was to work in parallel. I assigned Courtney as project manager. Jeff Levinsky was the engineering manager and Danielle Sunshine, an assistant product manager, also began work on the project.

The CD-ROM Wave

Separately, I studied sales trends among different classes of software, looking for those driven by technology waves. These waves result from newness overcoming whatever existed before, and their effect is analogous to a wave at the beach pushing a surfer to the shore. When successful new technologies move along the S-curve from their flat, erratic beginnings to the phase of exponential growth, they give complementary products an added push in the market. The more fundamental and broad-based the technology, the larger the wave and the bigger the push.

When I plot a strategy, I always want as many things as possible in my favor. I want to be riding waves, not swimming against them. Although it is extremely difficult to anticipate a successful technology before it enters the market, once established by actual customer purchases, the waves are readily apparent if you look for exponentially increasing sales. My analysis led me to believe that there were three technology waves simultaneously passing through our markets: a CD-ROM–driven multimedia wave primarily reflected in the sales of educational and entertainment software, an interconnectivity wave of exceptional duration and persistence reflected in the accelerating growth of e-mail software, and a broad-based Windows wave that was beginning to slow.

The CD-ROM–driven wave was of the most interest to us, for CD-ROMs provided a means to deliver genealogical data to our customers. While CD-ROMs had been around for almost a decade, they had attracted a very limited following, but now all of that had changed. As entertainment programs used more and more sophisticated graphics, it was not uncommon for leading-edge games to fill a dozen floppy diskettes. Such products were expensive for the manufacturer to produce and a nuisance for the customer to install. CD-ROMs allowed the manufacturer to cut costs while adding ever more detailed graphics, including video. They also made it a breeze for customers to install the program. Thus, after a long gestation period, CD-ROMs created their own demand in several ways from both ends of the product pipeline. Consequently, CD-ROM drives were now standard equipment on computers sold for home use, and upgrade kits for adding CD-ROM drives to existing computers were inexpensive and readily available. Our own surveys showed that 40 percent of home computer users now had a CD-ROM drive.

On the software side, there was an educational program called Carmen Sandiego that exemplified this trend. In December of 1992, approximately 5 percent of its sales were on CD-ROM; by December of 1993, that had exploded to 24 percent of sales. Similarly, the CD-ROM encyclopedia program Microsoft Encarta grew from almost no sales the year before to one of the most popular home programs in December of 1993.

After these exciting Christmas results, retailers were quickly dropping some diskette-based programs to free up more shelf space for the new CD-ROM programs. The retailers' behavior was a good example of how these waves become self-reinforcing phenomena. Walking through the crowded CD-ROM exhibit area at the Intermedia trade show in San Jose, I could also feel people's excitement. I told Eric Holstege, our new vice president of engineering, to load our engineers in a car and take them to the show. I wanted them to be excited as well.

Management Focus

It was enlightening to compare my thoughts on company strategy with what I saw other companies doing. In January 1994, I attended the Demo '94 conference in Palm Springs, California. At the exhibition, there was a little backup utility program being developed by a company with millions of dollars of venture capital. The program had a snowball's chance in hell of succeeding, but the amount of management talent applied to the enterprise was awesome. In contrast, we were trying to spread our thin but talented resources across diverse families of products in both the home and business markets.

Those two markets had many differences, including different channels of distribution and different product requirements. To my knowledge, Microsoft was one of the only other companies succeeding with products in both the home and business markets and they were orders of magnitude larger in size. So, when I looked at all the energy going into products like that backup utility, a program that had a fraction of the complexity of Brochure Maker, I realized we were not focusing our efforts nearly as much as other companies.

Our Family Tree Maker product line appeared to possess a great deal of untapped potential. We also could exploit important technology waves to tap that potential, and if other companies were any indication, we had been spreading ourselves too thin. All of these facts indicated that we should increase our focus on Family Tree Maker. However, to complete my analysis I also needed to evaluate whether other opportunities were even better. I chose to approach this issue by first looking at our success in selecting new product areas. It seemed to me that if we were good at picking products and if there were substantial opportunities for the taking, then we might want to consider an alternative to focusing on Family Tree Maker.

The Art of Selecting New Products

Obviously, as we considered new products, we did not want to repeat past mistakes. It was clear that either our selection criteria or our use of them was not perfect because we had had several failures in the past. To evaluate our methods, I summarized the degree of success for the products we had begun, if not completed, coding.

Among our successes, I had developed Org Plus because I had seen a very clear customer need based on my firsthand experience within Hewlett-Packard and observations of Hewlett-Packard customers. They had been paying too much money for poor solutions to their organization chart needs. Org Plus filled the need by offering a significant productivity improvement at a low price, and it was highly successful. With Family Tree Maker, we also saw a very clear need, based on our firsthand observations of Org Plus customers who were attempting to use the program to make trees. It too was highly successful. Uncle Sam's Budget Balancer had modest expectations and a low cost, so I gave it the benefit of the doubt and called it successful.

Among our failures was the phone book maker. By the time we canceled the project we questioned whether it had sufficient product differentiation from other products that had come on the market since the project's genesis. The need we saw for the Banner Blue Movie Guide turned out to be a phantom relative to our high expectations. It was a "movie buff" product for the small number of people interested in selecting the perfect movie to watch or rent. It also made a great gift, selling reasonably well during the holiday season, but having almost no sales during the rest of the year. Later, Microsoft had introduced a competitive, multimedia program on Windows which bled off all the leading-edge buyers. Not surprisingly, multimedia features were very attractive in a program about movies! However, we could not justify additional investments in the program to bring it up to speed. Brochure Maker's many problems I discussed earlier. Thus, our success rate among our major market initiatives was three for six, or 50 percent—only two for five, or 40 percent, if I left out Uncle Sam's Budget Balancer.

Had we made errors of omission? Had we declined to pursue ideas that turned out well for others? I looked at the ideas we had seriously evaluated with a full product prospectus. Only one of those ideas, a travel planning program with maps and facts about interesting destinations, became a successful, actually a very successful, category of products. However, I considered us correct in declining this idea because we had no expertise in the area and the successful companies, DeLorme and Rand McNally, did. Other companies had tried all but one of the other ideas with limited success, so it looked as if we were not making errors of omission. Our biggest problem seemed to be that we had imagined several markets that did not really exist.

After all of this analysis, I thought there was sufficient evidence to update our new product selection criteria. Since 1989, when we developed the first version of Family Tree Maker, we had modified our product selection criteria to require that a product have built-in barriers to competition. We had also monitored our choices to make sure that we were not, for example, developing only new products to the exclusion of upgrading current products.

The correct decision not to proceed with the travel planning program suggested adding another criterion, one that required management to have first-hand experience with the problem area. Indeed, our lack of knowledge of the lithographic printing process had caused us problems while developing Brochure Maker. In addition, the Brochure Maker fiasco had shown how important control was to us. Admittedly, this related to the kinds of people we were, but the idiosyncratic nature of some criteria seemed entirely appropriate. We were not writing a management textbook; we were establishing a process that worked for us.

The other changes I made were more subtle. What constituted a solution to a single, known customer problem was really a question of the level of abstraction used to describe it. If we concentrated on the word *single*, we were concentrating on the wrong thing. Certainly Family Tree Maker solved more than a single problem and we were considering adding to its repertoire. What we wanted was a solution to a problem that was differentiable and one that consumers recognized they had. Finally, I wanted the criteria to incorporate my long-held belief that any solution had to represent an order of magnitude improvement. It had to be ten times better.

Revised New Product Criteria

1. The product solves a differentiable, known problem—a task people perform in spite of the difficulty—providing an order-of-magnitude improvement.

2. Our management offers special expertise.

3. The product has no significant competition.

4. It makes good use of the computer.

5. It meets profit objectives. Typically this means that the product requires one calendar year of development time or less (as required by the market), and that it has reasonable support costs.

6. It has built-in barriers to competition.

7. We have control over all key technologies and relationships.

8. It represents a balanced addition to the product portfolio. This results in a mix of new programs, upgrades, and ports to new platforms, and leverages existing marketing channels.

Of course, even though we were learning from experience, it would have been dangerous to believe that we would now have greater than 50 percent success when picking a new product. The market was changing every bit as fast as we were. Fifty percent was actually a good mark.

Were there great product ideas just waiting for us to discover them? I built a table of the top ten personal productivity software categories for home use, the sales of which represented the lion's share of the total market. Below the top ten categories, sales fell off quickly. I then noted the date when the first successful product had appeared in each category. It was clear from this table that approximately one new category broke into the top ten every year. We already owned one of the categories with Family Tree Maker. With hundreds of competitors and only one big, new category appearing per year, the odds of us uncovering the next hot product were not high.

Given our limited resources, I concluded that there were greater odds of increasing the company's success by focusing on Family Tree Maker than by developing new products in new markets. We already had a winner and we had uncovered new opportunities for exploiting it. We needed to focus.

Investment Bankers

While performing this analysis, I was discussing exit strategies with three investment bankers and a friend who worked in the area of mergers and acquisitions. Although I had not made any final decisions, my inclination was that I would want to sell the company at some indeterminate time in the future. Therefore, most of my questions were about an acquisition.

In this group of people, there was universal agreement on several points. First, in the technology arena, the acquiring company looks for revenue velocity and momentum, not profitability. Although our profitability was excellent and a definite plus in our favor, most acquiring companies assumed that they would run the business at *their* profit level. Second, there was no company who would want both Family Tree Maker and Org Plus. Acquiring companies were generally looking to fill some kind of strategic void, so they would want one product or the other. Finally, timing was everything. The selling company wanted to look hot relative to the market direction. That was the best way to attract multiple offers that would in turn drive up the price.

So, preparing the company for my exit also argued for focusing our efforts. I decided that what looked like a dilemma (a company wanting only one of our product lines) really was not. Org Plus was a tremendously profitable "cash cow" and we would just accept it as such. It had stagnant sales, but because of its high profits it was worth more to Banner Blue than it would be to someone else. The Family Tree Maker product line only represented 35 percent of Banner Blue's sales during 1993, but if it continued its accelerated growth rate of the past year it would represent the majority of our sales in short order. I wanted to focus most of our resources toward making that happen. The primary risk I identified was an increased seasonality to our business because Family Tree Maker sold in much higher volumes during the holidays than it did during the rest of the year, but that seemed manageable.

Banner Blue's Revised Strategy

In my entire professional career, I had never seen so many events, trends, and judgments point in such a consistent and clear direction. We had a unique opportunity, the knowledge to understand it, and the resources to exploit it. All we had to do was execute and I was supremely confident in our ability to do so. It created a rare sense of exhilaration and I was resolved to make the best of Banner Blue's good fortune. I quickly turned all of this thinking into a revised company strategy that ultimately served as our guidepost for the next several years.

The simple, straightforward strategy called for Banner Blue to focus on the Family Tree Maker product line, broadening the market by redefining the product category to encompass capabilities never before seen. Our primary objective was to reduce the amount of time that the customer had to spend on researching his family. Our secondary objective was to attract younger people to the Family Tree Maker product line. To free additional resources for this effort, our objective for the Org Plus product line was simply to insure that it ran on new operating systems as they appeared.

Family Tree Maker Deluxe

I was extremely aggressive in carrying out this strategy. By the end of February 1994, I had decided that we should introduce and ship a new CD-ROM–based Family Tree Maker product in May 1994, just three months away. I wanted this development effort for what we would call Family Tree Maker *Deluxe* to continue in parallel with the new version of Family Tree Maker for Windows, version 2.0, scheduled for completion in August 1994. Thus, within months of each other, we would broaden the market in two ways: by helping people find their ancestors with CD-ROM–based Family Tree Maker Deluxe and by enabling them to store photos, audio clips, and video clips with Family Tree Maker for Windows 2.0. In a sense, we would take advantage of the CD-ROM, multimedia wave both coming and going, by shipping information on CD-ROM and by allowing the user to organize the multimedia information that their computer could now handle. Then, I wanted to ship a revised version of Family Tree Maker Deluxe in time for the holiday selling season.

I briefly considered shipping a single version of Family Tree Maker Deluxe during 1994, but decided against it. I knew that we would make many mistakes in our initial design for such a revolutionary product and I wanted to correct those mistakes based on user feedback before the holiday season. I also knew that we had to master several new technologies just to produce a CD-ROM product. Forcing the first version to ship in May would shake out unanticipated problems early, giving us a cushion of time to recover before the holiday season if we stumbled.

To produce Family Tree Maker Deluxe we would have to select the archival and how-to information and negotiate rights to use it. We would also need to learn how to produce a CD-ROM and modify our installation programs so that the user could load the program onto their computer. Fortunately, our primary disk duplicator, DisCopyLabs, was already capable of producing this new media. These just represented the new tasks—we also had to design and program means for accessing the genealogical information, provide packaging, write advertising copy, and sell the program to the channel. Quite a list for just three months' time.

My early concept for Family Tree Maker Deluxe matched up well against our new product criteria except for three areas that were not as strong as we liked: our management expertise, barriers to competition, and our control over key relationships. While we were experts in genealogy software, we were not experts in genealogical research. However, we recognized that even if we did not sell genealogical information on CD-ROM, we would still need to learn more about genealogical research simply to meet the needs of our existing customers. As the functionality of Family Tree Maker moved beyond "just printing trees," knowledge about genealogical research became increasingly important to the design of many new features. We also lacked experience in the world of CD-ROM applications, but since the industry was moving towards CD-ROMs as a distribution media, we had to learn this technology anyway. So, Family Tree Maker Deluxe required the same improvements in expertise that management would need to make no matter what.

As far as barriers to competition were concerned, we had discovered that most genealogical data was in the public domain, so the only barriers were our head start and our channel strength—the quicker we acted the better. At the same time, it was very important that we develop more proprietary information sources over the long haul to increase those barriers to entry. Finally, in the area of relationships, we thought we would have to negotiate many deals to obtain data, and we did not like the implications of this. Although no single relationship would be as complex as the one with our partner for Brochure Maker, the more relationships we had, the more difficult it would be for us to remain in control until we established ourselves as the leader. A savvy negotiator could easily play us off against competitors. Again this supported the argument that we should obtain exclusive and proprietary information sources over the long term.

Our desire to obtain proprietary information had us all reconsidering Jeff's idea of a clearinghouse for customers' trees. Someone suggested simply collecting all the customer trees on a CD-ROM and I decided that would be the first alternative to investigate. We called it the World Family Tree. During 1993 we had positioned the idea as a club that the user could join and did some canvassing to see what people thought. Unfortunately, there was little interest. However, the results from Courtney's broadening survey made me realize that we should position the World Family Tree as a productivity tool to help customers find additional ancestors and family members, not a club. If we also provided a means for participants to contact each other, we would be creating a gigantic marketplace for family information with many commercial possibilities. When we had previously described the idea as a club, we were forcing the user to figure out for himself how the product would create value. Sometimes the words describing a product are vitally important to its ultimate success, especially when the product represents an entirely new concept. We decided to do a new test market during the summer to see if my new analysis was correct.

Now that Family Tree Maker Deluxe had a firm and challenging schedule, I re-evaluated the composition of the development team. Courtney, age 25, had managed Family Tree Maker for DOS 3.0 and done an outstanding job. She was at ease dealing with people she had never met before and this was an important skill for convincing people that they should give us the rights to their information. Jeff, age 35, was a technical wizard and prodigious programmer. I knew we would need both skills at some point on this project, so Courtney and Jeff were a good match. We did not find anyone willing to give us the rights to how-to information at a reasonable cost, so we decided to write our own. We added our technical writer, Kim Mullin, age 23, to the team. She and Danielle, also 23, would collaborate to produce the how-to guide.

Except for Jeff, they were very young for a project of this importance, but Courtney and Jeff both knew the Banner Blue way of doing things and I was confident of their success. Indeed, we had more favorable results teaching our philosophies to a young person in an entry-level position than we did changing the pre-existing philosophies of an experienced individual joining the company at a senior level.

Throughout its duration, this project exemplified the value of having a mature product development life cycle. There was never an argument about the procedure for designing and building Family Tree Maker Deluxe, substantially reducing the scope and difficulty of the problem. Bright, young people like those on this team could step in and apply all their energy, without distraction, to the actual creation of the product. At the same time, the life cycle gave me assurance that they would succeed and the tools I needed to monitor their progress along the way.

I had created a striking contrast to the environment I experienced at Symantec. I had a small, focused team with leadership previously proven under stress. The team acquired additional members over time to test the product and perform a variety of necessary functions, but this group of four constituted the core. It was an ideal setup.

With a strategy, a tactical plan, and a product development team in place, it was time to communicate our new direction to the entire company. At the March 9, 1994, company meeting I gave what I called the "wave" speech. I reviewed the marketing information and technology trends I had analyzed. I demonstrated several new CD-ROM products that had become successful in the preceding months. Then I showed a hand-drawn overhead slide of a big wave with four stick-figure images of surfers: one riding the wave, one swimming behind, one ducking under, and one wiping out. "We're going to be the one riding this wave," I said, "no other position is acceptable."

When asking people to do what will require a supreme effort, I considered it imperative to explain why. In this case the reason was clear, believable, and more fundamental than my personal desire to succeed. The new and fast-selling CD-ROM products would replace the aging and slow-selling DOS products on the shelves of our retailers. There was not room for both. We either stepped up to the market's new challenge or we shrunk in size as our DOS sales disappeared. To add some perspective, credibility, and confidence, I compared our opportunity to those successfully exploited by several other companies in the past, including our own success moving from DOS to Windows. Finally, I offered to reimburse employees for putting their own photos on a Kodak Photo-CD and provided other incentives for people to learn the many new technologies they would need to master simply to test our new products. The speech energized our fifty-three employees.

The Family Tree Maker Deluxe team was in full stride and addressing their most important issue—what data to include in the program. They started by obtaining agreement on criteria the data had to meet. The desire was for information that provided instant gratification to the user, the ideal being that they would actually find their entire family tree in the box. Since the ideal was impossible, a more down-to-earth criterion was for a high hit rate. In other words, the average user would find a good number of individuals in his family when he searched our data. We also had to obtain and integrate the data into the program in a short period of time and at an economical cost. A single CD-ROM held as much information as 1700 of the floppy diskettes for my first computer, purchased eleven years earlier, yet as the team did its research they quickly found that obtaining a high hit rate required even more data storage, even if they compressed the data.

To solve this problem, Jeff proposed the concept of a meta-index. Much of the electronically available genealogical information was in the form of an index to paper or microfilm records such as the

United States census, and even these indexes took up vast amounts of data storage space. The meta-index would be an index to these other indexes. It would give the user information such as, "Erastus Fowler is in the 1840 Census Index for Ohio." The user would have to purchase another CD-ROM to obtain the actual census information. At a cost of adding a second step for the user, we could include many more names on the CD-ROM because the amount of space required for each name would be extremely small. The hit rate and resulting user satisfaction would be extremely high. Unfortunately, there was no way the team could construct a meta-index in the time available. The best compromise seemed to be a national phone directory that would include living relatives for all but the most recent immigrant, supplemented by something like the 1790 census which would have relatives for everyone who could trace back that far. There were only four million inhabitants of the United States in 1790 so that census was reasonably small in size.

Courtney had been negotiating with two companies that sold national phone directories on CD-ROM. Her objective was to obtain the products for a royalty of approximately a dollar per copy, but both companies wanted much more. Separately, the team had found that Automated Archives in Orem, Utah, had acquired the vast majority of genealogical data on CD-ROM. At some point in March, I became the primary negotiator with them. Paul DeBry was the president of Automated Archives and I found him very interested in working with us. Unfortunately, Paul also wanted more money than we were willing to pay. Then, in one of our conversations, Paul told me in passing about a new product that they did intend to sell at a very low price. They called it the Master Name Index. It was a catalog listing the names of one hundred million people and the data they had available for each one. The product was just about complete. Their plan was to sell it very inexpensively as a means to stimulate sales of their data CDs. I immediately called Courtney and Jeff and said, "Automated Archives has the meta-index!"

On April 8, 1994, we consummated an agreement with Automated Archives and abandoned negotiations with the phone directory companies. In my interest to erect entry barriers, I successfully convinced Paul that the Master Name Index as a catalog had no intrinsic value—it was the sales of his data CDs that had value. However, I was willing to pay for the Master Name Index if we had exclusivity. The agreement gave us the exclusive rights to the Master Name Index for $1.25 per copy with a minimum commitment of $1250 per month.

We sweetened the pot by agreeing to pay $2.50 per copy for upgrade sales to our installed base. Of course, the exclusivity and low pricing was negotiable in the first place because we owned the genealogy software market and we agreed to become a distributor for Automated Archives' forty data CDs. Our users would obtain a hit, then order the data CD, and that was where Automated Archives would make its money. It was a good deal for both of us.

Now we had five weeks to complete the program. Jeff had to integrate the Master Name Index with Family Tree Maker for Windows. Working as long as eighteen hours a day, he was actually able to mock up several alternatives for the user interface while writing a sophisticated piece of code to handle browsing. The user would be able to click a button to search the Master Name Index, although he would have to use a separate piece of software from Automated Archives called the GRS to view any of the data CDs purchased separately. Then Jeff successfully sorted through all the new technologies required to produce our first CD-ROM.

Meanwhile, Kim and Danielle produced the equivalent of a full-length book on how to do genealogy, then successfully put it in a format that allowed users to access it from the program. Courtney coordinated the activities of everyone on the team and worked feverishly to produce the required packaging and marketing materials. We decided to simply put a sticker describing the new Family Tree Maker Deluxe features on our existing package, since we would be revising the product again only several months down the road. Producing a box from scratch would take too long and cost too much. On May 19, 1994, we sent Family Tree Maker Deluxe to the CD-ROM duplicator, just three months after we committed to the project. The young development team had delivered.

Selling Family Tree Maker Deluxe was the first test of our new sales organization. We were asking them to sell the program into the retail channel, knowing that we also had to tell the retailers that we would take the expensive step of asking them to swap out their inventory for a new version just several months later. Making it worse, June and July were the slowest sales months of the year—not the time when retailers wanted to be adding to their inventory. Alma and Julie quickly discovered that the secret to the sale was to look for the family of the buyer in the Master Name Index when demonstrating the program. The odds were very high that they would find an ancestor the buyer recognized, so it made for the most unique sales pitch a buyer had ever seen and it left some people in tears of disbelief. It also made for a lot of orders. We shipped over 14,000 copies worth $610,000 before the end of September 1994.

During June, I flew to Utah to meet the Automated Archives people face to face and Paul flew to California to see our operations shortly thereafter. With the press of time, we had done all our work by phone until my visit. The big question for both companies was whether anyone would buy the Automated Archives data CDs.

A Break in the Action

I needed some rest and relaxation so I scheduled a three-day racecar driving class at Laguna Seca Raceway, near Monterey, California. I found that keeping my car on the track as I sliced through a turn called the corkscrew was a great way to clear my mind of everything else. However, I told Connie that I would never be a good race driver—I had too much to live for.

At about the same time Connie and I decided to purchase a new home in Carmel. We had agreed that when I exited Banner Blue, we would move our primary residence to Carmel. From time to time we had looked at property, since our existing home in Carmel was only big enough to be a vacation home. Surprisingly, a unique, older estate came on the market and we decided to buy it even though we had no idea when we would actually be able to effect our move. To make the down payment on the home, I sold a small amount of my stock in Banner Blue to Lynn Brewer, my first supervisor at Intel in 1974 and now Banner Blue's only outside director.

Shortly after purchasing the home, we began to investigate potential schools in the area for Amber. Since they all had waiting lists, sometimes quite lengthy, we decided to apply to the two schools we liked the most in anticipation of our eventual move.

Stock Options

Also during June 1994, I initiated a process to change the way we offered stock in Banner Blue to employees. In the past, we had offered senior employees stock grants. The disadvantage was that the employee had to pay income taxes on the grants as if they were income. What was simple for the company was financially burdensome for the employee. I wanted to switch to a traditional stock option plan, wherein we gave the employee the right to purchase stock at what we all hoped was a price less than market value. Acquiring the right to purchase stock was not a taxable event. Stock option plans involved a complicated application and approval process with the state, so I also decided this was a good time to look for a new lawyer.

Legal firms are much like accounting firms—junior employees perform much of the work. As I worked with my accountant over the years, I learned another advantage of working with the senior partner: he could answer many of my questions in seconds, eliminating the need for a junior employee to become involved. I paid more per hour, but overall it cost less because it took less time. The information was also more timely and accurate. When the senior partner needed to delegate the work, I wanted him to review the results before passing them back to me. I just considered that to be good quality control. Unfortunately, that is not how our current attorney liked to work with us.

I had accumulated a file folder full of potential attorneys from various sources and decided to call Shirley Buccieri at Gibson, Dunn, and Crutcher. Shirley's resume intrigued me because she had worked as an engineer before becoming a lawyer. I thought we might hit it off, and we did. It even turned out that her engineering experience had been in my home town of Warren, Ohio, where she worked in the same engineering department as my father. I hired Shirley to prepare our stock option plan.

Testing the World Family Tree

Meanwhile, our other projects were heating up. I hired an MBA student for the summer, Allyson Beasley, to investigate creating a service that our customers could use to obtain genealogical documents from libraries. She also was to evaluate whether or not we could round up enough family trees from our users to make the World Family Tree a viable product.

Her first task was to survey more software users who had not purchased Family Tree Maker to judge the interest level in these potential products. The initial results were positive. The idea of the service was that once the customer obtained a hit in Family Tree Maker Deluxe, they could further verify the validity of the information using the Automated Archives data CDs. Then, they could visit a library to obtain a copy of the document or contact us to do the work for them. It was a service consistent with our strategy of reducing the time it took our customers to complete their research. Unfortunately, it looked as if it would be extremely difficult for us to make money, so we shelved the idea. The test of the World Family Tree, however, far exceeded our expectations.

Our large installed base was a significant advantage for the World Family Tree because if the idea appealed to our customers, we could quickly amass an enormous database. Like the snowball effect with sales volume, the bigger our database, the more valuable it would be in attracting even more customers. Any competitor would have to start essentially from zero. After processing the survey, we did a mailing to several thousand of our users, asking them to send us their family tree on an enclosed diskette. Our sales pitch was that if our many users shared their family trees, everyone would benefit. It was a message that we had honed in the first survey:

1. Extend your family tree when you access the family trees of others who share your ancestry.

2. Help others who may be searching for information that you have.

3. Protect your family history from loss or damage.

4. Preserve your family history data so that it can be accessed by your descendants.

We received a higher response than expected in this test, so we decided to proceed with the World Family Tree as soon as possible.

Managing a Large Development Project

At the same time, the parallel development team was in the final push to complete Family Tree Maker for Windows 2.0, a much larger development project than was Family Tree Maker Deluxe. A big problem had been the design of the user interface.

I had designed the first version of the program, but with my energies directed towards company strategy I did not want heavy involvement in the design of 2.0. We decided to give the opportunity to a young developer who had been successful at his every task so far. He had actually designed and managed a much smaller program and his critiques of our other designs were always right on target.

Our product development life cycle, successful as it had been with the challenging circumstances of Family Tree Maker Deluxe, required the designer of the program to quite literally hold the entire program in his head. Of course, he recorded his design in a lengthy document for others to critique, but we had no holistic mechanism for presenting the program in its entirety and at one glance. Our new designer was just not able to hold all the interacting pieces in his mind's eye. This deficit led to many situations where he proposed an unnecessarily complex design element that was inconsistent with other areas of the program and difficult to create. Sorting out the ensuing problems led to lots of controversy.

The design of Family Tree Maker for Windows 2.0 also validated some key concepts of project management. In his book *The Mythical Man-Month*, Frederick P. Brooks, Jr., described what had become a law of large programming projects:

> In tasks that can be partitioned but which require communications among the subtasks, the effort of communication must be added to the amount of work done. Therefore the best that can be done is somewhat poorer than an even trade of men for months.

In other words, there is a nonlinear increase in the communication load for every person added to a project. If a two-person project requires one unit of communication time, a four-person project may require as much as six units of communication time. I would add that the skills required to effectively communicate in a large project are also qualitatively different from those required in a small project. This increase in the communication load as a team grows in size is a strong argument for having as small a team as possible. The four core people building Family Tree Maker Deluxe was ideal. Sometimes, however, a large team is necessary and that was the case with Family Tree Maker for Windows 2.0. Our designer's only experience had been on small projects where he communicated primarily with the project manager or his supervisor and no one else.

So, while our designer had shown promise in the areas of software design and project management, that promise was in the environment of a very small project. The increased complexity of the program itself and the inherently more sophisticated communications skills required for Family Tree Maker for Windows 2.0 simply over-whelmed him. Inadvertently, I had set him up for failure.

Because of this problem, I had to step in to adjudicate the de-sign, which made no one happy. I had other tasks I wanted to be working on, and the designer and the project manager saw me as un-dermining their authority, which had some truth to it. But they were not achieving what I judged to be necessary, and this was an impor-tant project. Our primary objectives as a company related to the quality and success of this particular program, so it was not an option to let the designer learn by failing. I had to step in whether they liked it or not.

To accelerate the development of this version, we had also de-cided to use more code supplied by third parties than had ever been the case before. We were aware of the risks, but even Microsoft was purchasing image-handling code from third parties, so we decided we would be crazy to write our own. Besides, it would be difficult for us to maintain the image-handling code as standards inevitably changed. The problem was that our standards for quality were higher than av-erage, and it was difficult to obtain the kind of responsiveness we needed from the vendor to fix his bugs. In the end, we got most of what we wanted; however, we never found a good solution to the problems inherent in purchasing code. I chalked it up to the cost of being on the leading edge. In such cases, it was very difficult to ex-ceed the standards of the industry. Even the underlying Windows code which we had to use was fraught with bugs.

In the plus column, we had made a major effort to automate many of the quality assurance tests for the program, and people in the company uniformly cited that as a big win. It helped us find and solve problems that would have been nearly impossible to locate with manual testing. On August 28, the team completed Family Tree Maker for Windows 2.0. It was on time and contained essentially all the functionality originally specified. About a month later, Jeff suc-cessfully revised Family Tree Maker Deluxe to incorporate all of the enhancements from 2.0.

The Right Person in the Right Job

How could we avoid more unfortunate experiences like the one in which the designer for Family Tree Maker for Windows 2.0 turned out to be the wrong person for the job? I thought we should be able to find a screening device to help us ascertain whether an individual was a good fit for a particular job. Banner Blue was effective at measuring an individual's job skills during an interview process, but not as successful at judging whether they had the appropriate personality for a job, even when the individual had been working for us for some time.

When we changed a person's job environment, it seemed that anything could happen and usually did. In some cases, like that of the designer for 2.0, the change was for the worse. In other cases, the change was for the better. For example, Kim Mullin was a Phi Beta Kappa graduate of the University of California at Berkeley. We hired her for a position in the marketing department, where she was unhappy and unsuccessful. After discussing the situation with her, we transferred her to a technical writing position where she blossomed, becoming a major contributor to Family Tree Maker Deluxe (she is also the editor of this book). Every job places different demands on the individual filling it, and every individual responds differently to those demands. I wanted a means to place each individual in an appropriate job without all the trial and error.

I had examined two services already and found them both lacking, but a little later in the year, my friend Monty Allen made me aware of just the service I wanted. He sent me an article about the Predictive Index, and I met with their representative Robert Ferrara during November 1994. Robert had me and several of my staff fill out a short questionnaire before the meeting. Then at the meeting, having never met any of us before, he told me with striking accuracy how we each approached our job, what tasks motivated us, and with which tasks we struggled. The demonstration sold me and I quickly signed up. We used the Predictive Index quite successfully.

The Order of Magnitude Rule

The problems we had with the large development team for the 2.0 project also led me to consider what I called my order of magnitude rule. Banner Blue had grown a full order of magnitude, from just myself to about ten employees, before I had to change my management style. Now at seventy-three employees, we were closing in on our second order of magnitude of growth. Techniques I successfully used to focus the efforts of thirty or forty individuals were not as successful for focusing the efforts of seventy people. I could foresee my techniques failing altogether by the time we reached one hundred employees.

Does a management technique fail when the organization has grown precisely by a factor of ten? Generally it does not. My order of magnitude rule is like most management rules of thumb, an approximation. In my experience, I could be extremely confident that something working well when the organization had a given size would still work when that size doubled or tripled. However, by the time the organization had increased in size by a factor of ten, my confidence was much lower (although some policies like profit sharing seemed to work equally well at every size as the organization grew). Rules like these simply give a manager a heads-up call, a signal to pay attention. They are not deterministic like the rules of classical physics, nor can they be.

When we had grown to be a company of ten people I found that I needed to spend more time communicating our direction. As you will recall, a new employee had disrupted our organization by filling a communication vacuum that I inadvertently created, so I developed new techniques that successfully solved the problem. As we grew to a company of one hundred, I was finding once again that I needed to develop new techniques to sell my philosophy in order to prevent losing it.

By 1994, there were often two levels of management between the frontline troops and me. This reduced the effectiveness of communication techniques like our company meeting, because employees spent a lot more time with their direct managers than they did with me in those large monthly gatherings. I needed to develop techniques to get the management team in sync with my thoughts.

One example of how the management team can be out of sync involved the new engineering VP, Eric Holstege. Eric and I had a continuing discussion about the objectives of good project management. Eric thought that the ideally managed project should have no crunch period at the end. The team would not add features after the initial spec was completed, and no one would ever have to work long hours as everything proceeded with even, well-planned effort throughout the project.

My feelings were quite contrary. Major changes in our market environment occurred on an extremely short time scale. Increasing our ability to handle changes created a competitive advantage; prohibiting late changes would create weakness. Quality assurance and documentation groups should strive to find ways to adapt to changes in specifications, not lobby to prohibit them. What we wanted to eliminate were changes caused by poor planning. I also felt that hard work was just as important. The more we could do with our resources, the more competitive we were. Extra effort was one of our key tools and we had to keep it in our toolbox. I saw good procedures as a way to obtain more from our efforts (through increased efficiency and reduced stress), not as a way to reduce our efforts.

These discussions were more than academic. In high-technology companies of the early 1990s, subordinates had a great deal of choice about where to work. They could obtain a new job in days, probably at a higher salary. If I successfully sold my position on issues such as project management and company direction, then I created a loyal, effective team. If I did not sell my position, then my subordinates, their subordinates, or both, would simply leave to find a company that they thought had better management (and no end-of-project crunch time).

When one former Banner Blue engineer read a draft of this book, he commented, "I never knew you thought this [about the need to handle late changes]." So, I truly did need to develop new techniques for effectively communicating my philosophies!

Acquiring Automated Archives

At the same time we finished Family Tree Maker for Windows 2.0, we received our answer about whether anyone would purchase the Automated Archives data CDs. We sold $17,000 of Automated Archives products in July 1994 and $36,000 in August. Some simple and realistic extrapolations convinced me that with Family Tree Maker Deluxe, we had produced what would become our most successful product ever.

At the end of August 1994, I called Paul to suggest that we strengthen our relationship. Automated Archives provided an outdated program called the GRS for viewing their data CDs, and they wanted to improve it. I suggested that Banner Blue incorporate CD-viewing functionality into Family Tree Maker, then give Automated Archives the rights to a demo version of Family Tree Maker to use in place of the GRS. This would give them and their customers a world-class program to view their data. In return and at a minimum, I wanted to extend the exclusivity clause in our agreement and obtain rights to use the Master Name Index in a potential online service.

Paul cut to the heart of the matter and asked whether we had an interest in purchasing Automated Archives. Paul's proposal was a stroke of good fortune, because acquisition was a desirable alternative that Alma and I had already discussed. I readily agreed that it made sense to evaluate an acquisition and on September 8, 1994, we signed a confidentiality agreement pursuant to merger discussions.

I knew that an acquisition would be extraordinarily time-consuming, so I hired Monty Allen as a consultant. We also needed an attorney whom we could trust implicitly. Our work with Shirley Buccieri had gone well, so I had Monty evaluate her ability to handle an acquisition, and he found she had exceptional qualifications. We determined that Curt Revak, my accountant of many years, was also able to contribute. The four of us and Alma comprised our acquisition team.

While a deal with Automated Archives began to develop, I also wanted to further explore a strategy for my exit from Banner Blue. On September 13, 1994, I attended the Digital Media Conference in San Francisco specifically to meet one of the speakers, Doug Carlston, the chairman and founder of Broderbund Software, Inc. Among a variety of other programs, Broderbund published one of the top two personal productivity programs, Print Shop, which made greeting cards, calendars, and banners. I thought that Family Tree Maker would complement their existing products, making them a likely purchaser of a company like Banner Blue. I suggested to Doug that we get together for a general discussion of business strategy, being very careful not to imply that the company was for sale because at this time it was not. He agreed, but I instead got a follow-up call from Steve Dunphy in their business development group.

Steve and I met for lunch and I suggested that Broderbund might profit from distributing Family Tree Maker to the educational market and perhaps to international markets as well. Given the strategic fit between our product lines, I also suggested that we were open to other ideas, up to and including a potential acquisition. Unfortunately, Steve round-filed us. I followed up with a letter to Doug, but to no avail. I would have expected Broderbund to seek us out as a hot company in their market area. Instead, when opportunity knocked they slammed the door.

Meanwhile, Paul wanted to talk to me in person to discuss the price for Automated Archives. He told me they wanted a lot for the company and he felt it was best if he carefully reviewed their reasoning for me face-to-face. We began our due diligence evaluating their financial statements and set a meeting in Utah for September 29, 1994. Over the phone during the ensuing weeks, Paul continued to reiterate how important it was to have a face-to-face meeting to discuss the price. Paul had sold a company before and he obviously knew what he was doing, yet his insistence on the face-to-face meeting had me extremely concerned that he would want more than we could pay, more than his company was worth, or both.

While we waited for the meeting, Alma and I focused on three strategic issues of the acquisition:

1. If we did not purchase Automated Archives, would an exclusivity agreement for the Master Name Index give us sufficient control of our business?

2. Was the Automated Archives information sufficiently proprietary that it created an entry barrier, justifying the high price?

3. Did we have sufficient resources to manage Automated Archives?

We concluded that the answer to the first question was no. Automated Archives was already talking to other companies about putting information online and we had no control over their pricing. Now that we had broadened and redefined the market, anything that had to do with genealogical data was part of Banner Blue's core business. It was clear that if we simply remained a distributor, they might make many decisions that could adversely affect our business. In order to build a great genealogy software company, the software and the data belonged under the same corporate roof.

We had confirmed that more than half of Automated Archives' information, such as a listing of people who had received death benefits from the Social Security Administration, was in the public domain. Banner Blue or any of its competitors could duplicate the information, implying that it did not constitute much of an entry barrier. On the other hand, there was a good amount of information that was proprietary; and more importantly, duplicating the information that was public domain would take time and resources. In a fast-changing, technology-based business, time and resource limitations are always the enemy. It was better for us to have the data in hand, allowing us to work on creating stronger entry barriers, than to have the data in the hands of a competitor.

Finally, we decided we did have the resources to manage Automated Archives, but only if Paul stayed. His employment contract would be a very important part of the agreement. Strategically, the acquisition would guarantee us control, would lengthen our lead over potential competitors, and was manageable. It made sense.

At long last, we flew out for the face-to-face meeting. Paul and Jay Potter, Automated's vice president of engineering, owned most of the company's stock. After briefly meeting in their office, we adjourned to Paul's house. Paul's wife Rita brought us some delicious, homemade apple pie to make us comfortable. My impatience getting the best of me, I wondered if Paul would ever get to the price.

At the request of Monty and me, Paul first clarified their motivations for selling. Paul himself felt no urgency to sell. He thought the company's prospects were extremely bright and he explained why in detail. More than once he told me that if Banner Blue acquired Automated, the data business would grow to be bigger than the software business in a matter of years. Paul wanted to stay on after the acquisition, because he loved genealogy. Jay, on the other hand, wanted to liquidate his holdings in the company for a variety of reasons that they explained. The two of them decided that a sale was the best way to accomplish Jay's desires. The side benefit to Paul was that he could turn over all of the operations tasks to Banner Blue, leaving himself free to concentrate on acquiring additional data.

After weeks of build-up and a long discussion of the bright prospects for Automated Archives, the conversation finally turned to the asking price. For three weeks, I had fully expected Paul to ask for an astronomical sum, far beyond the true worth of the company. When he finally stated their price ("and we won't take a penny less"), it was half of the number I had feared. Paul had done a masterful job of psychologically preparing me to feel good about a price that I otherwise would have considered very high had he just blurted it out when we began our conversations in August.

At Paul's request, Monty and I discussed how we thought we would integrate Automated Archives operations into Banner Blue. Our plan was to leave Paul in charge of data collection and processing in Utah while transferring manufacturing and customer support to California. We collected some additional information we needed to evaluate the acquisition and then concluded our meeting.

Automated Archives had a complex history; therefore, we decided with Shirley that the acquisition should be an asset purchase, which means that we would purchase the physical and intellectual property of the company without purchasing the company itself. This method of purchase reduced the risk of incurring any unseen and unknown liabilities associated with the Automated Archives corporate entity itself. Monty worked with Paul's attorney and Shirley to write the sales agreement while continuing to perform due diligence. He also spent a great deal of his time reviewing the many agreements that Automated Archives had signed to acquire the data they were selling.

By the end of October, Monty, Shirley, and Paul had worked out a financial structure for the deal. Banner Blue would fund the acquisition from cash on hand, issuance of some new stock to Paul DeBry, and future earnings. On November 14, we signed a letter of intent to purchase Automated Archives, and the drafting of the closing documents soon began. The frustrating thing about any such negotiation is that a large portion of the effort goes into hammering out items that ultimately have no import. Shirley had the experience and the business acumen to help minimize these items, so she would just tell us when something was not worth arguing about. Unfortunately, Paul's attorney fought hard over many issues that we did not think were worth fighting over.

The final documents were three and one half centimeters thick. The asset purchase agreement was the largest document, including employment contracts for key employees, the security agreement, and twenty other schedules and exhibits. Other documents were the bill of sale, assignment and assumption agreement, receipts, compliance certificates, promissory notes, releases, assignments, consents, and government registrations. As the team drafted the documents, I wondered how much of it was really necessary, but as I came to understand each component I saw its importance. We finally had agreement on all issues on December 27, and in a very kind gesture, Paul sent me a special pen to sign them. The next day, we signed the documents in the offices of our respective attorneys.

Our Finest Year

Nineteen ninety-four had been our finest year. Our accomplishments gave me more satisfaction than I had had at any time since the first two years of Banner Blue's existence. We began the year with hardly a CD-ROM drive in the company and did not even decide to do a CD-ROM product until late February. We ended the year by acquiring the assets of a CD-ROM company from internally generated funds and also achieving 30 percent of our sales with CD-ROM products. We had indeed ridden the wave.

Family Tree Maker Deluxe sold 70,000 units worth $2,879,000 and the Family Tree Maker line as a whole sold 201,000 units worth a total of $6,727,000, including the Automated Archives data CDs we distributed. This represented growth of 102 percent in units and 167 percent in dollars—our focus on Family Tree Maker had paid off. Family Tree Maker revenues climbed from 35 percent of the company's total in 1993 to 62 percent of the total in 1994 and the company's growth as a whole exceeded 50 percent to reach $10,930,000. Pre-tax profits remained above 30 percent.

Our family also had a great year in 1994. During February, I encouraged Amber to ride her bike without the training wheels. We practiced at my office parking lot because it was so large and flat. There were a few crashes, and consequently Amber did not consider bike riding to be much fun. Finally, the third time we went for a lesson she just pedaled off, circling the Banner Blue office building twice before stopping.

Later in the year, I showed Amber the new Family Tree Maker for Windows 2.0 box. On the back was a Family Tree Maker Scrapbook screen shot, and it included a picture of Amber in her Halloween costume at age five. She was very upset. "Daddy, kids are going to think I look silly. I look like I'm four years old." I told her she was about that old when I took the picture, and that she looked cute. "Grown-ups will think I look cute, but kids will think I look silly." From then on I had to get her permission for any pictures I used.

Connie stepped up her volunteer efforts at Amber's school as well as leading Amber's Brownie troop. She took a class so that she could be a part-time music teacher in a volunteer program called Music for Minors. She conducted the first concert by her students during 1994, getting tremendous satisfaction from all the hugs afterwards. Connie also found time to do some painting, and her artwork appeared in a special show at the Olive Hyde Gallery in Fremont.

Unfortunately, Santa would no longer come down our chimney, another sign that Amber was growing up. One day in December, she came home from school and told Connie, "Now tell me the truth. Nicole told me there is no Santa Claus—she said your parents do it."

When Connie admitted the truth Amber said, "You mean you guys have to pay $80 for that doll?!" (She was referring to the American Girl doll, Kirsten, that was on her Christmas list.) Several days later she was listening to the carol "I Saw Mommy Kissing Santa Claus," when she chuckled and said, "The boy doesn't know [that Santa is his daddy]!" All week Amber asked for good night kisses from Santa.

TABLE 3
BANNER BLUE SOFTWARE SUMMARY 1984-1994

Year	Net Sales	Sales Growth	Profit Before Tax[1]	People[2]	New Programs	Total Releases[3]
1984	$0			1		
1985	$92,820		23.8%	1	Org	4
1986	$884,829	853.3%	38.5%	5		6
1987	$1,814,917	105.1%	36.9%	8		7
1988	$2,044,275	12.6%	32.5%	10	Org Plus Advanced	14
1989	$2,757,579	34.9%	21.0%	16	Family Tree Maker	10
1990	$3,410,661	23.7%	18.6%	19	Org Plus for Macintosh Data Exchange Utility[4] Laser Fonts Disk[4]	19
1991	$4,660,481	36.6%	23.2%	25	Org Plus for Windows Banner Blue Movie Guide Family Ties[5]	27
1992	$5,674,820	21.8%	27.9%	35	Brochure Maker Uncle Sam's Budget Balancer	10
1993	$7,113,215	25.3%	30.4%	42	Family Tree Maker for Windows Microsoft Organization Chart Biography Maker Direct Elect[6] Exercise in Hard Choices[7]	20
1994	$10,929,533	53.7%	30.1%	55	Family Tree Maker Deluxe Microsoft Organization Chart for Macintosh Family Ties for Windows[5]	31

[1] As a percentage of net sales.
[2] This count of full-time employees represents an average number for the year. It includes temporary employees, full-time contractors, and summer hires.
[3] Total product releases include new programs, upgrades, and rolling releases during the year.
[4] Accessory program for Family Tree Maker.
[5] This program was manufactured for sale by another company.
[6] A version of Brochure Maker designed for candidates for political office.
[7] A special version of Uncle Sam's Budget Balancer for the Committee for a Responsible Federal Budget.

6

Selling Out

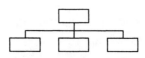

With our most successful year behind us, I turned my thoughts to an exit strategy. Once I had asked a successful entrepreneur how he decided when it was time to sell, and his only advice was, "Trees don't grow to the sky." My interpretation of this statement was that you sell when it looks as if things cannot get any better—and that description fit our situation quite well. It would be hard for Banner Blue to exceed the growth rate of 1994, and just as important, the stock market was placing record high valuations on consumer software companies. Even if another company acquired us, stock market valuations were important because those valuations trickled down to private companies in a variety of ways. Private companies sell at a discount to public companies and it is better to have that discount applied to a larger starting number. Looked at another way, when a public company's own stock has a high value, the company can use the stock itself to purchase other companies at a lower cost than when stock prices are low.

It was only fitting that many of my initial thoughts about whether to sell Banner Blue were financial. After all, one of the key reasons I founded Banner Blue in the first place was to obtain financial independence. Now the company had attained a value where I could honestly say that I did not need any more—enough was enough.

Other considerations were also important. As I have already mentioned, my overall energy level was no longer what it was when I started the company eleven years earlier, and except for the recent Automated Archives acquisition, many of my daily tasks were becoming repetitive. I have many varied interests, most of which I suppressed as I single-mindedly focused on growing Banner Blue. At this point, I wanted to step back, enjoy my hobbies for a change, and carefully evaluate what I should do next. It was time to smell the roses.

It may seem strange to sell a company immediately after purchasing another, but it is not that unusual. Paul DeBry of Automated Archives expected me to sell at some time in the not-too-distant future. In fact, he had even suggested several companies that might have an interest in purchasing our combined organizations. Indeed, the purchase of Automated Archives had dramatically increased the value of Banner Blue by creating such an excellent entry barrier to competitors.

Banner Blue was on top of its game, the market was placing a high value on software companies, I had exceeded my financial objectives, and I was ready for a change. Everything said this was the time to sell.

Of course one way to sell the company was to go public, selling shares to individuals rather than another company, but my preference was still to have someone acquire Banner Blue. If we went public, we would obtain a higher valuation for the company, but with much lower liquidity. Given our relatively small size compared to most public companies, we would have a thinly traded stock and it would take me years to diversify my holdings. During those years anything could happen, and I would have to continue running the company, which I did not want to do. On the other hand, our negotiating position with an acquiring company was stronger if we had a credible threat of going public. We wanted a buyer to think we could easily walk away from the deal unless they paid top dollar. So, it was important to keep our options open, at least in public.

At about the same time, I began a series of helpful conversations with my board member, Lynn Brewer. In the time since we had worked together at Intel, Lynn had personally run large divisions of several companies, as well as an independent corporation. His most frequent advice to me was, "Ken, it's your company." Often I would describe to him the various forces playing on the company or a particular business situation and he would repeat that advice one more time. Now that we were discussing an acquisition, he said the same thing to me again.

Lynn was addressing my tendency to worry perhaps too much about what was best for my employees and not enough about what made sense for me. Lynn is one of the more considerate people I know, so he would be the last person to tell me not to worry about others, but he also wanted me to keep a balance among the various needs. As on several other occasions, I now wished I had expanded my board of directors to include more people, but I had never gotten around to it. If the others even had a fraction of Lynn's good advice, it would have been well worth the trouble.

Since it was clearly the time to move, Alma and I began a quest for the perfect deal—something that we quickly found does not exist. We decided to follow a twofold strategy: I would personally contact companies that we thought were a good match, and in March 1995 we would make a presentation at the American Electronics Association Winter Financial Conference for Emerging Growth Companies. The conference would be our "coming out" if you will, a financial and marketing presentation to leading investment bankers.

Another Call to Broderbund

As I reviewed software companies, looking for those that might be buyers, it seemed that Broderbund was still the best strategic fit for Family Tree Maker. Although Alma and I were both concerned about their lack of interest months earlier, all else being equal, the best strategic fit should result in the highest price. Why had they dropped us like a hot potato? I decided to call Broderbund's founder and chairman, Doug Carlston, and ask for a meeting with him personally. I did not want to be shuffled off to a subordinate again. I reached Doug on January 16, 1995. In our conversation and a follow-up letter, I summarized my position as follows:

> Banner Blue is in a position where we could choose to go public in the next 18 to 24 months. We have always been extremely profitable and our growth rate is much higher than the industry average. Although our genealogy products deal with the most traditional of human needs, we find it appropriate and profitable to satisfy those needs with some of the latest, hottest technology available. And, in December we acquired the assets of Automated Archives in Orem, Utah. This cements our access to the world's

largest commercial collection of genealogical archives—an outstanding entry barrier to potential competitors and a large source
of follow-on or aftermarket revenue.

At the same time, if we continue the course as an independent company we need to revamp our internal operations to allow
us to handle much higher volumes. And, while we have excellent
relations with our 3,200 retailers, there are a number of potential
outlets that will be difficult for us to penetrate. Combining with a
larger player would help us address these issues while providing
the same, if not better, liquidity than a public offering . . . .

Of course, Banner Blue is not under any pressure to be acquired at this time. We have plenty of cash and our business is
booming. We have taken sound strategic actions to protect ourselves from larger, potential competitors. But, there's a window
here. We face the need to make substantial internal changes to
prepare for the next phase of growth. If an attractive opportunity
presents itself before we make those changes, I will take advantage of it. After we make the changes, it's a new equation.

Doug wanted to know if Family Tree Maker was what he called
an "evergreen" product. I explained the strong interest people had in
their roots—they have always had it and they always would. As new
technologies developed, we could update our software almost indefinitely in order to satisfy this perpetual human need. Our archival
data was even more evergreen. Most of the genealogical societies we
worked with were over one hundred years old! The same data those
societies collected in 1820 was even more valuable now. I told Doug
I wanted to sit down with him personally, no more subordinates, and
he agreed to meet.

On February 1, I drove to Broderbund's offices in Novato, California, about an hour from Banner Blue. With Doug was Broderbund's vice president of business development, general counsel and
secretary (lots of titles, but just one person). It was the general counsel's organization who had round-filed us after the previous contact.
I believe Broderbund's president dropped in for a portion of the
meeting as well.

My objective was to raise their interest; I could ask hard questions at a subsequent meeting if one took place. I demonstrated Family Tree Maker and described our strategy in detail. Having satisfied
him that Family Tree Maker was high-quality and evergreen, Doug's
primary interest turned to Banner Blue's management team.

Broderbund had purchased a small company called PC Globe
two years previously and the young founder had died quite unexpect-

edly. There was no number two in place, so the company essentially evaporated. They did not want to repeat their mistake. I was proud of our people and told him without hesitation that Alma could step in for me. Doug asked about my plans and commented that it would be easy to lose interest after receiving a pile of stock. I replied that Banner Blue had always done well. I already had a second home and a sports car—the money would not go to my head. I would stay if they wanted me to, and at the same time my career plans were not to vie for a job running Broderbund.

On a personal basis, Doug and I hit it off. He was bright, a strategic thinker, and easy to talk to. We agreed to meet at Banner Blue on February 13.

Although I thought Family Tree Maker was a good fit with Broderbund, I had many serious questions about how the company was run. My agenda for the second meeting was to understand Broderbund's product strategy, learn about their acquisition history and plans, and ascertain whether they were serious buyers. Most likely buyers, including Broderbund, would offer stock for Banner Blue, so it was important to project what their stock would be worth down the road when I could actually sell it. I needed to understand their product plans to make such a projection.

The strategic vulnerability of their Print Shop product line was of particular concern because it represented about one third of company sales. Personal publishing programs were boxing in the product much like presentation graphics programs had boxed in Org Plus, while special-purpose programs like My Brochures were nibbling away at the edges of its market space. I also noted falling sales for their number-three product line, the Carmen Sandiego geography game. The success of their entertainment program Myst masked these problems, but entertainment programs had a notoriously short life. What would happen when Myst disappeared? Although Doug was a strategic thinker, his managers seemed to implement little of that thinking. Finally, I knew that Broderbund had a troubled acquisition history. By their own admission they had botched the acquisition of PC Globe and they had aborted mergers with Sierra Online and Electronic Arts. They had also failed to acquire Automap. After distributing the successful street map product for years, they let Microsoft purchase the company out from under them. I wanted to know why they had such a string of missed opportunities and to make sure that I did not become the next company on the list.

Only Doug arrived for the meeting at Banner Blue and I politely fired away. Doug told me that Broderbund was developing a personal publishing product of its own to expand the Print Shop line. He also felt their premium image would keep competitors out of the distribution channel, a wholly unrealistic appraisal, I believed. Doug thought they had "over-exposed" Carmen Sandiego with too much distribution, leading to the recent sales declines, but it was good to hear that Broderbund had the rights to the sequel for Myst and the project was already underway.

Discussing Broderbund's merger history, Doug explained that one of the co-founders of Sierra Online had decided against the merger, so he thought it was inappropriate to continue the process. He described the Electronic Arts merger fiasco as resulting from a crisis in leadership and culture shock. At the time, Doug was not actively managing the company because he was settling a divorce case that required him to appear in court every day for several months. As the merger proceeded without him, the participants found they had terribly different corporate cultures, ". . . like the Waltons [Broderbund] versus the Mansons." Broderbund backed out of the deal and paid Electronic Arts a $10 million cancellation penalty. Automap, Doug explained, was more valuable to Microsoft than to Broderbund because Microsoft wanted to apply the mapping technology to markets in which Broderbund had no presence.

In spite of these problems, Doug said that one of Broderbund's highest objectives was to grow their personal productivity line through acquisitions. I did not find Doug's explanations for their failures entirely convincing. Broderbund should have identified the problems with the Sierra Online and Electronic Arts mergers before they signed a letter of intent. They could explain away one failure, but three failures, combined with their earlier dismissal of Banner Blue, led me to believe that they had serious problems with their ability to evaluate a merger.

To ascertain whether Broderbund was a serious buyer, I asked Doug a number of questions that outlined the key features of a deal:

1. "Is there a good fit?" Doug said personal productivity products would remain Broderbund's primary focus, making Family Tree Maker a good strategic fit.

2. "What are you willing to pay?" Pending due diligence and additional negotiation, Doug felt a valuation in the range of

three to four times trailing twelve-months' revenue made sense. This is a common way to value a company in a merger, taking the sales for the previous twelve months and multiplying by an appropriate factor depending on the company's overall health. I had done research on valuations and a multiplier of three or four represented a premium price, appropriate for a company with our growth rate and profitability.

3. "Would you pay stock or cash?" Doug wanted to use stock in an arcane procedure called a pooling of interests. I made it clear that such stock would have to be tradable and free of restrictions.

4. "Would you want me to stay with the combined company?" Doug said they would want a multi-year, personal service contract with me.

5. "Can Banner Blue stay at its current location as a separate division of the company?" Doug answered that it could.

6. "How my employees are handled during an acquisition is extremely important to me. What are your plans?" Doug saw "synergies" playing out over the long term. In other words, his intent would not be to come in and immediately change our organization or lay off employees.

These were good answers, exactly what I wanted to hear. So, in spite of my concerns about Broderbund's business and their merger history, I decided we should continue our discussions. Doug explained that Broderbund's president, the general counsel, and Mike Shannahan, their new chief financial officer, would drive the negotiations.

Reflecting that night on the meeting with Doug, I concluded that the best way to address my concerns about their merger history was to push for a speedy process. At least if the deal fell apart, I would have done my best to minimize the time investment. Alma and I planned to continue seeking out other buyers as well. All the investment bankers I had met stressed the desirability of competing offers as a way to drive up the price. Of course, these two efforts were in conflict with each other. If the Broderbund deal moved quickly, there would be no time for another suitor to appear. But, if we got the deal we wanted, it would not make any difference.

Is There Anyone Else?

The Soft*Letter 100 was an annual list of the one hundred largest independent software companies, on which Banner Blue ranked sixty-fourth at the time. I pored over that and other lists time and time again to make sure we were seeking out all likely buyers.

Our most important criteria for a buyer revolved around the price they would be willing to pay, their actual ability to pay, and the liquidity of their currency. As I have already discussed, we assumed that a good strategic fit equated to a willingness to pay a high price. The ability to pay a high price and provide liquidity depended on factors such as the buyer's size and health. There were several companies with sales of less than $50 million that were a good fit, but they did not have the cash to buy us and their stock traded in such low volumes that we would have been unable to liquidate our holdings in any reasonable amount of time. We decided not to talk to them.

One other company we decided not to contact was SoftKey International. This company had itself been formed in a three-way merger, but they did not have the kind of in-house product development group that was a foundation of Banner Blue. Because our product development strategies did not match, I did not think they would be interested in acquiring us at a fair price. Unbeknownst to me, they were soon to purchase several large software companies structured along the lines of Banner Blue—they were changing their philosophy. I assumed that I knew more about them than I really did. I should have given them a call.

Very large software companies easily met our primary criteria and several of them, seeing their corporate software growth slowing, wanted to enter the consumer arena. Microsoft was a clear possibility. They were making major investments in consumer software, including the productivity segment, and they were the one company that would also see value in Org Plus since they were already selling a version of the program. In fact, Microsoft had announced an intent to acquire Intuit, the manufacturer of the leading personal finance program. I had talked to Patty Stonesifer, Microsoft's senior executive in the consumer area, the previous year and I decided to put out another feeler through a friend. The problem with a giant like Micro-soft was finding the correct person to talk to, then getting their attention. Any development with them would take time.

Word Perfect was another large company that had announced a strategy to enter consumer markets. Their location in Utah also meant they had many Mormon employees who valued family history, and I had a casual acquaintance with the manager of their consumer effort. I tried to set up a meeting several times when I was visiting our Automated Archives Division, but the manager never returned my phone calls.

If we overlooked someone, we were counting on presentations like the one at the American Electronics Association Conference to cause them to seek us, and indeed, two other companies did contact us about a possible acquisition. Ironically, one of the companies was Sierra Online, the company that almost had merged with Broderbund; however, neither of these contacts turned into serious discussions.

Meanwhile, in a phone conversation with Broderbund's general counsel, he indicated they could make a more firm commitment, such as a letter of intent, in two to three weeks, after completing some preliminary due diligence. He envisioned the entire process taking three to six months.

On February 23, 1995, I followed up with a letter to both Doug and the general counsel. I stressed that time was of the essence be-cause of the high stock valuations that would not last forever, Banner Blue's need to consummate new European distribution agreements (expensive to unwind if Broderbund purchased us), and a number of pending investments in new equipment and people (unnecessary if Broderbund purchased us).

On the same day, the general counsel sent Broderbund's non-disclosure agreement. In an act of good faith, I sent Broderbund our financial statements before we actually signed the non-disclosure.

Due Diligence

On March 2, after waiting almost two weeks, the general counsel faxed Broderbund's due diligence material request. Surprised by its contents, I showed it to Alma. He had sent the same request that Broderbund's law firm, Wilson Sonsini Goodrich and Rosati, had prepared three years earlier for the acquisition of PC Globe. It still had the original fax headers, referred to PC Globe throughout, had paragraphs crossed out even though they applied to us, and contained many handwritten comments in the margins from that earlier acquisition. The information Broderbund requested was routine, but in my mind it was incomplete. They wanted the basic corporate documents such as the articles of incorporation, complete stockholder information, stock options information, all contracts and license agreements of any sort, personnel policies, trademarks, patents, a list of employees with titles and salaries, and bank records. They did not ask for the important material: technical information and product plans.

To help with the due diligence work, we brought Banner Blue's controller, Bonnie Anderson, onto the acquisition team. Before joining Banner Blue, Bonnie had worked at another successful software start-up, the Learning Company. With her experience in entrepreneurial companies, it did not surprise Bonnie that I was entertaining an offer and it excited her that her Banner Blue stock was about to become liquid. We assigned different tasks to each team member and quickly began assembling the information.

Around this same time, Broderbund's general counsel asked us to defer the granting of Banner Blue stock options to a number of employees. Typically, an employee stock option consists of the right to purchase a certain amount of stock at a price set on the date when the employee receives the option. In most cases, equal portions of the option vest each year for three to five years. After shares of the option vest, the employee can buy the stock and sell it for a profit. In a fast-growing company with an increasing stock price, such options are a tremendous incentive for the employee to work hard, thereby helping to increase the stock price and his own potential profit. They also encourage employee loyalty, because vesting stops when an employee leaves the company. Broderbund's general counsel was afraid the grants could violate one of the pooling restrictions, although I countered that they had been in the works since well before Doug and I first met. I told him to expedite an answer from whomever he needed to talk to. After fruitlessly waiting several weeks for definitive information from the general counsel, we decided to grant the options whether it created a pooling problem or not.

Structuring a Deal

In early March, Mike Shannahan, Broderbund's new chief financial officer, became more involved in the process. He faxed us a revised and much more professional request for due diligence information, although it still did not include a request for technical or product information. Otherwise, we could see little activity on their part as we continued to feed them the information they had requested. Simple questions went unanswered and we had already passed the date when the general counsel had told us that Broderbund would send us a letter of intent. It was becoming clear that we would have to drive the process. With Broderbund's lack of responsiveness and history of failed acquisitions, Shirley suggested that we negotiate a break-up penalty.

Since Broderbund was a publicly held company, the procedures for a merger were much more complex than what we faced when we purchased Automated Archives, and the choices we made had important consequences for the liquidity of the Broderbund stock I received. Shirley guided me through the various options for structuring the deal and by mid-March, we had weighed each of them against the appropriate decision criteria. I will briefly describe several of these issues to illuminate their peculiar nature.

For example, Broderbund had to register the stock with the Securities and Exchange Commission before I could sell it. There were a variety of ways to accomplish this registration and we favored a method called an S-3 filing.

We also wanted the deal to be a tax-free exchange and that placed restrictions on how much stock I could sell and when. Unfortunately, the Internal Revenue Service was the controlling government agency in this case, and their guidelines were not specific. Plus, in many cases the courts had overruled them. I had to look at previous court cases with my accountant and make my own judgment. Complicating matters, if I remained an employee of Broderbund for a period of time, I would have additional restrictions on when I could sell stock. I would be an "insider" and the law effectively limited my sales to a short period of time after Broderbund released quarterly financial results.

If Broderbund would pay cash, these issues would disappear, but that was not to be. After all the years of hard work building Banner Blue, I now had to navigate a sea of arcane government rules and restrictions to convert that work to cash. Timing was more important than I ever imagined. I had focused on selling when the valuation for Banner Blue was at a peak and now I was realizing that the valuation of Broderbund was equally important. If Broderbund's stock price collapsed before I was able to sell, I would end up with nothing.

On March 17, I went to Broderbund's offices to meet with Mike and the general counsel. We discussed the form of Broderbund's coming letter of intent, stock registration, a break-up penalty, employment contracts, and whether the merger would require a federal government filing for the review of antitrust issues. The general counsel objected to an S-3, fearing that it would make it easier for a shareholder to sue Broderbund. Shirley did not take that concern seriously, but the issue of stock registration remained undecided. I made known my desire to structure the deal so that we locked the dollar value in at least until closing. I could control the price until then if not after. Broderbund refused to consider a break-up penalty, probably because they had just paid a large one when they called off the Electronic Arts merger and they themselves had doubts about whether the Banner Blue deal would go through.

The law favored me on the issue of employment contracts. Since the deal would be a pooling, Broderbund could not contractually obligate me to stay, but they could enforce a non-compete agreement and that was their desire. About a week later, Broderbund's president came down to Fremont and took me out to lunch. Since they could not put me under contract, he asked for my personal commitment to stay with the combined company for two years. I knew the question was coming and replied that I could perform any job for two years.

Although we were moving forward, our concerns about Broderbund's ability to execute remained, so I once again reviewed the list of potential buyers. On March 24 and March 28, I met with two additional investment bankers who had seen us at the American Electronics Association Conference. We discussed options for taking Banner Blue public and I did not mention that we were in merger negotiations.

While waiting to secure a letter of intent from Broderbund, I prepared a list of due diligence items I wanted to receive from them. It was clear that Broderbund's style was much more laid back than Banner Blue's and I wanted to get a handle on how and why they had been successful. On March 29, I requested the following information:

1. Company objectives for 1994 and 1995, with actual performance noted

2. Long-term company plan or objectives

3. Product development plans for the past 12 months, with actual performance noted

4. Product development plans for the next 12 months, including (but not limited to) the following: When is Myst II shipping? Do you have a long-term agreement with the authors of Myst? What is next for Print Shop?

5. Executive pay, bonus, and option amounts

6. Sales quota and projections by product for FY95, including performance to date

7. Fiscal year-to-date budget performance (at a summary level)

8. Any actual or potential legal actions against the company, not yet reported (e.g., Doug mentioned that the Federal Trade Commission had begun an inquiry of the system requirements for Myst)

9. Analysts' projections and any published stock recommendations over the past 12 months

Items (6) and (9) were publicly available (it was just more convenient to procure it directly from Broderbund), but the other information was not.

Other Pressing Business

The negotiations were taking most of my available time, but while I let many things slide, some important tasks had to be accomplished. We had to integrate Automated Archives into our operations and repackage their products. We renamed the Automated Archives data CDs, calling them Family Archive CDs to be consistent with our Family Tree Maker line. I also worked with Paul to negotiate an important contract for genealogy data.

And at our growth rate, there was no other choice than to keep hiring. With Alma now focusing on sales, we had developed a critical need for additional management in the areas of accounting and finance, purchasing, customer support, human resources, and operations. To cover these areas, we wanted to make an offer to Rob Armstrong, an individual Alma had worked with at General Electric, now living in Texas.

Although only a handful of Banner Blue employees were aware of our negotiations to sell the company, I felt it was only fair to discuss the situation with Rob since in his eyes it might greatly affect the desirability of the job. I decided to tell him more or less simultaneously with giving him an offer to become a Banner Blue vice president. I discussed specifically how we would structure his job if we stayed independent and alternatively if someone acquired us. Rob showed he was comfortable with uncertainty when he accepted the position not knowing who, if anyone, would own us six months down the road. He became an extremely successful manager in our organization.

The First Offer

On the same day, Broderbund's general counsel called to say that he was faxing a term sheet for our proposed transaction. It surprised me that he would not drive down to discuss the matter in person. When it arrived, among the boilerplate items was a request for a "no shop" agreement wherein I would agree not to solicit, initiate, entertain, or encourage competing offers. Much more importantly, the number of shares they offered was more than 25 percent below the low end of the range Doug and I had discussed and little more than half the high end of the range.

To make matters worse, they had not expressed the offer as a fixed dollar amount of shares as I had requested. The dollar value of the deal would oscillate until the deal closed. Broderbund had stiffed me and I was absolutely furious. I stomped back and forth in my office for over ten minutes, too angry to even call Alma or Shirley. Broderbund's delivery of their offer stood in stark contrast to the savvy presentation and setting of expectations by Paul DeBry when he announced his price for selling Automated Archives.

Microsoft Calls

As I continued to vent in solitude, the phone rang. I picked it up and Dan Williams, a product manager at Microsoft's Consumer Products Division, introduced himself. Dan loved Family Tree Maker and had been studying the market for several months. He said Microsoft wanted to discuss possibilities ranging from working together to outright acquisition. My face broke out in a Cheshire cat grin. Our nondisclosure prevented me from discussing our negotiations with Broderbund, so I simply told Dan they would have to act quickly. Dan had enough experience to know what I meant and said he could come down for a visit on Friday, just two days later. He would be leaving the next day for a three-week European trip, but he said if there was interest, discussions could continue with other individuals at Microsoft. I pulled Alma into a conference room and described the new landscape; then I called Shirley.

We decided to make a counter offer to Broderbund at the high end of the range Doug and I had discussed. I called Broderbund's general counsel an hour after receiving the fax to tell him he was not even close and that I would prepare a formal response. Although Banner Blue's growth rate and profitability were much higher than Broderbund's, I demonstrated in a letter sent the next day that we were asking for about half their market-value-to-revenue ratio, reflecting the discount at which a private company sold relative to a public one. I also provided information on comparable sales that further justified our valuation and told them that we had another interested party.

Via fax, we signed a non-disclosure with Microsoft, although we decided to carefully screen due diligence requests from them since they intended to compete with us. Then, after Alma and I reviewed our agreement with Broderbund, we concluded that we could tell Microsoft that we were in negotiations with another blue chip company as long as we did not identify which one it was. I told Dan that because he was not the only interested party, we would only consider a full acquisition at a high valuation and suggested that he bring down additional people for his visit the next day. Unfortunately Dan's managers were out of town, but he understood the urgency of the situation. I also hoped to coax an offer out of Sierra Online, but nothing came of it.

Dan arrived a half hour late to our meeting and did not bother to apologize. It was not the best way to begin our relationship. He dis-

cussed his own background, then told me that they had decided they
wanted to enter the family history market and Patty Stonesifer had
talked to Bill Gates about it a few days earlier. Dan explained that
Microsoft had done an analysis observing how people spent time in
their homes. From this they picked five areas in which they wanted
to develop products.

When I worked at Hewlett-Packard I had done a similar analysis
for white-collar workers in an office environment. In the end, it was
not valuable because it did not identify what the customer perceived
as a needed improvement. Just because someone spends time doing a
task does not mean they want to reduce the time so spent. For example, almost everyone eats lunch, but that does not imply that everyone
wants to spend less time doing so. Dan also described Microsoft's
desire to build bridges across the different home applications. Microsoft Office had recently accomplished this for business applications. Combined with extremely aggressive pricing, they had wiped
out competition in that arena. Now they were fervently trying to find
a way to redefine and dominate the consumer market.

Dan had used essentially every genealogy product on the market,
and he complimented me on Family Tree Maker several times. He
specifically mentioned our anticipation of the mass consumer market
for the product area, the fantastic user interface, our redefinition of
the market to include help for finding one's ancestors, our timing in
shipping new versions to market before the Christmas selling season,
and our excellent distribution (which he recounted in detail). He also
thought that the new image management features set the standard for
the home market. Then, in a display of astute product marketing that
I had never seen before nor since, Dan told me the product features
he anticipated we would include in our next version and he was 100
percent correct. Dan became more circumspect as he discussed how
he wanted to grow the market, but his general comments and forecasts were in sync with my own. He felt that genealogy was a wonderful window for people to view history and other life events and
issues. I wanted to hire this guy.

I asked why they would buy us and he said we had a great product and owning it would allow them to enter the market more quickly.
He also confided that our acquisition of Automated Archives was a
wake-up call to them, confirming that Microsoft had been quietly
investigating their business. Now we had the data and Microsoft
wanted it. Dan said they could not ship their own product until 1996
at the earliest, but they would have a product, one way or another.

As our meeting closed, I stressed our urgency to Dan and gave him some basic financial statements to deliver to Amar Nehru, a manager in Microsoft's Business Development & Analysis group, who would be coordinating their due diligence.

On Monday, April 3, Amar called first thing in the morning. He had returned from Europe the night before and read Dan's report. He had picked up some kind of virus, but wanted to have a brief conversation before heading home to bed. Amar explained that Mike Holm, the business unit manager for several home products, including their family history project, would be returning to the office on Wednesday. Amar would have Mike call me immediately upon his arrival. Then Amar began an exchange of due diligence information that was to continue for the next two weeks.

Telling Mom and Dad

About this same time I decided to call my parents in Ohio to let them know what I was doing. They both got on the phone at the same time. I told them, "Well, I just turned down an offer to purchase Banner Blue. I don't think they offered enough." I described Broderbund, whom they had never heard of, and told them that Microsoft had also expressed an interest.

My mom gushed about how proud she was, the way mothers often do. Dad, on the other hand, did not say a single word—he was absolutely, completely silent. I know my dad well enough to realize that my news had simply stunned him. I think it would have surprised him to find that Banner Blue was worth $1 million, let alone the numbers I was naming, so in spite of the many things my father taught me to enable my success, when success came, he had no idea what to say. As I talked on the phone I could not help smiling to myself, picturing my father with his eyes wide open and his mouth agape.

Of course, I had talked with Connie about the possibility of selling Banner Blue a number of times over the past couple of years. Now for the first time she began to believe it might actually happen, and she looked forward to the prospect of me spending more time with her and Amber.

Just before the Broderbund negotiations heated up we had a nice break as a family, something we wished we could do more of. Amber had expressed an interest in skiing so we embarked on an expedition to Sundance Resort in conjunction with a business trip to visit Automated Archives. Neither Connie nor I had skied in years, but we were quickly back in our respective form, such as it was.

Amber had never skied, so we concluded lessons were preferable to instruction from her impatient father. After a day and a half of training, her instructor said she controlled her speed well, turned nicely, and had been to the top of the hill with no problems. I asked Amber where she wanted to go and she pointed, "The big one." Mom groaned. After Amber and I boarded the chair lift, Amber turned to look at Connie in the chair behind and whispered, "Mommy's kind of scared." Amber and I flew down the hill, and after a long wait Connie caught up with us at the bottom. We all had a great time.

The Second Offer

On April 4, I finally heard from Broderbund when the president responded to our counter offer. He dismissed Doug's earlier comments about a fair price range. He also told me that Mike, the chief financial officer, had revised our sales projections and he thought we would achieve only $14.1 million in revenue for 1995 rather than our quota of $16 million, a 12 percent difference. My latest forecast to Broderbund had been even higher, over $17 million. Mike had also revised our rate of pre-tax profit to less than half of our projection.

I asked the basis for these revisions, but the president declined to provide any details other than to say that he could not justify growth of more than 30 percent to his board. Broderbund had not allowed for any improvement in sales or profits if the acquisition indeed went ahead. However, he did offer to increase the purchase price by 19 percent. He was unwilling to tie the price to a fixed dollar amount of shares, and he never so much as mentioned or asked about the other interested parties. In so many words, Broderbund's president described this as their final offer, take it or leave it. I decided to leave it—at least for a while.

Alma and I considered whether Broderbund's perplexing forecast for Banner Blue was a negotiating ploy and decided it was not for these reasons: Except for Doug (who really was not on the team), the Broderbund negotiating team had a grand total of one or two years' line experience. Broderbund's president and Mike, the chief financial officer, both had accounting backgrounds and the general counsel was an attorney. Thus, they had no marketing experience with which to generate and defend a meaningful forecast for our product line. In our estimation, they considered it more important to avoid mistakes than to close the deal; therefore, they took what to them was the logical step of basing a forecast for Banner Blue on the results they expected of themselves. They could safely and confidently say that if Broderbund was going to grow 30 percent, then Banner Blue could grow 30 percent. To them the only alternative was to rely on our forecast alone, which they knew was not the right thing to do.

Given our analysis, Alma and Shirley both thought I should go to Broderbund and make a presentation about the potential of the family history market and Banner Blue. We decided to look for an opportunity.

Putting Broderbund on Hold

On Wednesday, April 5, 1995, I spoke with Mike Holm, manager of the Microsoft business unit that included the team working on a genealogy product. He explained that he would be the individual driving the acquisition discussions. He asked a variety of questions and also asked for time to make an offer. We agreed to meet on Friday. He would come down along with Amar and Rick Thompson, general manager of the product group to which Mike reported and a direct subordinate of Patty Stonesifer.

I would have been foolhardy to sign a no-shop agreement with Broderbund when I had Microsoft begging us to give them time to present an offer. Instead, I called Doug Carlston with the intention of rattling his cage. I told Doug the story about how Paul DeBry had presented his price, and compared that to the work of the Broderbund team. I complained of the total disconnect between our first conversations and the response of his subordinates. I described the lack of responsiveness to every input and request. They sent the term sheet weeks after the targeted date; I responded to it within an hour while it took them four and a half days to respond. We had yet to receive a single due diligence item we had requested. I expressed disbelief that Broderbund's president "could not justify growth of more than 30 percent to his board" when our sales year-to-date were 90 percent above the previous year, and asked why there had been no involvement from their own marketing group. I told Doug we were not re-jecting their offer, but we were not accepting it either—I was going to give the other party time to make a proposal.

Doug responded, "I told you we didn't have much experience doing this." He repeatedly stated that Broderbund needed to learn how to do an acquisition. He thought most of my points were reasonable, but he also pointed out that he was not the "numbers guy" and he needed to trust his team.

Experience is a necessary ingredient of success, but every job requires aptitude as well. In my opinion, Broderbund had screwed up more mergers than the average manager experiences in a lifetime. Therefore, I did not think that experience was the problem. I told Doug that his team seemed to require a high degree of certainty about things. He indicated that he was indeed afraid that the company was taking on the personality of a bunch of "bean counters." He closed by saying, "That's one of the reasons I want someone like you here. An entrepreneur like yourself is comfortable with a much higher amount of risk." I continued to like Doug and I hoped he could shake up his team. However, Doug and I certainly had different styles. I would have stepped in and fixed things just like when I was a kid in my dad's shop, while Doug, with many successful years that honed his own style, acted like there was nothing he could do. Neither of us were likely to change.

At this point, Microsoft created a sharply contrasting image. Microsoft composed its team primarily with line managers, not support staff. The managers shared our vision for the product category and understood the market in detail. They were proactive, responsive, and aggressive. They had experience completing acquisitions. For our upcoming meeting, they asked me to make a presentation on the underlying basis for our projections—essentially the same presentation we *wanted* to make to Broderbund.

Since Microsoft was a knowledgeable competitor, my strategy was to tell the Microsoft managers anything they wanted to know, so long as it was unimportant or they could find the information somewhere else anyway. Conversely, I would not tell them anything that was important and that they could only find out from me. That way I would look responsive, but not endanger our business position. So, I gladly gave them our Family Tree Maker sales numbers since they could estimate those numbers from public sources anyway, but I did not tell them which Family Archive CDs sold the best because that information was not available from any other source and it was important. I did not want them to know that the best-selling Family Archive CDs at that time contained public domain data that they could acquire for free.

Microsoft Visits

We began our meeting on April 7 with a tour of Banner Blue. I was nervous because I did not want to have to explain to anyone whom I was leading around. Alma and I then took the Microsoft executives over to my house to have our discussion. In retrospect, it was all kind of silly, because if I had said "these people are from Microsoft" and then moved the meeting into a conference room, no one would have thought anything of it. After all, we had a large contract with Microsoft and I could have been talking to them about anything. I doubt one person would have guessed the true nature of the discussions. The way I handled the visit invited suspicion, although I do not believe anything came of it.

There were many stories about senior Microsoft executives loving to talk (at least in private) about how smart they were. While I was at Banner Blue, I too looked for smart people. It seemed obvious to me that a company should hire the smartest employees it could find, and I never imagined someone might have a different view. But one day, while attending a dinner at the Stanford University engineering department, I made a casual remark to the effect that we always tried to hire the smartest individuals we could find. A gentleman across the table, employed by a large Midwestern company, expressed disbelief at my statement. He felt that there were many qualities more important than intelligence. He did not convince me. I wanted intelligence and the right experience and personal qualities, because that was what Banner Blue needed to survive. It was nice that someone else wanted to hire the people we did not select!

If ultimately we competed with Microsoft, I wanted them to know we were not a bunch of pushovers, so I began the meeting with Microsoft by reviewing our staff. The vast majority of our employees were college graduates, with 25 percent possessing degrees from Stanford, UC Berkeley, Harvard, or the California Institute of Technology. We also employed a Fulbright Scholarship finalist and four members of Phi Beta Kappa. If Microsoft respected brain power, then they had better respect us.

I reviewed our business projections in the way Mike Holm had requested and discussed the overall family history market. When I

forecasted the sales of a Banner Blue product, I always tried to break
out the underlying components of growth. For example, in the case
of Family Tree Maker, I expected growth to come from porting the
program to additional platforms such as the Macintosh, offering the
program internationally, offering related products and services, and
continuing to broaden the market to include people not previously
interested in genealogy. On the other hand, I expected pricing to decline. By looking at these individual pieces I acquired much more
confidence in the overall forecast than I would have by simply projecting an aggregate number, and I found that an error in one component often offset an opposing error in another, improving the forecast's accuracy. Per my plan, I was careful not to divulge any
information Microsoft could obtain only from us. They seemed comfortable with my analysis, as they should have been, since my estimates were similar to their own.

I then turned the meeting over to Rick. Rick described his organization, which had total sales of almost $400 million, representing
two-thirds of the entire Consumer Products Division and a size almost three times as large as Broderbund. Mike alone was responsible
for $100 million of revenue.

The strategic focus of the Consumer Products Division was
threefold: online products, Bob, and international distribution. This
list pointedly did not include new applications software, even though
Microsoft was making massive investments in the area. "Bob" was a
product, not a person. It was a home manager of sorts with a radical
new user interface intended to integrate Microsoft's many consumer
products. Rick described Bob as a "holy war" between factions at
Microsoft that either favored the approach or did not, and his body
language suggested that he was much more skeptical of the Bob strategy than were Mike and Amar. (In the end Rick was correct, as Bob
disappeared from the market having made little impact.) He also described how they looked for opportunities to share code and develop
in a modular fashion—techniques of which I was a great proponent.
Finally, he said they were on the lookout for special synergies, like
the case with Automap. Confirming what Doug had told me earlier,
Rick liked Automap because the underlying technology tied into personal digital assistants, global positioning technology, and the travel
reference business—all markets that Microsoft was contemplating.
Although I did not agree with every element of Microsoft's consumer
strategy, it was far-reaching, forward-looking, and consistent.

Rick then turned to their family history project. He described their evaluation of the acquisition as a make or buy decision. At the time, they had eight people, including Dan, working on the new product while Rick's entire organization had authorization to increase its headcount by one hundred people before the end of the 1995. Rick said that our success meant that competing with us would consume more of their scarce resources, yet purchasing us would consume an even larger chunk of his authorized headcount. So, the way Microsoft managed its product groups, Rick explained, made it difficult for them to justify the purchase of a relatively mature company with an ongoing revenue stream like that represented by Family Tree Maker. They preferred to buy a company simply for its technology, before the company had significant sales and headcount. In this case, he said they would have preferred to purchase Automated Archives; we had simply beaten them to the punch.

Nonetheless, they did want to acquire us. Rick thought that in the case of Family Tree Maker there was a good fit with their online efforts and a good fit with Bob, although neither strategy needed Family Tree Maker to succeed. They had doubts about the product's success in international markets because of cultural differences.

I pointed out that our Org Plus product line was also valuable to Microsoft, but Rick did not give those products any more consideration than did Broderbund. Org Plus had no value to Rick's organization, and to get Microsoft's office products group involved at that time would have been more trouble than it was worth.

Rick said he would want to move Banner Blue to Microsoft's Redmond, Washington campus to facilitate code sharing. He also asked us to consider the alternative of serving as an information provider to Microsoft, acting as their developer and being paid with royalties. I dismissed that option as one without interest to us. At this point we broke to caucus, with Microsoft retreating to my front porch while Alma and I remained in the dining room.

When Rick, Mike, and Amar returned, Rick reiterated that serving as an information provider to Microsoft was an attractive option to them. As an alternative he offered to acquire us for an amount that represented about 77 percent of what Broderbund had proposed, in our choice of cash or Microsoft stock, pending due diligence and subject to discounts. Although at first glance this might appear to be a weak offer, the option to receive cash instead of stock was an advantage. He felt he could sell that price to his superiors and it was consistent with other acquisitions they had done over the past year.

Honest and straightforward, Rick flat-out said that someone evaluating the acquisition as the purchase of an income stream would pay more and the Broderbund offer proved him correct. I asked who would approve the offer and he indicated that it would be Patty Stonesifer, explaining somewhat facetiously that Bill Gates now focused only on things that would generate a billion dollars in revenue. We exchanged home phone numbers and adjourned our meeting.

Weighing the Offers

I had not yet received a single piece of due diligence information from Broderbund, although I had sent the request ten days earlier. So, I phoned the general counsel to find out why. He had lost our request and asked me to re-fax it.

Alma and I exchanged thoughts on Saturday. We had preliminary offers from our two top prospects and we were emotionally ready to do a deal, but we questioned whether we yet had a fair offer given market conditions at the time. We did not think we would be able to convince either Broderbund or Microsoft to raise their price significantly. We looked to the market to establish market value, while both buyers related to their own peculiar circumstances. Banner Blue was doing so well at the time that it was tempting to pass on the offers and try again in a year or so when some of the smaller companies might also be bidders. On the other hand, my calculations of market value were just that, calculations. Two bona fide, prospective buyers of the company had offered us comparable prices (adjusting for the fact that the Microsoft offer was in cash). Those two companies represented the *real* market, and they spoke consistently. As soon as possible, I wanted to obtain outside advice to help settle the price issue.

Looking at other aspects of the deals, both companies were a good strategic fit for Family Tree Maker, but which company would we want to work for? Microsoft had an outward-looking, results-oriented corporate culture that was much more compatible with our own than Broderbund's inward-focused approach. The Microsoft managers were assertive and had a high sense of urgency like us, while the Broderbund people were easygoing, with no sense of urgency. Unfortunately, Microsoft wanted to disassemble Banner Blue and move it to Redmond, while we thought Broderbund would treat our employees well and largely leave us alone. The bottom line for me was that after eleven years of building Banner Blue, it would be difficult to see it dismembered in one fell swoop. No matter how good the reasons for going with Microsoft, it was hard for me to like the idea.

Rick and I talked by phone on Sunday, April 9. He continued to try to sell me on the concept of serving as a development house and information provider to Microsoft because that would allow him to use his authorized headcount on something else. However, that really did not give me an exit and I had no interest in dropping my entry barriers for the benefit of an aggressive competitor.

After talking with Rick, I faxed a letter to Doug explaining how our first quarter results made me feel comfortable that we would exceed our projections in contrast to Broderbund's forecast. I suggested that I personally make a presentation to the Broderbund board at their meeting scheduled for April 11. I also asked him to put some pressure on his general counsel to be more responsive.

I was on the advisory board of the Software Entrepreneurs Forum with Ann Winblad, a venture capitalist who had founded and sold her own software company some years earlier. I could not tell Ann whom we were talking to, but I could lay out the facts of the two deals to obtain her opinion on their fairness. I also wanted to know how much I should worry about what was going to happen to the product after we sold. Since she worked with these issues every day, I knew she would have good perspective. She graciously offered to meet me for lunch.

Ann was quick and decisive with her advice. She thought the offers we had received were excellent and she would do the deal. "Don't look forward to what the deal could be if you do it in a year. Don't look backwards after doing the deal. Just do it. A bird in hand . . . deals have a way of disappearing." She also reminded me that Banner Blue's performance was not a certainty—our growth had been extreme and could cause problems that we did not foresee. She was aware of other negotiations going on that she could not divulge and repeated that we had received good valuations from both companies. Considering stock market levels of that time, Ann said she would take the cash deal. If we chose the stock deal, she said we should mentally prepare for a 50 percent stock decline. She considered the stock market to be "frothy" at the time and reminded me that Sybase shares had crashed just the previous week. She emphasized that the cleaner the deal, the better.

With regard to the other issues, Ann told me that once I signed away the company, the product was no longer mine and I would have no control over it. "Don't think about that as a criterion for making a decision. The feather in your hat is having built the company and sold it, not what happens afterwards."

Ann had given me exactly the information I was looking for. I accepted her advice to do the deal, putting aside any more thoughts of waiting a year. She had not said it, but there was a risk of becoming greedy as my competitive instincts took over during the negotiations. "Trees don't grow to the sky." The level of Broderbund's stock did not concern me as much as it did Ann.

Doug had not invited me to present at the Broderbund board meeting, and it was going on as Ann and I spoke. After I returned to the office I called Doug to get a report. As I feared, the board had expressed concerns about Mike's forecast—why should they pay a premium for such lackluster growth? Worse, the tremendous deceleration of growth in Mike's forecast led two board members to ask about the total market size—was Banner Blue running out of customers? It was a question that the president, general counsel, and Mike could not answer. I found it extremely frustrating to have my position represented by others when I knew I could do a better job. Not surprisingly, the board approved the acquisition without additional leeway on the price.

It was decision time. We wanted to sell, and we were fortunate to have two interested parties. Many companies only have one, if any. Nonetheless, we faced a pragmatic choice to select the best deal, warts and all—the perfect deal was not an option and rarely is.

Alma and I reviewed our objectives for the deal:

1. High valuation and liquidity

2. Strategic fit for Family Tree Maker

3. No relocation of Banner Blue

4. Good treatment of employees

5. Cultural fit between Banner Blue and the acquiring organization

It was arguable whether Broderbund's offer of volatile stock was worth more than Microsoft's lesser cash proposal. After all, Ann Winblad had said she would take the cash. Nonetheless, Alma and I ranked the Broderbund offer as higher, especially considering the complex terms Microsoft kept proposing for the deal. We thought that the strategic fit for the product and the treatment of employees would be about the same with either company. So, Microsoft's lower, more complicated offer and our desire to avoid relocation put Microsoft in the number two position, even though we thought they were a better cultural fit.

We would keep working with Microsoft in case Broderbund fell through, but we decided to concentrate on improving the valuation and liquidity of the Broderbund proposal. We thought we should be able to raise the Broderbund offer by 5 to 10 percent by focusing on a package of smaller items like the details of how to account for un-vested stock options. I called Doug to set up a one-on-one meeting.

Pushing Broderbund

Doug was in Mountain View, a short drive across the bay from Fremont, for a meeting on Thursday, April 13. We agreed to meet there for lunch. I reviewed our objectives with Doug and told him that if Broderbund could not move on the big things, they should at least move on the small things. I gave him a number of examples. I also expressed the importance of Doug's continued involvement since he understood the Banner Blue entrepreneurial personality bet-ter than his acquisition team. Unfortunately, Doug informed me that he was leaving for an extended Hawaiian vacation the next day. Doug was not going back to the office, but he said he would talk to his president and general counsel by phone from his car. I called the general counsel later in the afternoon, but Doug had not called him yet, so I reviewed what we had discussed.

At about the same time I spoke with Broderbund's general coun-sel, I received a more formal proposal from Mike Holm at Microsoft. Mike and I had several phone conversations running through Sunday, April 16. The deal they were proposing was becoming more rather than less complex and I had doubts about ever being able to consum-mate a definitive agreement based on the broad outline he proposed. I told Mike it was not attractive relative to the other offer. Mike tried to excite me about their plans for the product area, but he was swimming upstream.

I pressed Broderbund's general counsel for another meeting at their offices, only to find that the president was going on vacation on Wednesday, April 19. The general counsel was glad to have a meeting on Tuesday, but the president was too busy to attend. Busy doing what, I wondered. Doug had told me that acquisitions were one of their highest priorities, but evidently not high enough for anyone to adjust their vacation plans. I insisted that the president attend, knowing that they would not make decisions without him. The president and general counsel relented and we agreed to meet at Broderbund's offices. Shirley and I attended, meeting with Broderbund's president, general counsel, Mike, and Tor Braham, Broderbund's outside counsel.

I wanted to run the meeting, so I just took over. The gist of my introduction was this: We have an offer from the other suitor and it is a good one. It does not blow you out of the water, but it has some very favorable characteristics. In particular, it is for any mix of cash or stock we prefer. We feel we can do a deal with either suitor, but for the same reasons we originally contacted you, you are still our first choice. However, you need to show some flexibility—either the price or the liquidity has to go up.

To initiate some movement, I felt I needed to help the Broderbund team look outside themselves and understand our needs, something in which they had previously shown no interest. I had prepared a handout to compare our objectives with their own and I thought that by emphasizing our common ground, the concessions we desired would appear to be small and understandable. As I explained my handout, I suggested that it was important to discuss each other's requirements without becoming adversarial. Broderbund's president laughed, saying that it was an adversarial process by definition. I disagreed, noting that the two parties in any merger negotiation had to work with one another after the acquisition, so a process seeking mutual understanding would be more effective in the long run. My discussion got us nowhere. The Broderbund team continued to have no interest in where we were coming from.

I turned to my wish list. I had prepared for myself a table of twenty issues, with separate columns for the Banner Blue position and our negotiating points for each one. Alma and I had decided that we would focus on the price and liquidity, leaving issues like a board seat for myself until later, if at all.

In a surprising and unexplained reversal, especially considering that my initial attempt to find common ground had failed, Broderbund agreed to almost everything we requested. Conceptually, we had a deal, and I was completely dumbfounded. After months of pushing and prodding, all the pieces fell into place within a matter of minutes. I was really going to sell my company. In the car on the way back to Fremont I had a few moments to reflect on the founding and sale of Banner Blue, and I felt proud about the accomplishment it represented. However, that was the only significant time I had to consider my feelings over the next two weeks—there was too much work to do.

We agreed that we would throw out the term sheet and proceed directly to a definitive agreement on an expedited schedule. Most companies, including Broderbund, permit executives with inside information to trade stock only during a limited time after each public announcement of financial results. Therefore, we targeted signing by the end of April 1995, which would allow all of the negotiators to trade shares in July, after Broderbund publicly announced its financial results for the quarter ending in May.

Further, Broderbund agreed to two additional S-3 registrations over the course of two years, after which the stock would be freely tradable. They also agreed to pay us additional shares on top of those already offered to cover all unvested Banner Blue employee stock options. This one concession was equivalent to a 5 percent increase in the price.

We also discussed special situations involving salary and stock options for several Banner Blue employees. Negotiating these kinds of issues is difficult, because the other side will argue that no one would lose a deal just to satisfy a single individual. In the end, everyone involved in negotiating just wants to close the deal and issues involving a single individual become decided as if by lot. Fortunately, Broderbund continued to be cooperative and we reached tentative agreement on all the important cases (although, proving my point, on one of those cases Broderbund reversed itself no fewer than five times over subsequent days).

Finally, I asked Broderbund's general counsel one more time for the due diligence items since we had only received about half of what we requested. He explained that he could not give me the company objectives and results because they did not use management by objectives at the corporate level.

Now we just had to prepare several hundred pages of documents in less than two weeks. The same process had taken almost two months on the Automated Archives deal, but we had consumed much of that time arguing about trivialities. Shirley, Tor, and I all thought the task was doable.

Looking for additional reinforcement for our decisions, I decided to talk to other employees. In separate meetings on April 19, both Courtney and Hugo Paz (now one of our senior programmers) told me that they had no interest in working for Microsoft and they did not believe that we had hired anyone who would. Indeed, we had refined our recruiting pitch to compete against Microsoft in the market for employees. On the other hand, the news that their stock would become convertible to cash excited both of them. It relieved me to know that people I had worked so hard with for so many years thought I was doing the right thing.

On Thursday, April 20, 1995, I called Mike Holm at Microsoft and told him that I had a deal with the other party that was too good to walk away from. I explained that I did not see the sense in making a counteroffer to his proposal of several days earlier because I did not see how Microsoft could come close. Nonetheless, he asked for a little more time. The next day, Mike Holm called after talking to Patty Stonesifer and threw in the towel. He asked who the winner was, but I told him he would have to wait until we made the deal public. I sincerely liked the Microsoft managers—it was unfortunate they could not make a more attractive offer.

On Friday the 21st, a Broderbund development manager came to Banner Blue to do two hours of due diligence on our code. That was the only technical review they performed. Later that same day, Alma and I talked individually to every Banner Blue shareholder and scheduled a shareholder meeting for Monday. All were positive about the deal and for good reason—they would make a lot of money, at least on paper.

The shareholder meeting and vote was a formality. Since I held such a large proportion of the stock, my vote alone determined the outcome. In fact, I encouraged the small shareholders to vote no, which would entitle them to receive cash when the deal closed rather than risky, restricted stock. I explained to them that they should treat the vote as a personal financial decision. Nonetheless, in the balloting, only one shareholder voted against the deal in order to receive cash and only after I repeatedly reassured her that it would have no impact on her employment.

Negotiations on the final agreement and supporting documents were remarkably smooth. There were two issues on which Broderbund waffled all week, but we finally resolved them. On Wednesday, I faxed Broderbund's general counsel to ask him about three due diligence items he still had not sent. Finally, on Thursday I called him and dragged the information out of him over the phone. After a week of very late nights for Alma, both legal teams, and myself, we were ready to sign on Friday, April 28, 1995. The event was to occur at Wilson Sonsini's offices in Palo Alto.

Signing the Papers

On Friday morning, as Alma and I drove across the bay, we checked the stock. Broderbund was down two dollars and Microsoft was up, even though the United States Justice Department had announced on Thursday that they would try to block Microsoft's merger with Intuit. When we pulled into the parking lot, we checked the price again— Broderbund had recovered one dollar.

At many times, it seemed like the deal would not have moved forward without our strong, persistent pushing. Broderbund spurned our initial contact, and there were innumerable times when it seemed like they did not care whether or not the acquisition occurred. I suspect that this is relatively common in acquisition negotiations, especially when the firm being acquired is small compared to the organization doing the buying (we were less than 10 percent as large as Broderbund). The chief executive officer or some other sponsor of the deal says "do it" because it makes sense, but the trouble starts when the sponsor turns the process over to a group of implementers with a different, less strategic agenda and little stake in the outcome. In that case, the company being acquired has to be the driver or the acquisition does not happen.

The Wilson Sonsini building was extremely large, housing hundreds of attorneys and their support staff. To erect it they had bulldozed the Hewlett-Packard building I worked in when I first graduated from business school. We walked down a long corridor past one receptionist and then another, arriving at a conference room located in virtually the same location as my first Hewlett-Packard desk. I was going to sign away my company while standing on the very same piece of ground where I first learned about running a business almost twenty years before.

Broderbund's general counsel and Mike Shannahan were there with all the attorneys. We reviewed one or two lingering issues to make sure everyone was finally in agreement. By this point everyone just wanted to sign the papers, which took about two hours to accomplish. I took some photographs and then Shirley pulled me into the hall to tell me that she had accepted a position as general counsel for Transamerica Corporation in San Francisco. I had just lost the best attorney I had ever worked with.

The morning was strangely anti-climactic. After all the years of hard work, Banner Blue was no longer mine. Alma had tears in her eyes as we drove away from Wilson Sonsini. I had a feeling of numbness—I was emotionally drained after the months of negotiations and many decisions. While the process itself had been incredibly stimulating, the aftermath was like walking into a vacuum.

I dropped Alma off at the office, but I did not feel like going inside. It just did not seem to be the right thing to do. I wanted to be alone with my thoughts, not talking to employees. So I drove over to Amber's school where her science fair project was on display. When I finally located her presentation board, I found she had received third prize. Parental pride quickly took my mind off Banner Blue.

7

Employee Number 1559

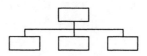

I slept fitfully the next few nights. I was feeling not just a letdown from the stress of deal-making, I also felt a loss. For the first time in many years I was missing a high-level objective, something to drive me forward day after day. Of course I had to manage the transition with Broderbund, but I saw that as a blip in my life's course. I lay in bed realizing that I had no idea of what *big thing* I wanted to do after fulfilling my commitment to Broderbund.

At the same time, I realized that I no longer had the control over my situation that was so important to my happiness. I was an employee again for the first time in eleven years, and would have to accept what that meant: a new culture imposed by others instead of the one I created, layers of approval, turf battles, heeding other people's wishes even when I did not agree, and more. This situation was every entrepreneur's nightmare and I knew that most people in my position did not stay long with the acquiring company. Would I?

Also worrying me were the many uncertainties I still faced: how would my employees respond to the sale, and at what price would I be able to liquidate my stock?

On the other hand, Doug had indicated to me almost every time we spoke that he looked forward to my involvement in the management of Broderbund, and for my part I thought that I had much to offer. Ironically, I expected that my experience with large companies such as Hewlett-Packard would be as valuable as my entrepreneurial experience, because Broderbund did not have many executives who had ever worked for another company, let alone a large, well-run company like they wanted to become. I also thought that I would be able to help them create a product strategy that would help fill the void when Myst sales inevitably declined. I was glad that Doug wanted my involvement, and from a business, personal, and financial standpoint, I had no regrets about the deal.

I decided that my goals should be to retain as much independence as possible in running Banner Blue and at the same time to participate in Broderbund's strategic planning process. Only with reasonable freedom would my new role as an employee be tolerable to me, while participation in the corporate strategy-making process might allow me to learn something new.

The Transition Plan

Over the weekend, I collected my thoughts about Banner Blue's transition to being part of a larger company. We had decided to make the announcement to employees and issue a press release on Friday, May 5. That gave me one week to act.

I decided our objectives during the transition should be as follows:

1. Minimize employee uncertainty caused by the merger

2. Replace the obsolete management control systems in operations (the software for processing orders and reporting relevant information to management) with those used by Broderbund

3. Turn our management focus to product development in both Fremont and Utah

4. Energize hiring in key areas of product marketing and engineering

I spoke with Mark Bailey, a friend responsible for mergers and acquisitions at another software company. His advice about minimizing employee uncertainty was to make as many decisions as possible before the announcement. Mark also sent me an article about the employee reaction to mergers. It advised the full and early communication of "all information, be it positive or negative, as soon as legally and practically possible." This struck me as good advice, fully consistent with my policy of openness.

I wanted to transfer customer service, data entry, inventory control, raw material procurement, manufacturing, and fulfillment to Broderbund as soon as practical. We already outsourced many of these functions, and those we performed internally we had staffed with temporary employees, so we could transfer them to Broderbund with minimal disruption to our organization. At the same time, this would allow us to take advantage of Broderbund's management control systems. At some point, we would also need to integrate our sales force with Broderbund's, but I wanted to leave all other functions essentially as they were.

Our salary levels and employee benefits package were comparable to Broderbund's, so I recommended that we make no changes until January 1, 1996, at the earliest. Benefits and salary administration were key tools we had used to define our corporate culture. By not switching immediately to Broderbund's salaries and benefits, we would be establishing a policy of independence that would comfort employees and serve as a precedent in other areas as time went on—now that I was an employee again, I wanted some management elbow room. Also, by moving the decisions on benefits far out in the future, it would allow Banner Blue management to focus on strategically important product areas. I would try to sell Broderbund's president on the idea that the gains from focusing on our products would far outweigh any losses from deferring the benefits integration.

The final two objectives, to focus management on product development and to energize hiring, did not relate to the transition itself—they reflected business necessity. Indeed, while I had been making deals for the previous eight months, our product development area had begun showing signs of my neglect. Product life cycle documents were incomplete and behind schedule, as was coding for the new version of Family Tree Maker. I would also soon discover that one of our junior managers was having a relationship with one of his subordinates, ultimately resulting in the loss of both employees. It was a matter of professional pride for Alma and me to deal with personnel problems, ship our new products, and meet the sales target upon which we had based our sales pitch for Banner Blue. I wanted Broderbund to feel they got their money's worth.

Broderbund's president and Patsy Murphy, Broderbund's Director of Human Resources, came to visit on Tuesday, May 2. The president accepted my recommendations and gave me a comfortably high purchase approval limit. In addition to the decision to delay any changes to our existing benefit package, Patsy suggested that we include Banner Blue employees in Broderbund's 401(k) retirement plan during the next open enrollment period beginning July 1. She thought employees would see it as a token of good faith. I thought it was an excellent idea and the president agreed. It looked as if we really would be able to maintain independence.

The Public Announcement

Doug, Patsy, and Broderbund's president came to Banner Blue on Friday, May 5, for the big announcement. I had already met with all of Banner Blue's managers earlier in the week. Before telling the troops, it always helps to have management fully apprised of and adjusted to a major change. That way they can help address any concerns that arise. People are often more comfortable talking with their immediate supervisor than with the head of the organization, not to mention that there was no way I could talk to everyone individually.

All of the employees gathered with us in the lunch room over pizza. I was extremely nervous. The only time I had been more tense was many years earlier when at a size of only ten people I had to announce that the accounting clerk and another individual were leaving because of our differences. I ran through the reasons for the merger, while at the same time engaging in some casual banter with the Broderbund executives to show the employees that we were all friends. Simultaneously, because Paul DeBry was out of town, Jeff Levinsky was delivering the same message to our staff in Utah. I emphasized that good treatment of Banner Blue employees was one of the most important objectives of the transition—especially since I was an employee again. I explained that we expected to have a spot for every regular employee (those who were not temporaries or contractors), but stated clearly that we could not guarantee it.

Next, before describing which departments would be affected by the merger, I explained that Banner Blue would maintain its identity, offices, and management. Benefits are a concern to everyone, so I was somewhat apprehensive that my plan to defer any changes for at least seven months would still cause concern. However, it did not, and our immediate enrollment in the 401(k) plan excited employees.

Reading the faces in the crowd, reaction to our sale appeared to be even better than I had hoped. The atmosphere was certainly not festive, but it was decidedly positive. My nervousness began to alleviate.

I personally promised my staff that we would strive to tell them everything we knew, when we knew it. If we had made a decision, but had a good reason for withholding the announcement, we would tell them what that good reason was. If we did not know the answer, we would say so.

To emphasize that we meant what we said about Banner Blue continuing as an independent organization, I pointed out that $250,000 of capital improvements previously approved by Banner Blue were continuing as scheduled and that we were honoring all outstanding job offers.

To take some of the edge off the day's events, I agreed to be the subject of a roast at the next company meeting. The Banner Blue roast was a staple of every employee's fifth anniversary with the company. Dan Handalian acted as the coordinator, writing a skit and dressing up to play the part of the employee, in drag with the appropriate wig if the employee were female. Sometimes the roast team prepared an elaborate video as well. One memorable time, the video had involved a mock robbery of our offices. The filming was so realistic that a neighbor called the police! I had never been the subject of a roast, somehow escaping on both my fifth and tenth anniversaries, so I figured this was a good time. I even challenged Dan to shave his head to match my own bald crown, and I bet anyone in the company willing to put up five dollars that he would not do it.

Afterwards, we passed out a memo detailing in writing everything I had just covered as well as background information on Broderbund and a Broderbund sweatshirt. We also assigned managers to contact every employee who was not at the office for the meeting, as well as job candidates. Then, every employee had an opportunity to speak with one of the Broderbund executives in small group meetings. Our purchase by a company like Broderbund, with its high profile and excellent reputation in the marketplace, seemed to reinforce to each Banner Blue employee that we too were a market leader. It made them feel good, and I do not recall a single complaint.

Since we could not guarantee all of the temporary employees a position after the merger, we thought it best to deliver that message in a separate meeting later in the same day. That way we had an opportunity to specifically address their concerns, which would be much different from those of the regular employees.

Of course, the temporary employees were extremely apprehensive. The atmosphere in that meeting was quite a contrast from the first. I do not gain any satisfaction from causing people anxiety, so it was nice to receive a congratulatory call from Monty Allen. He anticipated my feelings about the temporary employees and encouraged me not to worry about it, suggesting that people bounce back quickly from such things.

The Days Afterward

Shortly after the announcement, I found that there had been a leak. I later traced it to the manager who was having an affair with his subordinate. He had told her about the merger when we notified him as a stockholder. This gave her ample time to spread the information around, causing a great deal of unnecessary angst. The people who found out in advance did not have the benefit of the positive information provided in our general meeting. All they had was uncertainty. It is my opinion that two of the people who would later jump ship did so because they found out early and got all worked up. By the time they heard the whole story it was too late to allay their fears. There was not much more we could have done to ensure confidentiality—these things just happen. Unfortunately, the head of the organization is always the last one to find out about a leak.

A major change in an organization always triggers departures from people who might have been thinking about leaving anyway, and an acquisition is even more likely to do so. Banner Blue was no longer the same company they chose to work for in the first place—a small, independent start-up. Nonetheless, my objective was to minimize unplanned departures.

To help track our efforts to find positions for each regular and temporary employee, I kept a table listing each one. In the end, there was just one regular employee for whom the only possible position was in Novato. Rather than relocate, he decided to join another company. Regrettably, several other people left of their own accord shortly after the announcement.

As for the temporary employees, we gave them a minimum of several weeks' warning about when their employment would terminate, and we found permanent spots for some of them. To the best of my knowledge, the majority found another employer almost immediately.

Moving to Carmel?

At about this time we learned that one of the schools in the Carmel area had accepted Amber for enrollment. So I took a day off at the end of May to spend time in several of the classrooms, making sure that this indeed was the best school for Amber. I liked what I saw, but more importantly, her admission forced us to decide when to move to Carmel. If Amber did not attend in September, we could not be sure that she would be able to enroll the following year.

Carmel was even farther from Fremont than Alma's home in Novato and commuting on a daily basis would have been impractical for me. Once we decided that the school was right for Amber, Connie thought she and Amber should move to Carmel in August 1995 and that I should keep the house in Fremont, coming to Carmel on weekends until completing my commitment with Broderbund. It was not ideal, but I agreed and we began to implement the plan.

Of course, Amber did not like the idea of moving at all. She explained that she did not want to leave her friends, and she also pointed out that it was not possible to move because of Brownies. She wanted to "fly up" to Girl Scouts together with her Brownie friends. She was quite clear, "I'm not going to that school." At least we all knew where we stood.

The school had a short summer session that would allow Amber to meet her new classmates, so we enrolled her. One week they took a day trip to the Children's Discovery Museum of San Jose, not far from Banner Blue's offices, and I decided to surprise Amber by meeting her there. With hundreds of kids operating and crawling through the many exhibits, it took me more than thirty minutes to find her. Finally I rooted her out, and received a big hug for my efforts. We had lunch together before she returned to Carmel.

Even after making many new friends at the summer session, Amber still had misgivings about attending the new school. One day Amber told me that she could not change schools because she never had the opportunity to have lunch with the principal at Mission San Jose Elementary—a treat that the principal shared with a few students on a periodic basis. Sensing an opportunity, I called the principal at

Amber's new school, explained the situation, and asked if she would invite Amber to lunch. She readily agreed. When I told Amber, she liked the idea of going to lunch, and she agreed to collect her questions: Do they have a science fair? Do they have a talent show? Are there any other new students in her class? They went out for a pizza and Amber's resistance to moving dropped a tiny bit more, especially when she found out that there would be other new students joining the class.

Selling Stock — The "Least Regrets" Strategy

Alma and I got the details of the transition rolling, and then in July, Connie, Amber, and I took a vacation to visit my parents in Ohio. The first window during which I could sell my Broderbund shares opened while I was there. Given my concerns about Broderbund's prospects, there was no question in my mind about selling the stock, although my interpretation of the rules governing the tax-free nature of our merger limited my sales to approximately half of my holdings during this first window.

Broderbund stock closed at $51.75 per share on the day we did the deal. It had drifted down to the low forties before recovering into the low sixties during July. After the merger I had decided that my sales strategy would be to sell a large chunk of stock during each window, and I had already worked out the legal details of the transaction with my stockbroker. It was a "least regrets" strategy—if the price declined over time I could look back and be happy I sold a chunk at a higher price, but if the price increased I could feel comfort that I had not sold all my stock at a lower price in the past.

On July 5, I called my broker and told him to sell what amounted to approximately 20 percent of my holdings. A week later, the stock had climbed to $68.00 and I decided I should sell more—the price was far higher than what I was willing to settle for when we closed the deal. Remembering the entrepreneur's advice, "Trees don't grow to the sky," I paced the room for thirty minutes while making sure of my decision, and then called my broker and told him to sell an additional 20 percent. I must admit that it was satisfying to see those shares become dollars—it put a healthy grin on my face for quite some time to come.

The Roast

Upon returning to Banner Blue, Dan Handalian coordinated my roast. He wore a hat until right before the show to conceal whether he had in fact shaved his head. When he walked on stage he was as shiny as a cue ball. I immediately paid off all my bets, considering it one of the best investments I ever made. I think that the technical support department had enough money wagered that they would have held Dan down and shaved his head for him if he had not done it on his own. His hair stylist thought the whole thing was so funny that she shaved Dan for free, leaving just a wisp of hair in the front to simulate what I had left. In fairness to Dan, I was taking advantage of his team spirit in order to lighten things up during the transition period. If he objected, he never once complained about it.

The event started off with a video collage of my life, narrated by Paul Burchfield, one of our technical support representatives. In collusion with my family, they had gathered a group of pictures showing me horsing around in one way or another—pictures intended for other family members and no one else. It was a hilarious presentation, but the serious roasting occurred in the skit that followed. One of the first digs was a reference to the famous "5X multiplier rule." The feeling around the office was that if I said, "You should be able to do that in an hour," then the employee should multiply by five to estimate the actual time it would take, five hours in this example. Before the skit was finished, I had been roasted about the number of drafts I required before I was happy with someone's work (fourteen was the estimate); my love for information in a tabular format; my impatience; using three words to describe something that would take twenty-five words for someone to understand—then my exasperation that they do not understand me; the hunger that strikes me precisely at noon every day; my fondness for grapefruit, Hydrox cookies, and glazed donuts; my propensity to take a few French fries from anyone eating them in the lunch room; and working in the car while someone else drives.

Connie, Amber, and my sister Linda, living in Southern California, also played roles in the skit. They acted out a true story that everyone thought was side-splitting. I did not eat bananas until recently, never before liking the taste. Amber had been there when I picked up my first banana and washed it before eating it. As if washing a banana was not funny enough, I fumbled around trying to open it, finally asking for a knife to cut off the end so I could peel it. At the sight of this, Amber said, "Duh! Daddy, you're not even as smart as a monkey!" I guess it was very funny and I was laughing as hard as everyone else.

To end the evening, Julie Rice, our sales manager, presented me with a three-by-five-foot, framed collage of pictures from my eleven years at Banner Blue, then we all retired to a local restaurant for dinner.

Afterwards, Amber told me that before the practice session, Dan asked if he should write her lines on a card for her to use during the skit. "I told him, 'No, I'll remember them.' What's so hard about memorizing a few lines? He didn't think I could remember them just because I was a kid." We laughed that during the actual skit, Amber was the only actor who remembered all of her lines without prompting.

The Banner Blue Division Charter

The next day I put the finishing touches on a charter for Banner Blue. Broderbund was facing the issues of operating a remote division for the first time and I wanted to continue my effort to draw lines in the sand. After several conversations, Broderbund's president agreed to a document that defined our identity as "Broderbund, Banner Blue Division," enumerated the functional departments we would retain (unchanged from our first meeting), authorized us to maintain historical policies such as Bucks for Bugs, authorized us to develop products outside the area of family history, and gave me, as division president, the following authority:

1. The division president will have hire and fire authority within the corporate policies and within approved budgets and headcount plans.

2. Consistent with current sign-off levels, the division president may authorize the purchase, lease, and acquisition of property.

3. The division president may enter into contracts and agreements, or where appropriate authorize senior managers to do so.

4. The corporation president determines the division president's sign-off levels and limits for purchases and contracts. These are currently as follows: capital expenditures and operating expenses up to $50,000 and contracts up to $100,000.

5. The division president is to use his judgment to obtain goods and services in a way that makes the most business sense. He may choose internal or external sources as he sees fit.

6. The division president will have pricing authority for the division's products.

I saw the charter as a means to head off turf wars with other managers and it turned out to be helpful in this regard. Banner Blue was able to maintain remarkable operating freedom. Surprisingly, the president also allowed Banner Blue to retain its own profit-sharing plan based on the division results rather than those of the corporation. Although Banner Blue Division employees earned less profit sharing than other Broderbund employees the first year, this reversed in subsequent years, becoming a significant motivator.

Integration Continues

One of our objectives during the integration of the two companies had been to replace Banner Blue's obsolescent management control systems with those used by Broderbund. Bonnie, our controller, had for years wanted an integrated system that automatically placed information about every order received directly into the appropriate accounts in our accounting software. Because we had separate software for processing orders and for accounting, Bonnie had to run reports to obtain sales information, then manually enter those numbers into the accounting system. It was tedious work, subject to error.

On the surface, Broderbund's system appeared to be far superior. It was state-of-the-art, integrated software purchased from one of the leading vendors in the field. Unfortunately, after we switched to Broderbund's system, we learned the many advantages that we had taken for granted in our earlier system.

Broderbund's system was outside our control and very difficult to modify even when we were able to persuade the responsible parties to make a change. We got less information to run our business, it was often late and untimely, and we had reduced ability to obtain ad hoc information. Our earlier system was flexible and so easy to modify that almost everyone in the production and accounting departments had done it at one time or another. If we wanted to track the sales results stemming from a late-breaking product review, find out how many orders originated in Utah, or ask any of hundreds of other questions, we could generally procure the information we wanted with a trivial amount of work. Local control of operating data, available on a flexible, easy-to-use system, is worth its weight in gold. With the new system we got the integration we desired, but at the expense of many other things we needed.

Nonetheless, the merger of the two companies went much more smoothly than these things often do. Our plan to defer a major overhaul of the benefits package allowed us to make all changes in a very thoughtful way, with each one announced far in advance. The adjustments appeared over time in a way not much different from the routine modifications every benefits package experiences. Banner Blue retained its key employees and continued to operate as successfully as before. Most of our employees were happy as events unfolded. However, as the founder of Banner Blue, I found our cultural differences to be troubling.

Banner Blue was results-oriented, with hard-working individuals held accountable for their actions. Broderbund was role-oriented, with people expected to perform the tasks of their job description with neither reward nor penalty for the results actually achieved. With no special rewards for success and essentially no penalty for failure, many Broderbund employees did not work very hard.

On one occasion, Lisa Graves, a long-time Banner Blue employee, was talking to someone at the corporate offices and she mentioned that she would be in the office over the weekend to take care of some pressing issues. The person at corporate asked, "Are you an hourly employee?" Lisa responded that she was not; she received a salary. The individual at corporate responded, "Oh, up here only hourly employees work on weekends." Alma and I had a good laugh when Lisa told us the story, but quietly I worried about how these events would change Banner Blue.

Updating Banner Blue's Strategy

At this time, Banner Blue had its strongest management team ever, allowing me to concentrate on our strategic issues. I focused on four areas in particular: a market analysis of our existing Family Tree Maker customers, an improved product development life cycle for Family Archive CDs, a means to sell Family Archive CDs through our retail channel, and our first Web site. This work was a welcome distraction from transition issues and I enjoyed it thoroughly.

Driving our market analysis was a desire to know who purchased Family Archive CDs and why. I asked my entire direct staff to read *Crossing the Chasm* by Geoffrey A. Moore, a book about marketing and selling technology products to mainstream customers. Courtney led the discussion about the book and did much of the work to apply Moore's thoughts to our situation. We found we could break our market into four subsegments, targeting different messages and products to each one.

Improving the product development life cycle for Family Archive CDs was a major project involving new life cycle steps, new management control systems, new vendors, and new personnel. The Family Archive CDs were different from our typical software programs because we were acquiring the data that went on the CDs. Then to be useful, the data had to be readable by another program, in this case Family Tree Maker.

The problem was that we had inherited a dysfunctional product development life cycle for the Family Archive CDs from Automated Archives. The facts called for a consistent, standardized process for acquiring, processing, and reading the information; Paul DeBry had spoken of this need even before we had purchased the company. Instead, we had a haphazard process relying solely on Paul's judgment to acquire information and a rickety technical procedure for preparing the CDs, resulting in constant changes to the file format. Every time we tweaked the file format, we had to change the software that enabled the user to read the CD. It was expensive for us and annoying to our customers.

We already had sales data on our dozens of Family Archive CDs, so I used this information to develop a mathematical model for predicting the sales level of new CDs depending on the type of information they contained. There was still room for Paul's valuable judgment and industry contacts, but the model enabled us to do a much better job of prioritizing which data to acquire. At the same time, I asked Jeff Levinsky to rationalize the technical process and I assigned Rob Armstrong to manage the entire effort as an independent business unit within the Banner Blue Division. We all but stopped the development of new CDs as we began to implement the changes, but month by month the operation improved. During November 1995, we signed an agreement with Genealogical Publishing Co. to publish many of their works on CD, and we shipped the first two volumes of the World Family Tree. By 1997, the business unit was running like a clock, publishing an average of one new Family Archive CD every week.

During 1995, we sold all of our Family Archive CDs via direct mail. I wanted to find a way to sell them through our retail channels; however, very few of the individual titles sold in high enough volume to make this practical. Instead, I suggested that we bundle several of our most popular titles with Family Tree Maker, selling it at a higher price, but still for far less than the combined total of the individual pieces. Of course, we would at the same time leave the existing, unbundled version of Family Tree Maker on the market. Back-of-the-envelope calculations showed that we would actually obtain more revenue and profit for the Family Archive CDs by including them in the bundle than by selling them separately at a higher price. This was possible because 100 percent of the customers purchasing the bundled product would be paying for the Family Archive CDs, albeit at a lower price, instead of a much smaller percentage who would order them through direct mail at the full price. It was a great deal for the customer and for Banner Blue.

The product bundle had another favorable characteristic. Our most popular Family Archive CD at the time contained Social Security data that was in the public domain. I knew it was only a matter of time before a competitor also obtained the information and included it with his product. By including this Family Archive CD with our own product, we pre-empted competition. In a competitive marketplace, it often pays to eat your young, so to speak. We called the product Family Tree Maker Deluxe Ensemble and scheduled its introduction for the beginning of 1996—it turned out to be extremely successful.

With the assistance of two product managers, I mapped out the content of Family Tree Maker Online, a site intended for the World Wide Web. I especially enjoyed this project because once again I was working in an environment of pervasive newness. The Web at this time was even earlier in its development than was personal computer software when I designed and programmed Org.

Because there was no physical inventory for a Web product and it was so easy to program something, I found the Web to be an ideal medium for experimentation. We could cast off the old without penalty and substitute the new at low cost. With even less risk than for a packaged software product, I could implement my policy of a minimalist first release, including only the most essential features. For example, we planned a number of experiments to find the best way to sell our Family Archive information online, each experiment lasting a month or less. Since we were selling productivity, we eschewed trendy graphics and animation, focusing instead on the content that created value for our customers.

The techniques we had developed over the years for managing our packaged software business proved to be equally valid for our new businesses of developing content for Family Archive CDs and the new World Wide Web platform. Of course, each required some modifications to our existing product development life cycle, but they were relatively modest.

The Success of the World Family Tree

The human desire to know one's roots is an enduring one, not subject to fad or fancy, making genealogy an extremely popular hobby. Judging by the circulation of genealogy publications and the number of genealogy organizations as compared to other hobbies, I estimated that it was probably the third largest hobby in the United States behind coin and stamp collecting. It was certainly among the top five.

As successful as we had been, during early 1995 we were still just barely scratching the surface of this vast market. When we shipped the first World Family Tree CD containing family trees from thousands of our customers, we finally tapped into the mother lode.

The first two volumes of the World Family Tree immediately became our best-selling Family Archive CDs, yet it was the emotional response to our product that showed the true depth of our success. Many professional genealogists vocally disapproved of the CDs, fearing that most of the trees submitted by our customers did not meet their standards of proof and documentation. I actually thought this was a good omen for the product. The displeasure of the reigning authorities is always a sign of a revolutionary idea. The concerned genealogists feared that thousands of incorrect genealogies would electronically replicate without bound, missing our point that giving customers a starting point from which to begin their research had value in itself. Many of the printed genealogies in libraries also contain errors. We had simply modernized the media—or so we thought.

Thousands of eager customers immediately searched the World Family Tree and a large portion of them found links to their own family. They had new data, data that made their researching much more productive. But that was not all they wanted—they wanted to contact their newfound family members, the people who had contributed the trees. Hundreds of e-mails, phone calls, and letters made this point perfectly clear.

We had purposely omitted the name of each contributor because we knew that much of the contact information would become outdated as people moved. It was our intent instead to quickly establish a fee-based matching service using a separate database that we would update whenever contributors provided a change of address. Little did we know that customers would consider the contributor information to be the most valuable part of the World Family Tree, and they did not want to pay us twice to obtain it. Rob Armstrong convinced the management team of the futility of our original plan—we would have a tremendously successful product unless we chose to be greedy. So, we accelerated the preparation of the contributor database and planned to make it available free to World Family Tree customers via our new Family Tree Maker Online Web site. Until that was available, we immediately satisfied customers by providing the information over the phone.

As much as data for family trees, the World Family Tree provided customers a means to connect with far-flung and distant relatives. We received unsolicited testimonials from dozens of customers, thrilled that they had found a cousin somewhere else in the world who had helped them uncover their past, sometimes solving genealogical puzzles that they had studied unsuccessfully for years. One woman even found her father in the World Family Tree. Her parents had divorced when she was young and she had not seen him since she was about ten. Whenever they traveled, she would look for him in phone books, but to no avail. She found him in the World Family Tree, and they reunited. The World Family Tree touched the emotions of our customers like no other product we offered.

Triumphs and Troubles

Banner Blue closed out 1995 with annual sales of $17.2 million, 8 percent over our sales quota and within an eyelash of my highest sales projection during negotiations. I indeed felt as if we had given Broderbund its money's worth.

Unfortunately, my personal life was not going as smoothly. Our split household with me in Fremont and Connie and Amber in Carmel was becoming stressful for the entire family. I still attended all school functions, but Amber remained unhappy about leaving her friends at Mission San Jose Elementary School and I was not able to offer her or Connie much help in addressing the issue. Fortunately, Amber's new teachers told us that she was exhibiting no anxiety at school, and her grades were excellent.

The dual households were hardest on Connie. She would just have become used to running things her way during the week when I would reappear for the weekend, forcing everyone to get used to having two adults around again. I know others who have tried a similar arrangement, and it is never smooth, especially when the family has children. I do not recommend it.

Promoting Alma

Coincidentally, Broderbund's corporate offices were a ten-minute drive from Alma's home, and she would have liked to work there since the Banner Blue offices were more than an hour further. I tried to find a new position for her in Novato, but the only one available was too junior. I understand now that without a strong leader insisting on this kind of cross-fertilization between the executive suites of two merging companies, it simply will not happen. We were outsiders and the Broderbund executives did not want Alma in their offices.

I decided to look for a way to bring Alma on as my chief operating officer at Banner Blue. That would free me completely from day-to-day responsibilities and allow me to concentrate even more on the strategic product issues that I found so interesting. At the same time, promoting Alma would prepare Banner Blue for the day when I left. The problem was Alma's commute to Fremont. Under the current arrangement, she was only coming into the office a couple of days each week and working at home the rest of the time. However, as chief operating officer, she would need to come in almost every day. I knew she would not move closer and it was out of the question for her to drive ninety minutes each way to the office.

I proposed to her that I personally, out of my own pocket, pay for a driver and car to ferry her to and from the office. She could both read and make phone calls from the car while avoiding the stress of driving, and since her commute time was now *work,* she only needed to be physically in the office for seven or eight hours, including lunch. The personal expense to me was worth the reduction in stress. She accepted and started her new job on January 1, 1996, the same day we folded our sales force into the Broderbund sales organization. This arrangement worked extremely well for everyone.

Broderbund announced its fiscal first quarter financial results at the end of December 1995, so our second window to sell stock opened on January 4, 1996. Broderbund had reported their best quarter ever, but the rate of sales growth was starting to slow. Public sources such as the research firm PC Data were also reporting that competitors were making substantial inroads against Print Shop, Broderbund's largest product line. The stock price was down from its high in the seventies to about fifty-six dollars, and I took the opportunity to sell another large block of stock.

In the ensuing weeks, the stock price continued to fall. I was considering the sale of additional stock when Broderbund's general counsel abruptly closed the trading window, explaining that the president was going to preannounce that the fiscal second quarter results would be below analyst expectations.

Why Am I Unhappy?

By most external measures (excepting the falling stock price and split households) I should have been extremely happy, but I was not. My story was the same as that of many entrepreneurs who suddenly find themselves entangled in a larger, acquiring organization. While the president gave me unusual freedom to run Banner Blue as I saw fit, at least to this point in time, that made my position merely tolerable to me.

Used to a world of my own creation, I had resettled myself in a foreign land where the new rulers did not speak my language. Even after translation, every word uttered by one party carried a slightly different meaning to the other party, and it was not a comfortable feeling. Nonetheless, like any good entrepreneur, my response was to try to make things happen. After years of being in charge, I had what I will call bootstrapper's hubris. I expected people to listen to me. In my particular case, I wanted to see Broderbund change to be more like Banner Blue. Paradoxically, I sold the company with the intent of leaving, not with the objective of transforming Broderbund. After cashing out, why in the world would I care? There were three reasons.

First, I had committed to stay for two years and if I was going to be there, I wanted the organization to be something in which I could take pride. Unfortunately, I found Broderbund's strategy and its execution very disappointing.

The problems that Alma and I had identified during the merger negotiations were coming home to roost. The new product flow was weak, competitors locked in on Print Shop's vulnerability, Myst sales had peaked, and consumers were spending more of their computer time online rather than with packaged software of the kind Broderbund sold. The market environment was changing at a very fast rate, but in my opinion, Broderbund was missing an opportunity to adapt. At the same time, Banner Blue sales were up 45 percent during January 1996 after an even stronger December, confirming that Broderbund's problems came from a lack of foresight rather than market weakness.

Broderbund was like a lumbering airplane spiraling towards the ground. I had given my word that I would stay, so I wanted to get my hands on the controls before the big crash.

Second, I cared for financial reasons. As the stock price fell, it was costing me a great deal of money. I consoled myself with the knowledge that the stock I had already sold at high prices meant I was still ahead of the valuation when we signed the agreement, but the way things were going that would not remain the case for long. If I had to remain at Broderbund another year, I wanted to protect my investment.

Third, I cared about the environment my employees would have to live in after I left. In fact, there was a part of me that did not want to leave at all. I had strong emotional ties to many employees. A number of them had worked for me their entire professional career, and leaving them raised complex feelings that I was abandoning them.

Paul DeBry liked to kid me by saying, "Ken, when you sell your company, you don't own it any more." Truer words could not be spoken. I was unable to involve myself in the corporate strategy-making process, let alone effect any kind of change. Broderbund's president brushed aside my every attempt. When I called him and suggested that I had much to offer and could be of help if I were to join a team who was making a presentation on strategy to the board of directors, he told me, "Corporate strategy is not the division manager's role."

Because an entrepreneur often gets a pot of money when he sells his company, people see any complaints as sour grapes. I agree that my unhappiness just came with the territory—after all, I chose to go with a company that I knew had management problems. Unfortunately, wealth did nothing to soothe the pain from the suffocation of my ability to create and control.

There were many reasons why my efforts to make a difference at Broderbund failed. Though the specifics will differ from one acquisition to the next, I believe that at least some of the problems I encountered will surface in other acquisitions. I hope that by describing my situation, I can help entrepreneurs who follow me reach a better outcome than I did.

A number of difficulties stemmed from a tremendous difference in perspective. The first of these I will call the "bigger is better" syndrome. The big-fish company ate the little-fish entrepreneur. Employees in the bigger company often assume they are smarter, have better procedures, and so on. After all, how else would they have become bigger? Particularly galling to the entrepreneur, after a merger the big fish also often assumes that any good things that happen at the entrepreneur's company result from actions of the big fish, whether that is true or not. Generally, the bigger is better syndrome makes the big fish unreceptive to input from the little fish. What is important to remember is that we all can learn from each other, big fish from little fish, and vice versa. Unfortunately, this syndrome reflects basic human nature and nothing more. As such, it is difficult to avoid.

If an entrepreneur receives stock for his company, as I did, other differences in perspective become important, especially if the stock price falls. I viewed the stock as a reward for past work at Banner Blue—I looked backwards and bemoaned the fact that my reward was now tied to the performance of someone else. As Broderbund stock declined, my natural emotion as an entrepreneur was that Broderbund executives were screwing up, diminishing my payout. Broderbund executives, on the other hand, viewed the stock price as an incentive for today's work. They were looking forward, hoping to improve the price so that the options they held would be worth more.

An entrepreneur also wants the acquiring company to treat him as a large shareholder, an owner of the business. In my case (at least initially), the only active employee owning more stock than I was Doug, the founder. As a major shareholder I had to deal with stock registration rights and unusual accounting concerns. Yet, treating a subordinate employee as a large shareholder is a concept foreign to a corporation and its executives. I could not be both a division manager and an owner of the business in the president's mind. Could it work in some settings? Yes, but probably not very many. Subordinate employees do not own large chunks of their employer and large shareholders are not employees. An entrepreneur is neither pilot nor passenger—often corporate executives see him as baggage.

One particular incident illustrates the confusing nature of my position. Several months after the acquisition, I received a call from Mike Shannahan, Broderbund's chief financial officer, informing me that they would like the refund of a dividend Banner Blue had paid to shareholders before the merger. I thought he was kidding. I had organized Banner Blue as an S Corporation, meaning that the shareholders rather than the company paid all income taxes on our profits. We paid dividends to shareholders so that they would have the cash to pay the taxes.

We had fully disclosed all information about our dividends to Broderbund, and in this case, we even notified them before we paid the dividend. Either no one read the due diligence information we sent to Broderbund (a common occurrence in many acquisitions, I have since found), or perhaps Broderbund had come across new information that only now made them concerned about the dividend. At any rate, I quickly realized that Mike was not kidding. In so many words I told him to forget it. Later, Broderbund's president reiterated the request. I considered the whole thing absurd, almost comical. What were they thinking? Banner Blue no longer existed as a legal entity; how could it repay something? I protested to Doug, but later I got yet another call from Mike.

So, for the first of approximately five times during my employment with Broderbund, I sought counsel from my attorney to represent me against my own employer—a company in which I owned a major stake. In this case, the company had chosen to see me as neither employee nor major shareholder—I was something unique.

Fortunately my attorney helped make the issue go away. Based on her advice, I sent Broderbund's president a letter on August 8, stating that we should handle the Banner Blue dividend issue strictly according to our contract which specified conditions for indemnification. I asked him to tell me *exactly* which paragraph under which he was claiming indemnification (I knew that none of them applied). Or, I suggested that Broderbund could negotiate an amendment to the contract which they would need to do individually with each of the former Banner Blue shareholders since Banner Blue Software no longer existed. I never heard about the issue again.

Another reason why entrepreneurs often have difficulty making things happen at the acquiring company is jealousy. One Broderbund senior vice president told me to my face, "You earned more in one day than I've earned the entire time I've been here." He may have been kidding, but I did not think so. I replied that it took me a lot longer than one day to earn the money. I wondered how many other Broderbund executives were thinking the same thing. Jealous colleagues are unlikely to seek or value your advice.

Finally, entrepreneurs generally lack the personality and skills to play the corporate game. I knew from my experience at Hewlett-Packard that I do not like to sell a solution to others—I wanted to be in control and take action directly. That is not the strategy of most successful corporate executives, and it is unlikely to result in corporate executives following an entrepreneur's lead.

During early 1996, I remember discussing all sides of my situation with Alma. My personality made me feel that I could not walk away, that I had to stay and make some changes, but at the same time, I realized my attempts were futile. It was a time of complete frustration. I felt as if I was in prison and among close friends I actually referred to my two-year commitment as my sentence. When asked how it was going, I would say something to the effect of, "Twelve months remaining to serve. Then I'm out!"

The lesson to take from all this is simple in my mind. Given the inherently divergent perspectives and incompatible personalities of an entrepreneur and corporate executive, entrepreneurs should stay with the acquiring company for as short a period as possible, certainly no longer than required to ensure an effective management transition. Six months would have been more than sufficient in my situation; three months probably would have been fine. I thought I could stick with anything for two years, but I was wrong. I could not play a role contrary to my very essence. There is no benefit to either party in having an entrepreneur around, if he cannot be entrepreneurial.

If an entrepreneur must stay with the acquiring company for an extended period, he needs a power base, such as a board seat; an acknowledged, effective corporate mentor; and a clearly defined corporate role. I had considered negotiating to obtain a board seat, but in the end I did not pursue it, concentrating instead on the valuation of the deal. Now I was paying the emotional price.

Even if I had negotiated a power base, it may not have made a difference. The catch-22 for a bootstrapping entrepreneur is that leveraging a board seat is not likely to be one of the things he is very good at.

Thus, I learned that the commitment entangling and strangling me was one that I should not have made in the first place and would never make again. The problem was that the deal had closed only one year ago, so my agreement to stay for two years was only 50 percent fulfilled. Nevertheless, with the door to the Broderbund cockpit firmly locked, I found myself thinking about a way to bail out of the crashing plane. While I debated whether and how to negotiate an early exit, I got lucky, although it did not feel that way at the time.

The incident that I am about to relate illustrates almost every one of the difficulties I have just described, not to mention my complete frustration. It also highlights the magnitude of the personality difference that can occur between an entrepreneur and a corporate executive.

Inadvertently, the President Does Me a Favor

In spite of our disagreements about my participation in the formation of corporate strategy, the president and I had a very amicable relationship. He was the consummate gentleman and always professional in demeanor. Until this time, our differences were policy differences and that was all.

Then on April 17, I received an e-mail from Mike Shannahan inquiring about the compensation of a particular engineering contractor. In spite of his many significant contributions, this individual by his own choice was a contractor rather than an employee. He preferred the freedom and enjoyed having several clients. Since outside contractors provide their own equipment and facilities, pay their own Social Security taxes, and also pay for their own benefits, they generally receive an hourly rate at least 25 percent more than they would as an employee. In addition, the contractor was a senior contributor and he was working a lot of hours for us. All of this meant that we were paying him quite a lot. Yet I considered the contractor a bargain. He was a rare, superstar talent, as much artist as technician—he made a contribution that was irreplaceable.

In my reply to Mike, I explained the contractor's many accomplishments. Indeed, I considered the contractor to be a key reason for our success. I described why he was a contractor and talked about the project he was working on at the time, showing how he generated a tremendous return on our investment. Mike had asked in particular about reimbursement the contractor received for going to a conference, so I explained that he had gone at our request and the material covered was of no value to his other clients. I also reminded Mike that Banner Blue was under budget and meeting its revenue target. I did not get a reply from Mike, so I thought that was the end of it.

Then in my regular meeting with Broderbund's president on April 25, he turned gravely to his computer screen and told me that he wanted to talk about the contractor. He made it clear that he did not want to pay anyone this much money, rattling off a number that was more than 50 percent over what we ever paid the individual. When I told him we had never paid the contractor anything close to what he was saying, the president insinuated that I did not know what it added up to. I replied that I knew exactly what it added up to because I signed it off every month. I reminded him that the contractor had been working for us for several years. I thought it was a good investment when the money came directly out of my own pocket and I still thought it was a good investment when the money was coming from Broderbund.

I reiterated the points that I had made in my e-mail to Mike. The president stated forcefully that this was not a matter of budget or results. He explained that declining fortunes had forced other areas of the company to retrench, and a highly paid consultant at Banner Blue created the wrong appearance for those other parts of the company. I countered that if we reduced our most scarce resource, engineering talent, we would inevitably get reduced results. He said, "I don't accept that." I asked how there could be any other result. He suggested that, "others can work harder" and "recruit more effectively. I don't accept that you get less [output]."

My initial surprise gave way to anger—the president appeared to be provoking me. By this time, it was common knowledge in both the Banner Blue Division and Broderbund corporate offices that Banner Blue employees put in much longer hours than others in the company. Was he speaking without thinking, or simply trying to anger me?

I tried further to convince him of my position, but he made it clear there was no use talking about the issue. His solution was that the contractor was not to work more than forty hours per week. Having no recourse, I told him we would do what he wanted.

We had disclosed the contractor's compensation to Broderbund before the sale, and they had been writing the checks to him for eleven months, yet the president's comments implied that he considered this some kind of skeleton in our closet. In fact he actually said, "I hope there aren't any others."

With his last comment, I ranked the message he delivered to be the most insulting I had ever received. In my opinion, our disagreement went beyond a philosophical difference—the message I inferred was that I had done something devious or unethical. He could not even imagine my results-oriented, entrepreneurial perspective, and concluded that I had to be acting from a desire to deceive!

To further understand the falling out between Broderbund's president and myself, it helps to briefly examine several aspects of our contrasting personalities. I do this with the belief that neither his personality nor my entrepreneurial nature was inherently good or bad; rather, our opposing characters suited us for contrasting environments, performing quite different tasks. We looked at the world through completely different eyes.

He was the prototypical Broderbund employee and to the letter he reflected the Broderbund culture that he had helped form. Roles, rules, and procedures were the important things to Broderbund's president. His role was to define corporate strategy; my role was to stay out of it. One of his rules was that contractors should not get big paychecks and another was that they should pay their own way to a conference. Of course the president had objectives from time to time, but not being achievement-oriented, he did not insist on meeting them. If everyone played by his rules, but things did not work out, he may have found the reasons in external circumstances. Or, when I did not play by his rules, he could cite external circumstances for Banner Blue's success. Achieving was not as important as playing his role.

To the president, just being on the Broderbund team meant more than winning in the marketplace. I once asked the president why

Broderbund did not have a commissioned sales force. He explained to me that commissions were unfair and he just could not live with that. He cited the example of a sales person who might miss her quota through no fault of her own because a major customer went bankrupt. His thinking focused on the external forces that might disturb a quota system. He did not consider the incentive a quota might provide to encourage the sales person to make up for the bankrupt account. The president wanted everyone to be team players, sharing the heartaches and the rewards—no jealousy, no conflict—everything level, even, and unchanging.

I was results-oriented, encouraged competition among our team members, rewarded the top performers, and played to win. Obviously, my style diametrically opposed his, and our falling out was simply a matter of time.

Although I considered resigning on the spot and wondered whether that was his objective, I simply left his office as quickly as I could. Long before, I had learned never to make any irreversible decisions in a setting even remotely as emotional as this one. Nonetheless, as I hurried from the building to my car I repeated over and over to myself, "Get out. Get out. Get out of this company now!" So often I had wondered at people complaining and whining about their situation instead of leaving for something better. Now it was time for me to follow my own thinking.

I had tolerated philosophical differences and the incompatible personalities of the senior Broderbund executives, but the inference that I was unethical was more than I could take. I had mentally checked out some time ago; the president did me a favor by causing me to act. As I drove back to Fremont, I decided to negotiate an early exit with Doug.

In a way I had come full circle, from frustrated employee to successful entrepreneur and back. Starting with an idea, I had created a world at Banner Blue, building a product, establishing procedures, and forming an organization. Banner Blue was the embodiment of my business philosophy. I was on top and in control. Now I was at the mercy of people with a different character and philosophy. Although I had temporarily isolated Banner Blue from the Broderbund way of thinking, I was personally unprotected, ostracized, and no longer in control of my own fate. I hated the feeling and had to get out. And, the stressful family situation with Connie and Amber alone in Carmel made my dissatisfaction even worse.

After cooling off, I decided that instead of quitting outright, I should phase myself out by drastically cutting my hours and working a good portion of the time from my home in Carmel. After all, I had promised a number of individuals at the Banner Blue Division that I would continue to be a presence in the company and I wanted to insure that Alma could take my place after I left, if she wanted the job. This plan would also let me spend much more time in Carmel with my family.

I met with Doug and gave him a copy of my notes from the meeting with Broderbund's president. Half jokingly, I told Doug that, evidently, it would not be an issue if I were paying *two* contractors the same hourly rate for half as much time each. That would not create the wrong "appearance." Instead the president had limited my best engineer to forty hours a week during crunch time, *not* worrying about the appearance *that* created. I explained that I was going to work several days a week from my home in Carmel instead of going to the office every day, and I would also begin steadily reducing my hours.

Doug said he was terribly sorry about the entire episode and he thanked me for not quitting. He also approved my wind-down plan. He added that the strategic planning process had been very disappointing. I already knew that Doug was going to step down from his chief executive role, retaining only the title of chairman. He asked me to become involved in the search process for the new individual because he said I was the only other true entrepreneur in the company.

Ironically, while I struggled to find the best way out of Broderbund, Doug struggled to find the best way to stay. Broderbund had started as a family affair, with Doug's brother, his late sister, and his mother all playing a role in the company. Now Doug was the last family member still involved. He had used his outstanding vision and sense of urgency to build the twelfth largest personal computer software company in the world. Founding Broderbund four years before I had founded Banner Blue, he took action while I studied and analyzed the market, not worrying about making mistakes during a time when the young market made them easy to correct. It had been a virtuoso performance showing that there are many possible strategies to build a successful business.

Escape

Over the summer of 1996, Doug did involve me in the chief executive officer search. Broderbund's financial decline was accelerating and obvious to all. While Banner Blue Division sales grew more than 60 percent for the year, sales for the corporation as a whole declined for both the fiscal third and fourth quarters.

Privately, it astonished me that a company of Broderbund's size did not have a stronger system to insure the accountability of its employees—especially its executives. I considered the absence of a management-by-objective philosophy to be an important reason for Broderbund's declining fortunes, but that is another story.

Alma was doing an excellent job as chief operating officer for Banner Blue and month by month I increased her responsibilities to the point where I had little left to do. I talked to Doug during August about winding down my involvement one more notch and he agreed to let me cut back to one day per week.

Soon the board hired a new chief executive officer, Joe Durrett. In spite of wide agreement on the problems facing Broderbund, a variety of conversations confirmed for me that the company planned no immediate replacements among Joe's staff. In my opinion, Doug, Joe, and the board simply did not want to make the kind of changes it would take to reverse Broderbund's fortunes. So, when Joe asked how I could contribute, I suggested that the best thing for me to do would be to turn over the division to Alma and terminate my employment before completing my two-year commitment. Broderbund was no place for an entrepreneur. He agreed and that was that.

When I announced to Banner Blue that I was leaving, Joe attended so he could speak to the division, present me with a gift, and officially promote Alma to division president. Broderbund's president was too ill to attend, so he called the next day to apologize for his absence and wish me luck. My last day as Broderbund employee number 1559 was November 30, 1996.

I promised myself that I would take one or two years off to recharge my batteries. I was not sure what I would do next and I wanted to clear my head before making a decision.

A few weeks after my last official day, Alma arranged a reception for me at Banner Blue. She invited some of the first Banner Blue employees and vendors who had worked with us over the years. Connie also attended and read a humorous poem she wrote about my stepping down. Susanne McDonell, the technical support supervisor, presented me with a beautiful scrapbook containing organization charts for each year of the company's existence and many personal essays contributed by past and present employees, each one with memorable reflections or anecdotes from the time we shared together. I am including several selections because they provide a perspective unique from my own—the impression that I made on others during my years at Banner Blue.

Fintan McCabe is a print broker with whom I worked from the time before hiring my first employee.

> I have worked with many small software companies, but none quite as small as Banner Blue in the very beginning. I delivered the first Org manuals to Ken's garage, and honestly wondered if there would be a second printing. But I hoped there would be because Ken was so upbeat and positive, and he exuded a quiet confidence that bolstered that hope. Over the course of the next year, I was struck by Ken's optimism, energy, and work ethic. In contrast to many other principals in start-ups with which I've worked, Ken maintained a sense of humor that was always easily tapped. Despite the high stakes of undertaking his own company with his own funds, he never seemed to let the pressure get to him. Now, the situation may be different for those who worked closely with him, or his family, but from my perspective he was always the most cheerful and energetic person. Over the years, as Banner Blue grew, I continued to be impressed by his business sense, his hiring decisions, and his optimism. Ken made an impression on me in another regard, and this is a lesson I review every day: you can swim with the sharks without becoming one.

> —Fintan McCabe

Corinne Speer was the third employee I hired and the first to receive our five-year roasting. She left Banner Blue to complete her college education, then married someone she met at Banner Blue.

> It was fun working at Banner Blue. I learned to expect the best and work hard. I'll never forget preparing weekly deposits at Ken's kitchen table while the dog (Pooh Bear) was in there with me . . . Ken was always giving fatherly advice. I think it was important to him that we grow both personally and professionally. I remember when our monthly meetings consisted of going out for pizza and he would share with us various business ideas. He often talked about the importance of striving for excellence in all as-

pects of business and in our personal lives. He talked about the
value of the customer and how important they are to us. Then he
let us share some of our own ideas.

—Corinne Speer

Tina Nomura was the fourth employee I hired and she still works
at Banner Blue. She may be the only person who has ever complimented me for being patient!

In the early days Ken had a lot of patience. When I began working with Banner Blue I had no technical skills, but after a few
months of Ken's help, he had me handling technical support calls
for Org . . . Whenever I was stumped on a call . . . Ken was
around to help me out. I had to get all the information first . . .
then Ken would tell me what I should tell the caller.

Ken, I forgot how much fun we had in the early days and now that
you are leaving I will remember them often.

—Tina Nomura

I hired Cathi Fineran as technical support supervisor in 1988.
For almost ten years, she worked tirelessly for Banner Blue and became a major contributor on almost every product release.

Ken told me that technical support was a key position at Banner
Blue because it was the direct contact point with the customer. He
stressed how important it was not only to help the customers, but
also to gather information from them; to learn what they wanted
and needed. I thought this was great, but didn't really grasp how
significant it would prove to be. Over the years, from product to
product and upgrade to upgrade, I watched Ken use this "customer
perspective" as a driving force in both product and feature design
decisions.

—Cathi Fineran

Susanne McDonell also made a contribution to the scrapbook
which she assembled.

What I appreciate most about Ken is his philosophy on opportunity. Ken will give anyone a chance who shows enthusiasm, en-

> ergy, or excitement. What you may be lacking in formal training or in years of experience, Ken lets you make up for with drive and ambition. Many of us at this company have been promoted to positions or given opportunities that we would never have been afforded at other companies. Ken knows that it takes new people, new ideas, and hard work to make a company continue to grow and thrive. Ken invests his time, money, and opportunities in men and women of different cultures and different races—completely unbounded by stereotypes.
>
> —Susanne McDonell

The scrapbook was one of the most thoughtful gifts I have ever received. Events recognizing an individual's contribution to an organization are important to both the organization and the individual. A company founder is no exception.

Final Accounting

I finished my involvement with Banner Blue having sold a cumulative total of 2,000,000 units of software that generated revenue of $78,000,000. Under Alma's guidance after I departed, Banner Blue grew 40 percent during fiscal year 1997, just as we said it would.

As of early 2001, Microsoft had not introduced genealogy software. I suspect they determined that the entry barriers we erected were too strong, but I have no way of knowing.

Unfortunately, the core Broderbund products continued their sales decline as the stock price plunged into the teens. In June 1998 Broderbund's death spiral finally ended when the company announced its acquisition by The Learning Company at a fire-sale price. Then in December 1998 Mattel announced that it was acquiring The Learning Company. Finally, in 1999 Mattel spun-off Banner Blue as an independent company, Genealogy.com. In spite of the many changes in ownership, Banner Blue Software was still going strong almost five years after I departed.

TABLE 4
BANNER BLUE SOFTWARE SUMMARY 1984-1996

Year	Net Sales	Sales Growth	Profit Before Tax[1]	People[2]	New Programs	Total Releases[3]
1984	$0			1		
1985	$92,820		23.8%	1	Org	4
1986	$884,829	853.3%	38.5%	5		6
1987	$1,814,917	105.1%	36.9%	8		7
1988	$2,044,275	12.6%	32.5%	10	Org Plus Advanced	14
1989	$2,757,579	34.9%	21.0%	16	Family Tree Maker	10
1990	$3,410,661	23.7%	18.6%	19	Org Plus for Macintosh Data Exchange Utility[4] Laser Fonts Disk[4]	19
1991	$4,660,481	36.6%	23.2%	25	Org Plus for Windows Banner Blue Movie Guide Family Ties[5]	27
1992	$5,674,820	21.8%	27.9%	35	Brochure Maker Uncle Sam's Budget Balancer	10
1993	$7,113,215	25.3%	30.4%	42	Family Tree Maker for Windows Microsoft Organization Chart Biography Maker Direct Elect[6] Exercise in Hard Choices[7]	20
1994	$10,929,533	53.7%	30.1%	55	Family Tree Maker Deluxe Microsoft Organization Chart for Macintosh Family Ties for Windows[5]	31
1995	$17,281,949	58.1%	28.3%	80	World Family Tree	38
1996	$23,357,376	35.2%	NA	NA	Family Tree Maker Deluxe Ensemble Family Tree Maker Online Eureka![8]	39

[1] As a percentage of net sales.
[2] This count of full-time employees represents an average number for the year. It includes temporary employees, full-time contractors, and summer hires.
[3] Total product releases include new programs, upgrades, rolling releases, and Family Archive CDs during the year.
[4] Accessory program for Family Tree Maker.
[5] This program was manufactured for sale by another company.
[6] A version of Brochure Maker designed for candidates for political office.
[7] A special version of Uncle Sam's Budget Balancer for the Committee for a Responsible Federal Budget.
[8] A special version of Uncle Sam's Budget Balancer for the state of California's budget.

8

Reflections

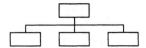

When I first considered entrepreneurship I had lots of questions: What personal qualities does it take to found a successful business and do I have them? What education and experience is the best preparation for becoming an entrepreneur? How do I find a good product idea? How do I obtain the money to start a company? Can I run a successful business, raise children, and still have a normal family life?

Each of those questions, it turns out, has many correct answers. My answers may not be the best for everyone, nor may they work in every situation, but collectively they worked for me.

Personal Qualities

Keeping that caveat in mind, here are the personal qualities that I believe contributed to my success: comfort with uncertainty, demanding standards, and force of will.

One of the key tasks of an entrepreneur is to anticipate trends in technology and the marketplace with sufficient accuracy and over a long enough period of time so that he can build an island of stability—a vision. With stable ground under foot, management by objective becomes an effective tool. Consider the opposite situation, without stable ground. If objectives change on a regular basis because of a lack of foresight about technology and the market, then the workplace becomes inefficient. Work accomplished today risks being thrown out tomorrow. At some point, if change is too frequent, the organization accomplishes no lasting work at all and the company fails. Effective leaders want people working on what *will* make sense, not what *did* make sense.

Creating a vision requires comfort with uncertainty. Indeed, one can also think of a vision as a means for the entrepreneur to internalize and remove uncertainty from an otherwise scary, unfiltered view of the outside world, enabling his employees to feel more at ease and permitting the company objectives to remain steady. Successful entrepreneurs are probably more comfortable with uncertainty than anyone else in their organization.

Personally, change and its inherent uncertainty attracts me because I enjoy building analytical, predictive models—descriptions of how things work that enable me to forecast conditions in the future. Business situations are normally so complex that the resulting predictions and forecasts are highly approximate; nonetheless, I believe that my models help me get the odds in my favor. The models represent how I construct a vision and the better my model, the higher my confidence of success.

Another important personal characteristic is my high performance standards. My parents raised me to always do my best, and the lesson stuck. I want the best employees, an elegant product, fast growth, high profits—only the best satisfies me.

Of course, high standards are both a blessing and a curse. When a company achieves high standards it becomes more competitive in the marketplace, and that is a blessing. On the other hand, a company can expend so much energy trying to meet a high standard that something more important suffers. Indeed, many good things come at the expense of other good things and a leader must trade one off against the other. For example, growth can be faster if a company lowers profits to spend more on marketing and promotion.

Time and again I saw the validity of the 80/20 rule, which says that 80 percent of the results come from 20 percent of the work. Surely this fact is key to making an effective trade-off between two good things. Unfortunately, the rule itself is not actionable because it does not indicate *which* 20 percent of the work gives 80 percent of the results. Rather, making a trade-off is a matter of judgment and experience. I scoured every decision looking for what would give the most bang for the buck. I also accepted a personal bias of insisting on excellence in the areas I enjoyed the most and where I had the most experience, such as product design. I think such a bias is fine in moderation; indeed, it often becomes the basis for a company's unique personality.

Gradually, I learned that I spent my own time most efficiently when I worked on things that made everyone else more effective: the company and product vision, market and product definition, product architecture, the product development life cycle, acquisition and allocation of resources, and improved methods of communication. It was better for me to hone the product development life cycle, so that every product design decision made by others was a little better than it otherwise would have been, than to involve myself in each design decision, trying to make it perfect. Entrepreneurs must look to leverage their precious time.

Another area where I demanded high standards was in the pace of our development efforts. Experience has taught me that in a fast-changing marketplace, competitors can come out of nowhere—recall that a new competitor emerged on my first day in business. Just as importantly, market insights and a leadership vision are fleeting. Consequently, I always scheduled projects as aggressively as possible, trying to insure that we made our existing products obsolete before someone else did it for us. Reflecting this emphasis, we spent an average of 16 percent of revenues on research and development during my years at Banner Blue.

Probably no other demand on my employees raised as much controversy as the constant push to develop new products as quickly as possible. Can I justify my impatience? Absolutely. For example, if I had not pushed for a three-month development schedule on our first CD-ROM product, Family Tree Maker Deluxe, it is likely that Microsoft would have purchased Automated Archives before we even considered it. In that case, the history of Banner Blue would have been much less significant and I would not be writing this book. If that was the only time it made a difference, then in my mind all of the other times were worth it. Usually a fire alarm is only a drill, but occasionally the fire is real. You only know for sure after the fact, so it is important to pay attention to each one. As Banner Blue sometimes raced against an unseen and perhaps nonexistent competitor, I occasionally became the enemy in the eyes of some employees who did not see the purpose of our haste. Lynn Brewer picked up on this phenomenon and gave me the good advice of always looking for an external enemy upon which to focus the company.

Nonetheless, people did not always follow a management directive just because I communicated that it was my desire for them to do so. Even when employees participate in the objective-setting process and financial incentives encourage them to perform, there is no guarantee that they will follow through. Every objective in the world I created as an entrepreneur conflicted with an objective in an employee's world at one time or another. Many times we encountered unplanned circumstances, requiring extraordinary effort to overcome, which is inevitable in a world with complex products and many players.

What closed the gap between employee desire and company necessity was well-informed force of will. I say *well-informed* because it was force of will not for the sake of same, but because it was necessary. When I believe that I must do something, there is no force that can divert me from the task. When the situation involves others, I am comfortable imposing my will on theirs. I consider it my responsibility. To meet an important objective, I was able to encourage, assist, direct, reward, replace, reassign, fire, and even step in for the employee not doing his job.

My employees accepted this because of the *well-informed* part of the equation. I did my best to insure that the objectives were realistic, necessary, and effectively communicated to the people involved. If the goals had been unattainable or unnecessary, people would not have taken them seriously—nor should they have. Taking it one step further, my judgment about these issues had to be correct most of the time, or people would have lost confidence in me as a leader.

Fortunately, when the entire organization sees the leader take objectives seriously, most employees do the same. Effective application of will power thereby reduces the need for it in the first place. The appreciative response of the company's most successful workers also encouraged me. When I stepped in to make something happen, they knew I was simply helping them meet their own objectives.

Education and Experience

When I founded Banner Blue, I did not have any experience running a business, but I had something equally important—a love of building and creating.

Fundamentally, company survival and growth are a function of product creation. No products, no sales, no company. I created and built hundreds of things before founding Banner Blue, I was responsible for shipping 225 products during my years at Banner Blue, and with a little luck, I will build hundreds of things during the balance of my life.

When I was growing up, I remember occasionally being concerned because my dad was not like the fathers on television. He did not teach me how to play baseball or take me to ball games—instead, he was always building something and showing me how he did it. I soon realized that he was simply teaching me about what my genes programmed me to enjoy. While others might see building something as an arduous task, I have avocations just to restore my energy so I can go back to building and creating. In fact, one of my favorite avocations is to read about scientific and technical advancements.

I say these things not to brag, but to demonstrate that I truly enjoy the things that helped me build a better product and allowed me to relate to the engineers I employed. The founder does not need personal expertise in every area of importance to his venture, but he should cover a good portion of the ground. In a technology-driven business, I believe it is imperative for the founder or the chief executive officer to understand technology at a deep and fundamental level. If a non-technical leader turns over technology leadership to a subordinate technologist, the risk is that the resulting technology vision ignores business reality. On the other hand, if a non-technical leader formulates the technology vision himself with only the advice of the technologist, he risks losing the technical subtleties and bad decisions result.

I strongly believe that there is no substitute for deep, relevant experience. In any human endeavor, the expert knows things without even realizing it. Sometimes we call it intuition. The person who has extensive, relevant experience has a competitive advantage over the person who does not, because all else being equal, the person with relevant experience will simply make better decisions. That is all there is to it; nothing more, nothing less.

My business education was also valuable. The Master of Business Administration program at Harvard rounded out my understanding of business, accelerating the day when I felt ready to strike out on my own. However, I do not consider an MBA indispensable by any means and I routinely tell people that many jobs provide a similar overview of business. It would probably be better for more young professionals to go back to school for a technical degree rather than an MBA.

Product Ideas

I found that as I developed expertise in an area, product ideas came naturally and without a lot of thought. This was especially true where I also had personal experience as a customer for the potential product. The more challenging job was to separate the profitable from the unprofitable ideas, a task I had intended our product selection criteria to solve.

Regrettably, I put far too much emphasis on the product selection criteria and not enough on market analysis. I never repeated the Porter five-force analysis that I performed as part of my due diligence before founding Banner Blue. I quite simply forgot how valuable it was. I am sure it would have prevented at least one of our errant attempts at diversification.

Paradoxically, while the best product ideas seem to come from personal experience, the best validation comes from *outside* one's personal experience, colleagues, and friends. The broader I cast my net for information, the more successful were my plans.

Financing—The Advantages of a Bootstrap

It seems that most people believe the only way to fund a start-up is to obtain venture capital. That was never true in the past any more than it is today. Of course, some opportunities require far too much capital for self-funding, but certainly not all. I was fortunate to recognize that bootstrapping my company would give me something that I found very important—greater control.

When an outsider makes a large investment in a business, he typically wants a say in the composition of the board, business alliances and combinations, future financing arrangements, and of course, the managers and management of the company. Not only that, he typically wants his money back as fast as possible. Banner Blue had the luxury of building a solid foundation of people and procedures at a pace that suited our talents and market requirements rather than a pace arbitrarily imposed by an outsider trying to quickly recoup his investment. When opportunities presented themselves, we were ready to exploit them.

There is also an inherent disadvantage of raising money—it can take an unbelievable amount of time. Although it never seemed like I had enough time, the freedom from raising money and tending to investors gave me much more time to spend on strategic and operational decisions than I would have had otherwise.

Over the years I have learned that a bootstrap has additional advantages as well. First, without outside investors, the entrepreneur gets to keep a much bigger piece of the pie. Table 5 shows a typical scenario after several rounds of venture funding. If the only difference between the companies is the source of funding, then the entrepreneur who bootstrapped his company realizes much better financial results. However, this scenario is not realistic because the typical venture capitalist will not invest in a company with prospects for sales of only $10 million. Most venture capitalists want to see a company quickly grow to at least $50 million in sales.

TABLE 5
COMPARISON OF FUNDING SOURCES—SCENARIO 1

Type of Funding	Founder's Equity	Employees' Equity	Investor's Equity	Company Sales	Market Value	Founder's Net Worth
Bootstrap	85%	15%	0%	$10 million	$20 million	$17 million
Venture capital	15%	15%	70%	$10 million	$20 million	$3 million

It stands to reason that there are more opportunities that will grow to $10 million in sales than there are opportunities that will grow to $50 million in sales. So, while it might look as if the entrepreneur with venture funding in Scenario 2 (Table 6) has almost pulled even with the bootstrapping entrepreneur, the reality is that his odds of achieving this level of success are lower.

TABLE 6
COMPARISON OF FUNDING SOURCES—SCENARIO 2

Type of Funding	Founder's Equity	Employees' Equity	Investor's Equity	Company Sales	Market Value	Founder's Net Worth
Bootstrap	85%	15%	0%	$10 million	$20 million	$17 million
Venture capital	15%	15%	70%	$50 million	$100 million	$15 million

Another advantage of spending one's own money is that it naturally encourages financial discipline. By definition, a bootstrap must have a profit-making business model, and profits provide the freedom for a company to invest in new products as well as the ability to survive a strategic mistake or market downturn.

Sometimes bootstrapping is the only possible business model for a company. As colleges increase the number of classes about entrepreneurship, more and more students desire to start a company the day they graduate. In most cases these budding entrepreneurs are too young or inexperienced to obtain venture capital—a bootstrap often becomes the only alternative.

Perhaps the most subtle advantage of a bootstrap comes from the necessity of doing things yourself. You will find areas where you are better than anyone you could hire, or at the very least you will be a better manager of the area when you ultimately delegate it or fulfill it outside your company. Banner Blue experienced this in advertising, and Banner Blue's resourceful and on-time development philosophy exemplified how limited resources created a lean elegance from necessity.

Balancing Work and Family Life

Family life contains many unexpected surprises, as the loss of one baby and the early birth of my daughter demonstrated. I found I could balance the demands of a family, including the surprises, with those of being an entrepreneur—but there was no such thing as "having it all." Good things come at the expense of other good things. Everyone must prioritize and make choices like in all other areas of life.

Communicating my business vision and objectives at home was as important as communicating them at the office. Doing so removed uncertainty for my family in the same way it removed uncertainty for my employees. My informal contract with Connie regarding the founding of Banner Blue was my first step in accomplishing this. I am sure Connie would agree that I could have done a better job of communicating the month-to-month objectives; but when I did, home life went much more smoothly.

I also tried to imagine myself looking backwards from some time in the future to insure that I did not neglect my family on one day in a way that I would regret the next. I placed special importance on attending events, making a point not to miss a birthday, anniversary, doctor's appointment, school meeting, school performance, or dinner at home.

In fact, I tried to create regular family events. The risk for the entrepreneur is to be there without really being there, preoccupied with matters at work. That is the benefit in making a common occurrence like a family dinner into more of an event. If I gave a few minutes' thought ahead of time to what I wanted to talk about at dinner, then interaction with my family came naturally even if the day's events made me tired and stressed. As Amber got older we turned every Friday into family movie night, a tradition we continue today. We choose a movie together, then eat pizza in front of the television while watching the video.

Surprisingly to me, the sale of Banner Blue was a disappointment to Amber. Whereas I grew up thinking I would work for a large company, she thought she would work for me—and maybe she will. At the same time, while it took me quite some time to become comfortable with the idea of starting my own company, Amber comes up with ideas for new companies on a regular basis. I created a home environment where for her, starting a company is the natural thing to do.

Reasons for Success: Consistency, Good People, Timing

In large part, I think Banner Blue was successful because its people, product strategy, and business philosophy were consistent with each other and with the times in which we operated. For example, our product selection criteria were consistent with a low-capital, self-funded start-up; our people were generalists who enjoyed an organization with low departmental barriers; and we balanced our demands on employees with excellent benefits and career opportunities. Consequently, as we made the myriad decisions that define a company—fortunately more right than wrong—success came because all the different pieces fit together.

I was fortunate to work for an extremely ethical, mature, and well-run technology company, Hewlett-Packard, before I founded Banner Blue. Hewlett-Packard provided an excellent model to build upon, as, like an architect, I worked on fitting the various pieces of Banner Blue into a whole. Consciously and subconsciously, I copied much of my personnel policy, product strategy, and business philosophy directly from them.

I tried to capture the essence of our philosophy in the welcome letter for Banner Blue's employee handbook. I wrote it in 1991 at the request of Candace Bregman, our Vice President of Marketing at the time.

Welcome to Banner Blue Software! This brief letter gives you an overview of what you can expect from your company and what we expect from you.

The microcomputer software industry is extremely fast-paced. The average life of a product is only 12-18 months before a major revision is required. One has to run just to stay in place! Since our founding in 1984, many competitors have come and gone. Yet, Banner Blue has been extremely successful. Here's why:

Business Philosophy

Banner Blue's business philosophy is simple and effective:

1)   Financial conservatism—pay as you go and don't borrow money. This principle is especially important in our hiring decisions. We only hire people *after* our business has reached a level that pays for their salary. This helps us maximize job security. We have been profitable every year of our existence.

2)   Technical creativity and quality—build unique products that people haven't made before. Our first product, Org Plus, is a perfect example. It was the first program to automate the production

of the common office organization chart. Over the years we have maintained its leadership position with regular improvements. It won "Best of 1986" and "Best of 1987" awards from PC Magazine. And, in December 1991, six years after it first shipped, PC Magazine gave Org Plus its coveted "Editor's Choice Award." They said, ". . . Org Plus Advanced is still the most versatile chart maker available, and it performs better than the competition at virtually every task."

3)   Hard work and commitment—do what you say you're going to do, when you say you're going to do it. We believe that software projects can be completed on schedule, and we prove it several times a year.

These guidelines have allowed us to become the leader in each market we enter while at the same time financing our continuing growth.

Work Environment

Every employee has a key to the office, a symbol of our trust and a symbol of your responsibility.

Our office environment is warm and friendly, but no-nonsense. It is the obligation of every employee to help maintain this environment. Banner Blue finds office politics distasteful and we do everything we can to discourage it.

Banner Blue is a goal-oriented organization. We write down our objectives, then we make them happen. Business decisions are based on facts and our best business judgment; our employees are rewarded on merit.

Benefits and Rewards

We have been able to follow our business philosophy with great success and we have maintained the positive work environment described above because of the substantial contributions by our employees. In return, we feel it is important to reward employees accordingly:

1)   Banner Blue does everything it can to create opportunities for its existing employees. Whenever possible, we train and promote from within.

2)   We have an aggressive profit-sharing plan that is one of the best in any industry.

3)   Our medical and dental benefits are outstanding.

4)   We offer a unique computer purchase plan that reimburses each employee for their own personal computer purchases.

5)   We turn each new product introduction into a fun contest, paying each employee for the bugs they find and the product improvements they suggest.

Banner Blue's future success is dependent on your commitment. With your commitment, Banner Blue will continue to be an outstanding place to make a career.

            Kenneth L. Hess
            President

Of course the quality of the person who read this letter also was a major contributor to our success. We only hired someone when they met our high standards, preferring an empty position to a bad fit. I can honestly say that when I left Banner Blue, our team of people was the finest with which I have ever worked.

Banner Blue also had good timing on two important occasions. I spoke of how my 1994 analysis of waves passing through our market led me to develop Family Tree Maker Deluxe. Looking back, I believe that my first program, Org, also rode a wave when sales of application software began to grow faster than sales of personal computers themselves.

The power of a wave passing through a market is difficult to overestimate. In some industries these waves are cyclical and driven by the economic cycle. In technology markets the waves tend to be unpredictable—like tsunami created by an earthquake. For Banner Blue, waves created by the economic cycle were mild, barely measurable in comparison.

Catching a wave is analogous to the "bold stroke" described by many generals. Correctly timed, the proper strategic action can compensate for numerical inferiority and hide many small errors in execution. In fact, producing the right product at the right time can carry a company for the product's entire lifetime—as much as seven years in the software business—no matter how many illogical decisions managers make along the way. Once again, this highlights the importance of thinking about the big picture.

Of course, the ability of a single bold stroke to elevate a company to a higher plane suggests that some managers can stumble upon that one big correct decision entirely by chance, and in my experience they sometimes do. This can become a trap, because success brings adulation that makes the recipient of such good fortune even less likely to listen to the advice of others—why should he; he is much more successful than they are. It pays to retain some humility, just in case fortune was more kind than one realizes!

Celebration

People frequently ask how I celebrated when I sold the company. There are two answers to that question. Connie, Amber, and I took a wonderful vacation to Hawaii to celebrate the sale. The other answer is more complex. I sold something I loved because I was tired—in my mind, it was not the kind of event I most enjoy celebrating.

I am a *builder*. In my own quiet way, I celebrate when I build something of which I am proud. Among my accomplishments at Banner Blue, I was most proud of my first product, Org; our first CD-ROM product, Family Tree Maker Deluxe; and what the company itself grew to be.

Org was a product that, by all rights, I never should have completed. However, my blind faith in my design and engineering skills allowed me to plow ahead, solving programming problems that might have scared me off had I known better. The program had a simple, elegant user interface that was a breeze to use, but internally some parts of the program were patched together with little more than the programmer's equivalent of baling wire. Nonetheless, it worked and I made it reliable. Then it sold! I ran ads and it sold and sold and sold. Org put me in business.

Family Tree Maker Deluxe was also special to me. During the years before that product, I had often wanted to figuratively "put the pedal to the floor," making Banner Blue into something really spectacular, but there was always something awry. We seemed to have insufficient resources or questionable product ideas. Then during early 1994, the technology, the market forces, and our resources all fell into place, allowing me to envision how we could redefine the genealogy market and our company. I felt like a racecar driver leading the pack as he exits a slalom into the home strait, knowing all he has to do is press the accelerator as hard as he can to win the race.

And I pressed hard, asking a group of twenty-year-olds to build the company's most important product in just three months, and they delivered. We were firing on all cylinders, initiating a string of events that doubled if not tripled the market value of the company within a matter of months. Now, that was exciting, something to celebrate!

Indeed, every time we shipped a product we had a Bucks for Bugs celebration, awarded special bonuses to key people, and held a banquet or luncheon. Accolades and applause were in abundance.

So, it was the products that truly *made* the company, and the actual brick-by-brick construction of the company that made me proud, not the company's sale. I celebrate such things by stepping back to admire them, analyzing them, studying how I can improve them the next time around. Writing this book is my celebration of Banner Blue.

Personal Thoughts About Entrepreneurship

Starting a company is an intensely creative activity. Beyond the creation of new products, the entrepreneur creates new rules rather than following those already existing—he creates wealth and power rather than taking it from someone else.

The process was fun for me because it let me do the things I enjoy doing (analyzing, creating, and building) and it was a natural fit with my personality (I know what I want, I want it done right, and I wanted it yesterday). The potential risk never bothered me because I always played the odds, and the responsibility never burdened me because I had learned to carry it as a youth. Whether these things are true for any other individual, only he or she can answer.

It is interesting that one of my primary motives for starting a company was the thought of accumulating wealth. Yet, the final impetus to actually found the company was a desire for control and freedom. Then after running the company for many years, I once again thought about the wealth issue and decided that I had enough, only to confront the issue of control once more during the time I worked for Broderbund. Now having had time to reflect on the entire situation, I find that I miss running a company. All I can conclude is that wealth does not have much to do with my happiness—creating things and controlling their development does. Certainly for me happiness comes from accomplishment, and thinking about past accomplishments is not nearly as satisfying as achieving new ones. I suspect these things are true of most people.

Can another person do what I have done? Absolutely. The technology, distribution channels, and markets have all changed substantially, but the principles of founding a successful business are essentially the same. The technology, distribution channels, and markets also changed *while* I was running Banner Blue, but my business principles successfully adapted the company each time. I have no doubt about the validity of the principles looking forward. Founding a company today might require the entrepreneur to address a different market, but that is what business principles help evaluate.

Looking back, there are a few things I would change if I had the opportunity to start Banner Blue all over again. In the heat of battle, it was too easy to forget the principles that initially made the company a success. Consequently, I based some of our new product decisions on limited market analysis—an embarrassing admission because I consider such analysis one of my strengths. I would be vigilant to avoid making that mistake again.

Of less importance, I would give more thought to a potential exit strategy at the time I founded a company. Inevitably, circumstances would change before the time to exit came, but I had not even considered it when I founded Banner Blue, so I had to start from zero when it was time for me to leave. If the actual exit involved selling the company, I would be very cautious about agreeing to stay with the acquiring company beyond a short transition period. If the transaction required longer tenure, I would want to have a position of reasonable power in the acquiring company, such as a board seat.

This list of things I would change is short, not because I think everything I did was perfect, but because my results were better than I ever expected. I just hope I can obtain the same results again.

Revolutionary ages sometimes teeter on politics, sometimes war, and sometimes religion, but it is technology that drives our age. Since we cannot control the nature of the times in which we live, I consider myself extremely fortunate to have been born in the right place and at the right time to take maximum advantage of my personality, natural talents, and experience.

Yes, I worked very hard, but I was also plain lucky to be born in the United States with its free-enterprise system. I was lucky to have parents that taught me timeless values and many invaluable skills. I was lucky to attend college at Stanford and accept my first job in the heart of Silicon Valley where entrepreneurism is a way of life. I was lucky to have the support of a long-suffering wife while I slaved away at Banner Blue. And, I was lucky that the markets evolved in a way that enabled me to capitalize on the changes. Greater people than I have had lesser accomplishments, merely for the lack of such good fortune.

To my mind this is a wonderful time, highly favorable to bootstrapped startups in a variety of markets. Our time is one in which thoughts in the entrepreneur's brain, transformed through a single computer requiring limited capital, can create vast wealth as if from nothing at all. In this realm of the pure entrepreneur, large organizational size retards the creative process and homogenizes the end result. The world is upside down. Today's world belongs to the entrepreneur.

Appendix A

Lessons Learned

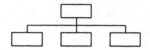

This is a summary of the important lessons I have learned about business and how business relates to my personal life. In most cases, the body of the book develops these lessons in more detail or places them in context. Whenever that is the case, I have identified the relevant pages.

Page(s)

The "Work Products" of Leadership

1. One of the key tasks of leaders in an entrepreneurial   18, 241
    organization is to anticipate trends in technology and
    the marketplace with sufficient accuracy and projected
    far enough into the future that they can build an island
    of stability—a vision. With stable ground under foot,
    management by objective becomes an effective tool.

2. Personally, I am most effective and possess the most confidence when I can build an analytical, actionable model of the relevant business area, taking into account all the important forces. This allows me to plan and predict. It is how I create a vision, although there are many other ways.

9, 14, 221, 242

3. The process for implementing a leader's product vision is as important as the vision itself. At Banner Blue we called this process the Product Development Life Cycle, and it contained the following steps, procedures, and documents: product selection criteria, product objectives and requirements, product specifications, schedule, budget, marketing plan, quality assurance plan, and management approvals. A good process makes everyone more effective, even letting junior employees succeed where senior people might fail without one.

24, 42, 122, 138, 157, 164, 221, 243

Activities of Leadership

4. Leaders must proactively create and nurture an organization's culture. If the leaders do not, someone else will, probably to the leaders' detriment.

92

5. Leaders must communicate their vision. It is important for everyone in an organization to know the company's strategy, each to his or her level of understanding.

157

6. Leaders must study developments and obtain opinions outside the organization as well as inside; therefore, a diverse network of contacts in every functional area of the business is invaluable. Since asking for advice is essentially asking for a favor, contacts should see some possibility of a *quid pro quo*—they should be friends who know you will return the favor, members of a trade organization, or individuals who see the legitimate possibility of a business relationship. Ideally, to obtain the most useful advice, contacts should represent an organization approximately the same size as the leader's. Indeed, leaders may even find it difficult to obtain a meeting with individuals in an organization an order of magnitude larger because such contacts will not see the value to themselves.

7. Leaders must be vigilant to avoid the "heat of battle" syndrome wherein the deluge of day-to-day demands overwhelms any thoughts about the big picture. I learned to make big-picture thinking one of my objectives, blocking out time for it on my calendar.

Requirements of Leadership

8. The leader of a technology-driven business should have a deep understanding of the key technology. If a non-technical leader turns over technology leadership to a subordinate technologist, the risk is that the resulting technology vision ignores business reality. On the other hand, if a non-technical leader formulates the technology vision himself with only the advice of the technologist, he risks losing the technical subtleties and bad decisions result.

9. The ability to impose your will is a vital prerequisite for leadership. To meet an important objective, leaders have a responsibility to encourage, assist, direct, reward, replace, reassign, fire, and even step in for any employee not doing his job.

Management by Objective (MBO)

10. Clear, measurable objectives help insure that every   113, 236
employee is working towards the same ends and with
the correct priority, that every employee is doing the
right things as determined by the managers of the
company.

11. Comparing results against objectives is the only non-   72, 95,
subjective basis for performance evaluation.   113

12. Failure to meet an objective most often results from its   112
neglect rather than difficulty in performing the task;
therefore, regular, written reports reviewing progress
towards objectives aid achievement more than anything else I have found.

13. Peer pressure helps some people meet their objectives,   112
but not others. The same is true of bonuses tied to
objectives.

Managing the Company

14. Managers should insist on profit as the primary objec-   71, 142
tive of the organization. In the short term, a lean,
profitable company can weather storms that other
companies cannot. In the long term, every company
requires profit for its survival. A requirement for
profit also helps foster discipline throughout the organization—so it is a good idea to emphasize profit
from the very beginning.

15. Companies and projects should have the appropriate   14, 164
scale at all times. There are many one-person businesses that an ill-guided founder tries to turn into a
ten-person business. That is a strategy of failure, just
as it is to starve a large opportunity. Everything has its
natural size.

16. Market focus is extremely important, because inde-   149
pendent of competitors' overall size, the company that
masses the most resources at the point of attack wins.

17. Fundamentally, sales growth is a function of product creation. No products, no sales.   245

18. For each order of magnitude increase in the size of a company (1, 10, 100, 1000 employees), management must adapt and change its means of internal control and communication.   93, 166

19. An accounting and management control system has many figures of merit, including: accessibility, ease of modification, and integration of key information sources. At Banner Blue, we found that local control of the operating data, on a flexible, easy-to-use system that did not require special training to access or modify, was more valuable than an integrated system managed by remote experts.   219

20. I contracted out things that we could do more cheaply on the outside, that were outside my management expertise or style, or that had a very uneven demand for labor. On the other hand, I found it valuable to do our own advertising and public relations because it made our managers more effective communicators of our product plans, both inside and outside the company. We also self-insured for employee dental benefits because it was easy and saved money. Rather than following the conventional wisdom on what should be contracted and what should be done in-house, I examined each case on its own merits.   72, 79, 90

21. Measure and track everything.   69, 87, 220

22. The board of directors is an excellent source of business expertise. It should comprise at least five members, with more outsiders than insiders.   179

Watching the Purse Strings

23. A straightforward way of managing headcount is to target an aggressive ratio of sales revenue per employee as compared to other successful companies in the industry, regardless of their size. Banner Blue targeted $200,000 in sales per employee.   71

24. Many people inside and outside the company want to spend *company* money because of what it does for *them*. You must ask what spending the money does for the *company*.   91

25. The best investment you can make is to spend money wisely. There is no return on money frittered away.   18

Hiring and Firing—Employee Fit

26. A startup is a great place to learn, but no one has time to teach. Employees must be self-starters *and* self-teachers.   95

27. Every job requires a slightly different personality. For example, the personality of a successful salesperson is generally quite different from that of a successful accountant. I found reputable, standardized personality tests to be extremely helpful in ascertaining a candidate's fit for a given job.   165

28. Different companies have different cultures, and employees cannot always adapt. For example, people who were effective working for me at Hewlett-Packard were not always effective working for me at Banner Blue.   96, 117

29. Just because a job candidate attended a prestigious school or worked at a successful company does not mean that they contributed to that prestige or success. You must ask what they know and what they accomplished.   73

30. I always try to hire the smartest people I can find who are also a good fit with my other criteria.   197

31. Giving unique privileges or extraordinary compensation to a new hire engenders jealousy, even at the executive level (perhaps especially at the executive level).   116, 118

Benefits

32. Offering excellent benefits compared to other compa-   71, 251
    nies in the industry is the *quid pro quo* of demanding
    performance standards.

33. Aggressive profit sharing is one of the most valuable   71, 119
    benefits to the company *and* the employees, because
    when properly implemented it demonstrates that eve-
    ryone is in the same boat, increasing productivity si-
    multaneously with compensation.

34. Benefits should be easy for employees to understand   119
    or they lose their value, potentially becoming counter-
    productive. For example, no employee, including my-
    self, knew how much Banner Blue's initial profit
    sharing plan would pay until the close of the year.
    Although employees liked profit sharing, they did not
    significantly alter their behavior. I modified the plan
    to make the amount of the profit sharing award more
    visible throughout the year and every employee ad-
    justed his day-to-day actions accordingly.

35. You should increase benefits steadily over time, be-   119
    cause employees take last year's new benefit for
    granted today. It is especially important to take this
    into account when establishing the initial level of a
    new benefit. For example, it is better to add coverage
    to a new insurance plan every year than it is to provide
    full coverage all at once. Avoid reducing benefits at
    all costs.

36. Cash is the ideal way to deliver bonuses of moderate   78, 111
    size because of the additional impact and favorable
    memory it creates.

37. Providing every employee a key to the office is a sym-   251
    bol of trust that pays back many times over.

Managing Employees

38. It is more important for subordinates to respect a man-   5
    ager than to like him. Fortunately, admiration nor-
    mally follows respect.

39. Managers should reward employees based on market conditions and merit as measured by performance against objectives, not seniority. This focus keeps the top performers happy and reinforces a results-oriented philosophy. 72, 113, 141

40. In spite of occasional jealousy, internal promotions build loyalty among an organization's top performers, but for every person promoted there is someone else who thinks the job should have been theirs. As a courtesy and in an attempt to obtain their support, I always privately pre-announce promotions to those individuals likely to feel disappointment. 98

41. When publicly announcing a promotion, I always give a detailed explanation of why I am promoting the individual. This lets others strive to emulate the person's achievement rather than complaining about it. 98

42. Some things are so deep that they never change. It is better to enjoy and capitalize on someone's personality than to make a futile attempt to change it. 86

43. Each person possesses different skills and motivations; consequently, it is necessary to manage each person differently. 116

44. Subordinates working extra-hard and extreme hours need their manager's moral support. In this case the manager's simple presence at the job site becomes his most important work. 139

45. When a manager asks people to make an extreme effort, it is good to have an external enemy, such as a competitor, to justify the request. Otherwise, the manager himself risks becoming the enemy. 243

Organizational Structure

46. A flat organization with low barriers between departments, staffed with well-rounded, multi-talented people, enables small, flexible, and productive project teams. 70, 138

47. Physical closeness is important to minimizing barriers   93
    between departments. Distance inherently creates dif-
    ferences and factions.

Analyzing the Numbers

48. A number has meaning only in comparison to another   31
    number. Common and valuable comparisons include
    those made to forecasts, targets, budgets, competitors,
    historical quantities, estimates of potential, lifetime
    totals, grand totals, cumulative totals, and projections
    based on a model. For example, all of my initial sales
    forecasts showed sales of personal computers relative
    to total potential sales, a comparison that yielded much
    more information than either number by itself. Gener-
    ally I do many comparisons to find the one that offers
    a special insight.

49. If in doubt about how to analyze a market (or a tech-   9
    nology), I learned to drive down to the lowest possible
    level in search of an element *common* to all the pieces.
    Then I compare each of the pieces, looking for a *dif-
    ference* in the behavior of the common element. Fi-
    nally, I come back up level by level, analyzing each
    one for interesting information.

50. You should never base a forecast on an aggregate   197
    number; instead, break it down into component parts,
    each one thoroughly understood.

51. Whenever I generate an estimate (a projected value for   31
    a number I cannot know with certainty), I try to arrive
    at a value using more than one independent method.
    The closer the separate estimates, the more confident I
    am of the result.

52. I always examine the sensitivity of an analysis to   31
    changes in the value of every variable and assumption.
    If an analysis is highly sensitive to a number that is
    hard to estimate (small changes in the number produce
    large changes to the outcome), then the analysis may
    not have much value.

Product Strategy

53. To create something new, you have to know everything that already exists in the same area. Otherwise,
it is not even possible to know whether the creation is
new. To create something better, you also have to
know why an earlier inventor did things the way he
did. In short, to create something new, you must be
the world expert in your field.   3

54. Technology waves result from newness overcoming
whatever existed before, and their effect is analogous
to a wave at the beach pushing a surfer to the shore.
When successful new technologies move along the S-
curve from their flat, erratic beginnings to the phase of
exponential growth, they give complementary products
an added push in the market. The more fundamental
and broad-based the technology, the larger is the wave
and the bigger the push. When I plot a strategy, I always want as many things as possible in my favor. I
want to be riding waves, not swimming against them.   136, 148,
                                                        157, 252

55. It is very expensive to convince someone they have a
problem when they are not aware of it, whereas people
who know they have a problem are already looking for
a solution.   20, 92

56. To successfully replace a customer's existing method
for dealing with a problem, you generally must offer a
solution that is ten times better. A 20 percent improvement does not even get a customer to raise his
head from what he is doing. A 200 or 300 percent improvement may get him to look a sales person in the
eye. A 1000 percent improvement causes people to
reach for their wallets.   23, 152

57. For a totally new market: limit the initial product to
the essential features—keep it lean and simple. Then
listen to customer feedback and upgrade quickly.   21, 62,
                                                         92, 110,
                                                         135, 223

58. I always try to make my own products obsolete before   222, 243
     someone else does it for me. To maintain its market
     position and price, every year a technology product
     needs 30 percent more features, functionality, or per-
     formance that customers want.

59. When upgrading or enhancing a product, it is good to   128, 134,
     give existing customers what they want, but it is even   146
     more valuable to explore the needs of potential cus-
     tomers, those not currently purchasing the product. If
     possible, meet their needs as well, broadening the ap-
     peal of the product.

60. A rule of thumb for determining whether to include   134
     additional features in a product: If it is possible to
     communicate a rich, extensive feature set to the cus-
     tomer, then a product obtains higher entry barriers,
     gives better value to the customer, requires less shelf
     space, and achieves higher sales volume. If it is not
     possible to communicate the feature set, you are better
     off with separate products.

61. There is danger in integrating separate products before   123
     the underlying technologies stabilize, for improve-
     ments in the separate products may negate any advan-
     tage of integration.

62. It is difficult to exceed the quality norm of the soft-   136, 165
     ware industry because you must build on top of the
     operating system and use third-party code to speed de-
     velopment or offer competitive features. You are at
     the mercy of the quality inherent in these third-party
     products.

63. Sales volume begets additional sales volume.   135

Choosing a Technology

64. You should never use new technology simply for the   135
sake of using it—customer needs should determine the
appropriate technology. Interestingly, however, to be
competitive and on the leading edge of those trying to
solve a customer problem, you will often end up using
leading-edge technology, keeping both customers and
your own engineers happy.

65. For product features where compatibility is an issue   47
(printers, file formats, etc.), you must always support
the mainstream technologies. On the other hand, you
will rarely have the resources to support all marginal
technologies. I found that it is a much better investment to support new, developing technologies that
have a small market share rather than trailing-edge
technologies that are probably dying and that have a
small market share.

Product Development

66. A product development team should be absolutely *as*   164
small as possible to get the job done.

67. Do not rely on opinion when facts are cheap. Proto-   30, 106,
types, mock-ups, and test beds are invaluable tools for   137
testing technical assumptions and verifying conclusions.

68. In software development, good product architecture   41, 135
preserves the freedom you need to enhance the product
in future versions and therefore deserves top management attention. Developers should plan carefully and
leave as much freedom as conceivable, or throw away
the first version when the program is still relatively
small and start over.

69. Subordinate the design to the available materials and   116
    subordinate the product feature set to the schedule—
    focusing on being *resourceful* and *on time*. This phi-
    losophy helped me obtain the greatest possible func-
    tionality at the lowest possible cost. Unnecessary
    customization of components raises costs and in-
    creases risk. Extending the schedule burns cash and
    risks overshooting your marketing insight. To imple-
    ment this philosophy, you should know the priority for
    every feature and complete the important ones first.

70. All else remaining equal, increasing a development   167
    team's ability to handle changes to the product specifi-
    cation creates a competitive advantage; prohibiting late
    changes creates weakness.

71. "Bucks for Bugs" (paying a bonus for each bug found)   76, 111
    is an outstanding motivator for product testers and an
    excellent way to train the entire organization on a new
    product.

Marketing

72. Customers are self-selecting and carry unique precon-   63, 122
    ceptions, making their feedback much more valuable
    than that of friends and colleagues a professional hap-
    pens to know. I learned to use a variety of mecha-
    nisms to collect customer feedback, including surveys,
    canvassing, and technical support calls.

73. Prospective customers can only extrapolate very small   89, 125
    distances from their current experience, making sur-
    veys a weak tool for testing innovative products. Per-
    sonal experience with customers offers superior in-
    sights.

74. Sometimes the words used to describe a product are   122, 156
    vitally important to its ultimate success, especially
    when the product represents an entirely new concept.

75. Direct marketing offers many avenues of experimenta-   59, 122
     tion for honing a message or selecting a price. In
     many cases, it is less expensive and more reliable to do
     an experiment than it is to do additional market re-
     search. Split-run advertisements are one of the most
     common techniques, but you can use almost any other
     customer contact; we often tested product registration
     cards. The key is to establish an effective control or
     baseline for the purposes of comparison and to meas-
     ure all variables without exception.

76. I found it tremendously valuable to enter a new market   103
     underneath the radar of my competitors, without pre-
     announcement and fanfare. In my mind, the rules are
     similar to those of a battlefield. The unarmed man
     who jumps up and down making lots of noise is the
     one who attracts the big guns of the enemy. It only
     makes sense if used as a misdirection or to fulfill a
     death wish. I prefer to wait until I can let my own
     guns do the talking—when I have a strategically tar-
     geted product ready to ship.

77. Getting press does not guarantee success. There is   7, 32
     almost no correlation between the amount of press
     coverage about a new product and its ultimate market
     acceptance.

78. You do not need to cave in to every demand of a dis-   52, 91
     tributor if the product is unique or a market leader.
     The reality is that an innovative, new product is as
     valuable to the distributor as it is to the manufacturer.
     If one distributor cannot see the importance of a deal
     that is positive for both parties, another will.

Special "Deals" and Joint Ventures

79. Most prospective deals never come to fruition—they represent the proverbial goose chase. It is best to screen them out early because there is no sense in negotiating if it will come to nothing in the end. One tactic is to quickly present an aggressive price to see if there is anything worth discussing. More often than not, the other party is looking for a windfall and this tactic immediately scares them away. 132

80. Special deals or joint ventures with another company are one of the easiest ways to lose focus. Most deals consummated to make a few incremental dollars end up being a distraction at their best and a time sink at their worst. 132

81. Banner Blue's best deal (the purchase of Automated Archives) was strategic and preserved our ability to create and control the product. Banner Blue's worst deal (Brochure Maker) was strategic and did not give us full control of the product. For other organizations, product control may not be the key issue, but it was for us. When making deals, heed what is important to your company culture. 121, 168

Buying and Selling a Company

82. If you decide to sell a company, do it when prospects cannot get any better. "Trees don't grow to the sky." If you decide to buy a company, beware of this feeling on the part of the seller. 177, 202, 216

83. Purchasers of technology companies typically shop for revenue velocity and momentum. In other words, they want fast-growing sales. Good profits add value, but the purchaser will probably assume that after the acquisition, the acquired company will make the same level of profit as the rest of their organization. 153

84. Competing bids are important to getting the best price for a company. Given that the number of potential buyers for any particular company is fairly small, go to great lengths not to overlook someone.   183

85. Consummating a merger requires an experienced, first-class attorney who is compatible with the owner or founder.   162

86. *Someone* has to drive a merger. It is as likely to be the acquired company as the acquiring company.   186, 207

87. The due diligence process is often very mechanical—the acquiring company requests massive amounts of information, but does not read much, if any, of it.   229

88. Setting the proper *expectations* for price and other emotionally charged issues is one of the most important aspects of negotiating a deal.   169, 190

89. The timing of a sale needs to take into account the value of the company on the day of the transaction *and* the estimated value of the "currency" received at a time when you can convert it into cash. You should mentally prepare yourself for a 50 percent decline in price when taking stock.   187, 201

90. If an acquiring company wants to retain a company founder after the transaction, the founder should insist on a minimal time commitment. It is rare for someone with an entrepreneurial personality to feel comfortable in a larger organization. He should seek a board seat or other position of power if a long time commitment is necessary.   230, 231, 255

91. Perfect deals are extremely rare.   202

92. Stock goes up and stock goes down. It is important to sell it with the same discipline that earned it.   216, 226

93. Any major change, such as the sale of a company, will cause some employees to leave. All you can hope for is to minimize the loss.   214

94. The best way to minimize employee uncertainty and undesired turnover is to make as many decisions as possible before the public announcement, disclosing all information, both good and bad, as soon as possible. 210

On Being an Entrepreneur

95. You do not have to be a big risk taker to be an entrepreneur, but you do need to be comfortable with uncertainty and show confidence in its face. 196, 242

96. Competition is natural, important, and a driving force behind every entrepreneur. I want the best in everything. 234, 242

97. Discipline, determination, perseverance, and hard work make up for a lot of mistakes. I know because I made plenty. 37, 109, 150, 255

98. It's your company. 178

Personal Life

99. Communicating your business vision and objectives to your family is as important as communicating them to the company. My informal "contract" with Connie regarding the founding of Banner Blue was my first step in accomplishing this. 28

100. You cannot control life events. Life is sometimes fragile, sometimes robust, and always full of the unexpected. The early birth of my daughter is an example of how such an event can totally pre-empt business plans. 44, 81

101. You can balance the demands of a family with those of being an entrepreneur, but there is no such thing as "having it all." You must prioritize and make choices. I try to imagine myself looking backwards from some time in the future to insure that I do not neglect something today that I will regret tomorrow. I make a point not to miss a birthday, anniversary, doctor's appointment, school meeting, school performance, or dinner at home.

102. Happiness comes from accomplishment.

Appendix B

The Product Development Life Cycle

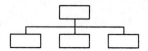

The process for implementing a leader's product vision is as important as the vision itself. At Banner Blue we called this process the Product Development Life Cycle. A good process makes everyone more effective, and even lets junior employees succeed where senior people might fail without one.

One could write an entire book on the Product Development Life Cycle, so what follows is necessarily somewhat schematic. I do not discuss who performs each step or who serves as the decision maker, because I found these things to be highly dependent on an organization's personnel. For the sake of simplicity, I have also omitted several sign-offs where managers approve the work the team has performed. (I insisted that any major changes made after a sign-off had to receive another approval.)

The Steps in the Product Development Life Cycle

Generally, we started the life cycle steps in the order shown below; however, there was normally a great deal of overlap and always substantial iteration—work at one step causes the team to redo work at the previous step, sometimes many times over.

Throughout the process and before the formal quality assurance process kicked into high gear, we used mock-ups, test beds, experiments, usability testing, and performance testing to verify the robustness of the design and the quality of the code.

Although I designed this Product Development Life Cycle for a software company, one can draw analogies with almost any business.

TABLE 7
BANNER BLUE'S PRODUCT DEVELOPMENT LIFE CYCLE

Life Cycle Step	Description
Prospectus	This document serves as a means to compare prospective product ideas. It contains: • Comparison against new product criteria • Market analysis (this should include Porter's five-force analysis) • Analysis of demands on each functional department in the company
Product Objectives	At a high level of abstraction, the product objectives identify the product's market, key functionality, performance, and targeted ship date.
Product Requirements Document (PRD)	This document puts the project objectives into a working format, containing: • Restatement of product objectives • Product description • Description of market opportunity • Detailed analysis of competitive products • Minimum product capabilities, feature by feature • Minimum hardware requirements • Performance requirements • Optional requirements specifying whether each is important, highly desirable, or desirable
Core Marketing Statement	The Core Marketing Statement is a draft advertisement or upgrade letter to make sure the product sizzles. It also serves as an excellent communication tool throughout the project.

External Product Specification (EPS)	This specification describes the operation of the product from the user's viewpoint, containing: • Drawings of each screen in the program as it would appear to the user • A mapping of the behavior of every input such as a keystroke or mouse action • Incorrect, out-of-range, and potential error conditions and the program's response The External Product Specification combined with the Internal Product Specification described below represent the "blueprints" for a product.
Internal Product Specification (IPS)	This document describes the programming necessary to meet the specifications of the Product Requirements Document and the External Product Specification. It contains: • A description of the data structure and key variables • The overall product architecture • Functions with their arguments and return values • Important algorithms
Master Schedule	The Master Schedule should comprise tasks lasting no longer than several days. If the time resolution is more coarse, then the potential for error skyrockets. Typically, we updated this schedule every week.
Project Budget	The budget specifies the dollars available to complete the project.
Coding	This step comprises the actual building of the product.
Test Plan	The test plan specifies how quality assurance will verify the performance of every feature.
Testing	This step implements the test plan.
Beta Test (optional)	Occasionally, we also tested the program with customers.
Release to Production	This step reflects the judgment of senior management that the program is ready to ship to customers.

New Product Criteria

After a number of revisions over the years, Banner Blue's new product criteria were as follows:

1. The product solves a differentiable, known problem—a task people perform in spite of the difficulty—providing an order-of-magnitude improvement.

2. Our management offers special expertise.

3. The product has no significant competition.

4. It makes good use of the computer.

5. It meets profit objectives. Typically this means that the product requires one calendar year of development time or less (as required by the market), and that it has reasonable support costs.

6. It has built-in barriers to competition.

7. We have control over all key technologies and relationships.

8. It represents a balanced addition to the product portfolio. This results in a mix of new programs, upgrades, and ports to new platforms, and leverages existing marketing channels.

Sample From a Product Requirements Document

This sample contains extracts from the Product Requirements Document for Banner Blue's program, Family Tree Maker for Windows, developed for Windows 3.1 during 1993. It describes the requirements for a feature to search a customer's database to find an individual meeting user-specified criteria.

Find Individual

Required: The feature can search every field for every individual and marriage record.

The feature can navigate back and forth among the individuals meeting the search criteria.

The search criteria themselves will be smart about the data type of the field being searched.

Important: The feature can search using multiple criteria.

Desirable: Kinship will also be available as a search criterion (i.e., search for all first cousins of NAME).

Desirable: The feature can search on embedded or linked objects.

Sample From an External Product Specification

This sample contains extracts from the External Product Specification for Banner Blue's program, Family Tree Maker for Windows, developed for Windows 3.1 during 1993. The entire document was 127 pages long.

Find Individual

The philosophy of the Find Individual command is to find too much rather than skip over what the user is looking for. Find Individual is accessible (currently) from the Family Page and the generic paginated views.

A key point is that this command is Find *Individual*. Many aspects of the behavior relate to finding a (single) person. For example, if several fields for one individual meet the criteria, the command navigates to the person once, not to the fields in succession.

The Answer Set

The program incrementally generates an answer set from the search criteria, allowing the user to navigate through the "found" items as they are located. Thus, if the user changes something in the answer set such that the search criteria is not met, it remains in the answer set until a new search is started. On the other hand, if someone modifies an individual not yet found so that they no longer meet the criteria, then they are never found.

If someone is deleted, they are dropped from the answer set. If a matching marriage or a matching object is deleted, the involved individual(s) remain in the answer set. In the specific case of a marriage, we would navigate back to the male, or the female if the male is deleted. (If this causes special problems, it's so obscure that it's not worth much work.)

If someone is added to the database during a search, they are found (if they meet the criteria) and their IND hasn't been searched yet. To the user, they may be found, they may not be found.

A new search is defined by any editing of the search criteria or by activation of the Restart button (which re-runs the search with the existing criteria). The criteria are remembered until explicitly cleared by the user. Thus, doing a search in the Index of Individuals destroys any other ongoing search.

Search Types and Criteria

Info presentation will be the same as in Family Tree Maker for DOS (move to each Family Page or Album Page in order, or in the index, move the highlight). A table below indicates what to highlight when searching on a given item from a given location. The dialog box hovers on screen until the user cancels. It moves out of the way depending on what field is highlighted when found.

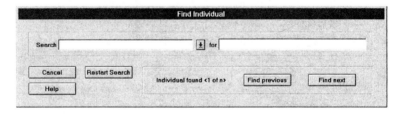

The Change Item to Search dialog is list of fields and other items as shown below. [To be designed.]

Field Name	Type	Quantity per Person	Search Type
Name	48 char alpha	1	Text
aka	48 char alpha	1	Text
Birth date	Comment/event	1	Date
Birth location	Comment/event	1	Text
Birth source information	Source	1	Text
[This table continued with an additional 48 items.]			

Search Type	Valid Search Criteria	Finds
Text	Any alphanumeric character(s)	Any field containing the string (not case sensitive, not whole word)
	!=	All non-empty fields
	=	All empty fields
Date	Month-Day-Year	Exact match & in range (abt, bef, aft, etc.)
	Month-Year	Any day in M-Y & in range
[This table continued with an additional 35 items.]		

[This portion of the document described additional special conditions and specified what field or screen area to highlight when an individual was found.]

Desirable: Kinship will also be available as a search criterion (i.e., search for all first cousins of NAME).

Future: The feature can search using multiple criteria.

Future: The feature can search on embedded or linked objects.

Appendix C

Pro Forma Income Statement

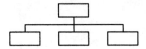

Over the years, Banner Blue's expenses were remarkably steady as a percentage of net product revenue. A good portion of returns resulted from taking back old versions of a program whenever a new one shipped. Indeed, we had few returns for any other reason. Sales and marketing expenses went primarily to advertising during the early years, but they became increasingly weighted towards sales and sales promotions as time progressed.

TABLE 8
BANNER BLUE PRO FORMA INCOME STATEMENT

	Percent of Net Product Revenue
Gross Product Revenue	104
Less Returns	4
Net Product Revenue	100
Cost of Goods Sold	18
Gross Profit	82
Operating Expenses:	
General & Administrative	12
Sales & Marketing	20
Technical & Customer Support	7
Research & Development	16
Total Operating Expense	55
Profit from Operations	27
Other Income (primarily interest)	1
Pretax Income	28

Appendix D

Product Awards

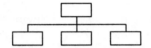

In addition to the awards listed below, Banner Blue products received dozens of outstanding product reviews. Org Plus and Family Tree Maker also had regular and long-running appearances on a variety of industry best-seller lists. I have included awards for part of 1997 because they resulted from work for which I was responsible before leaving the company.

TABLE 9
BANNER BLUE PRODUCT AWARDS

Date	Product	Award
January 1987	Org Plus	*PC Magazine*, "Best of '86"
November 1987	Org Plus	*PC Magazine*, nominated for "Technical Excellence Award"
January 1988	Org Plus	*PC Magazine*, "Best of '87"
December 1991	Org Plus	*PC Magazine*, "Editors' Choice Award"
March 1993	Uncle Sam's Budget Balancer	Software Publishers Association, "Codie" finalist for "Best Educational Tool Program"
August 1994	Family Tree Maker	*Home PC*, "100 Top Products of the Year Editors' Choice Award"

August 1995	Family Tree Maker	*IndelibleNews! Guide to CD-ROMs*, "IN!-ovation award"
February 1996	Family Tree Maker	*Computer Life*, "The Best of Everything Award"
June 1996	Family Tree Maker	*Computer Life*, "First Annual The Best of the Best of Everything Award" (Top 20 Software Programs for 1996)
June 1996	Family Tree Maker	*Family PC*, "Top 25 for 1996"
February 1997	Family Tree Maker Online	*PC Magazine*, "Top 100 Web Site"
March 1997	Family Tree Maker Deluxe Edition II	Software Publishers Association, "Codie" winner for "Best Home Productivity Software Program"
June 1997	Family Tree Maker	*Home PC*, "Top 100 Programs"
July 1997	Family Tree Maker	*Family PC*, "Top 50 Products"
September 1997	Family Tree Maker	*PC Magazine*, "Top 100 CD-ROMs"

Bibliography

Brooks, Frederick P., Jr. *The Mythical Man-Month: Essays on Software Engineering.* Reading, Massachusetts: Addison-Wesley Publishing Company, 1975.

Caples, John. *How to Make Your Advertising Make Money.* Englewood Cliffs, New Jersey: Prentice Hall, 1983.

Heckel, Paul. *The Elements of Friendly Software Design.* New York: Warner Books, Inc., 1984.

Hess, Kenneth L. "Picking the Best Display: An Easy-to-Follow Guide." *Electronic Design* (August 19, 1982): 139-146.

Kernigan, Brian W. and Dennis M. Ritchie. *The C Programming Language.* Englewood Cliffs, New Jersey: Prentice Hall, 1978.

Marks, Mitchell Lee and Philip Mirvis. "Merger Syndrome: Stress and Uncertainty." *Mergers & Acquisitions* (Summer 1985): 50-55.

————. "Merger Syndrome: Management by Crisis." *Mergers & Acquisitions* (January/February 1986): 70-76.

Moore, Geoffrey A. *Crossing the Chasm: Marketing and Selling Technology Products to Mainstream Customers.* New York: HarperBusiness, 1991.

Ogilvy, David. *Ogilvy on Advertising.* New York: Crown Publishers, Inc., 1983.

Porter, Michael E. *Competitive Strategy: Techniques for Analyzing Industries and Competitors.* New York: The Free Press, 1980.

Index